FILM, FORM, AND CULTURE

FILM, FORM, AND CULTURE

SECOND EDITION

Robert Kolker

Chair, the School of Literature, Communication, and Culture
Ivan Allen College
Georgia Institute of Technology

Boston   Burr Ridge, IL   Dubuque, IA   Madison, WI   New York   San Francisco   St. Louis
Bangkok   Bogotá   Caracas   Kuala Lumpur   Lisbon   London   Madrid   Mexico City
Milan   Montreal   New Delhi   Santiago   Seoul   Singapore   Sydney   Taipei   Toronto

McGraw-Hill Higher Education 🕸

*A Division of The **McGraw-Hill** Companies*

FILM, FORM, AND CULTURE

Published by McGraw-Hill, an imprint of The McGraw-Hill Companies, Inc. 1221 Avenue of the Americas, New York, NY, 10020. Copyright © 2002, 1999 by The McGraw-Hill Companies, Inc. All rights reserved. No part of this publication may be reproduced or distributed in any form or by any means, or stored in a data base or retrieval system, without the prior written consent of The McGraw-Hill Companies, Inc., including, but not limited to, in any network or other electronic storage or transmission, or broadcast for distance learning.

Some ancillaries, including electronic and print components, may not be available to customers outside the United States. This book is printed on acid-free paper.

4 5 6 7 8 9 0 DOC/DOC 0 9 8 7 6 5 4

ISBN 0-07-240715-8

Editorial director: *Phillip A. Butcher*
Sponsoring editor: *Allison McNamara*
Senior marketing manager: *David Patterson*
Associate project manager: *Catherine R. Schultz*
Lead production supervisor: *Heather D. Burbridge*
Media producer: *Shannon Rider*
Coordinator of freelance design: *Mary Kazak*
Lead supplement producer: *Marc Mattson*
Photo research coordinator: *Judy Kausal*
Cover design: *Joanne Schopler*
Cover image: *Copyright © 2001 VCG/FPG International. All rights reserved.*
Cover movie shots: *Copyright © 2001 Photofest. All rights reserved.*
Typeface: *10/12 Palatino*
Compositor: *GAC, Indianapolis*
Printer: *R. R. Donnelley & Sons Company*

Library of Congress Cataloging-in-Publication Data

Kolker, Robert Phillip.
    Film, form, and culture / Robert Kolker.—2nd ed.
      p. cm.
    Includes bibliographical references and index.
    ISBN 0-07-240715-8 (alk. paper)
    1. Motion pictures. I. Title.
PN1994.K573 2002
791.43—dc21   2001041025

www.mhhe.com

For Linda

PREFACE

The response from colleagues and students who have used the first edition of *Film, Form, and Culture* has been both gratifying and helpful. Based on their responses, we have made a number of changes that will hopefully result in a text and CD-ROM even more useful and comprehensible for your film course.

In the text, I have retained the coverage that teachers and students appreciated, including an introduction to the cinematic shot, a description of the collaborators who work to make a film, a discussion of genre, an overview of the history of representation, and a look at "other screens" (television and computer). I've kept the cultural studies chapter, which introduces students to the methodologies of historical and cultural analysis through a comparative reading of Hitchcock's *Vertigo* and McTiernan's *Die Hard*. (Colleagues tell me that students particularly like that chapter!) The cultural reception of film is treated throughout. The response from readers is that the book presents sophisticated ideas in contemporary film criticism in an accessible, readable style appropriate for undergraduate students.

NEW TO THE SECOND EDITION

The second edition of the book expands into areas suggested by the many reviewers and colleagues who've given me both formal and informal feedback on the original edition. The text has been reorganized for a better flow of ideas. I have expanded and clarified some of the more difficult concepts and added two major sections: one on documentary films—from Flaherty to Errol Morris—and one on women filmmakers—such as Maya Deren and Julie Dash.

A number of features have been added to the text to make it easier for you to integrate the book and the CD-ROM in your course:

- Each chapter now ends with a boxed section on how to integrate the CD-ROM segments with each chapter of the text.

- A glossary of film terms has been added to the text that covers terms from both the text and the CD-ROM.
- An index of CD-ROM contents has been added to the book to make it easier for you to integrate the two in your syllabus and to assist with assignments.

THE *FILM, FORM, AND CULTURE* CD-ROM

Unique to this book is an interactive CD-ROM in which clips from films are analyzed closely, more closely than can be imagined through the still images common to most film texts. Through images interactively designed with explanatory text, stills, and animations, the reader will become intimately familiar with the basic elements of editing, montage, shot structure, point of view, mise-en-scène, lighting, and camera movement. The CD-ROM can be used alone and/or easily used in conjunction with the text.

The *Film, Form, and Culture* CD-ROM has been expanded in the new 1.0.3 version. A section on "sound" has been added to the music segment, with examples from *Citizen Kane, Nothing Sacred,* and *Meet John Doe.* The unit illustrates how sound is used to concentrate the viewer's attention on dialogue, how it functions as an expressive element that complements the visual, and how it works as one of the methods of continuity cutting. There's also a new section on genre, focusing on film noir. Using clips from *Detour* and from the films of Anthony Mann, the section demonstrates how genre operates in terms of thematic and visual patterns, examines the gender issues of noir, and discusses noir's overwhelming sense of isolation and fear.

Film, Form, and Culture remains a unique introduction to film (and new media) for students in a variety of courses. It is the only introductory text with an interactive CD-ROM and one of the few that discusses not only the basic issues of film construction but the way film is constructed for and by the culture in which it is made. It thinks about film as part of the world it inhabits. I hope it will remain a good reading (and viewing) experience for both instructors and students.

Robert Kolker

Georgia Institute of Technology

Atlanta

ACKNOWLEDGMENTS

I would like to express my thanks for the many useful comments and suggestions provided by the following reviewers: Jeffrey Renard Allen, *City University of New York—Queens College*; Richard Ascough, *Queen's Theological College*; Anna Banks, *University of Idaho*; Jon G. Bentley, *Albuquerque TVI Community College*; Richard A. Blake, *Boston College*; Gerald Boyer, *Maryville University*; Bill Clemente, *Peru State College*; Robert A. Cole, *State University of New York—Oswego*; Jeffrey S. Cole, *King College*; Michel deBenedictis, *Miami–Dade Community College*; Shekhar Deshpande, *Beaver College*; Pamela S. Ecker, *Cincinnati State Technical & Community College*; Susan Felleman, *Southern Illinois University*; Cliff Fortenberry, *Mississippi College*; Mark Gallagher, *University of Oregon*; Mikhail Gershovich, *State University of New York—Old Westbury*; Marsha Gordon, *University of Maryland*; Melody Graulich, *Utah State University*; Ann Green, *Jackson Community College*; Darren Harris-Fain, *Shawnee State University*; Bruce H. Hinrichs, *Century College*; Margot Starr Kernan, *Maryland Institute College of Art*; Salah Khan, *Pacific Lutheran University*; Tammy Kinsey, *University of Toledo*; William Klink, *Charles County Community College*; Börn Krondorfer, *St. Mary's College of Maryland*; Patricia Lacouture, *Salve Regina University*; Gerry LaFemina, *Kirtland Community College*; Sandi S. Landis, *St. Johns River Community College*; Christina Lane, *Ithaca College*; Sandy Maliga, *Minneapolis College of Art and Design*; Gina Marchetti, *Ithaca College*; Gaetana Marrone-Puglia, *Princeton University*; James D. Marsden, *Bryant College*; Michael Minassian, *Broward Community College*; Jerry Naylor, *Iowa Wesleyan College*; Devin A. Orgeron, *University of Maryland*; David J. Paterno, *State University of New York—Albany*; Reneé Pigeon, *CSU—San Bernardino*; David Popowski, *Minnesota State University—Mankato*; Don C. Postema, *Bethel College*; T. J. Rivard, *Indiana University East*; Brooks Robards, *Westfield State College*; Patricia C. Roby, *University of Wisconsin—Washington County*; George S. Semsel, *Ohio University*; Sharon R. Sherman, *University of Oregon*; Thomas J. Shoeneman, *Lewis and Clark College*; Mark Smith, *Northwestern Michigan College*; Sherry S. Strain, *Keystone College*; Ralph Swain, *Briar Cliff*

ix

College; Stephanie A. Tingley, *Youngstown State University*; Frank P. Tomasulo, *Georgia State University*; Amy Villarejo, *Cornell University*; William Weiershauser, *Iowa Wesleyan College*; J. Emmett Winn, *Auburn University*; Andrew A.Workman, *Mills College*.

Many people were involved in the making of *Film, Form, and Culture*. My film students, patiently working with me over the years (most especially those in my fall, 1997, Intro to Film class), helped me hone and clarify my ideas. Mike Mashon indirectly provided the name of the book. Marsha Gordon did important research on its behalf, and Devin Orgeron helped check out the facts. David and Luke Wyatt read the manuscript, and their comments made it better. Stanley Plumly made me feel better with his encouragement. Other University of Maryland colleagues—particularly Sharon Gerstel, Elizabeth Loiseaux, Barry Peterson, Jenny Preece, Ben Shneiderman—helped with conversation, ideas, and facts. Marta Braun, of the Ryerson Polytechnical Institute, Toronto, supplied the image by Etienne-Jules Marey that appears in the text. Paul Schrader, Oliver Stone, and William Blakefield helped make the CD-ROM possible. Robert Lieberman, my agent, saw the book's potential and helped bring it to publication. At McGraw-Hill, Allison McNamara, Catherine Schultz, Heather Burbridge, and David Patterson were extremely helpful. I am also grateful to Stephen Prince, who gave me technical support; Patty Zimmerman, who offered information on independent women filmmakers; and Janet Murray, who simply gave incalculable moral and intellectual support.

CONTENTS

INTRODUCTION

Film, Form, and Culture asks you to think seriously about film, as seriously as you would about literature. It's a book about form and structure, content and contexts, history and business. It will give you some sense of film's history and its place in the greater scheme of things, especially in that envelope of words and deeds, money, art, artifacts, and daily life we live in that is called culture.

But why think seriously about film at all? Many people don't. In fact movies are among those things in our lives that we apparently don't *need* to take seriously. We go to the movies to be entertained, scared, grossed out; to make out, spend time, have something to discuss afterward. But we don't often want to think about movies as a serious part of our emotional or intellectual lives, or even treat them with the same intensity we use when we discuss sports or politics. Outside of a film studies course, we rarely hear other people engaged in a discussion of films that goes much deeper than plot or characters.

Even the people who review movies on television or in the papers are not as serious about their subject as other journalists are about sports, music, or painting. They make jokes and puns, stick their thumbs up or down, tell us the plot and whether the characters are believable. Reviewers, in fact, are often part of the show, a kind of overture to the film we may go to see or bring home on video. They are another part of the entertainment.

But the fact is that attention must be paid to film because most of us get our stories—our narratives and myths—from it or from its close cousin, television. In other words, since the turn of the century, people have turned to film as entertainment, escape, *and* education or as an affirmation of the way they live or think they ought to live their lives. But even if film were "only" entertainment, it is important to find out how it works. Why does it entertain us? Why do we need to be entertained? And what about the fact that film is part of world politics and policy? Some governments support filmmakers as a means to express their national culture to the world. Other governments have caused international incidents over film, particularly where copyright and piracy issues are at stake.

Hard to believe, but sometimes international policy concerning film can lead in turn to aesthetic consequences. After the end of World War II, in 1946, for example, a major agreement was drawn up between France and the United States: the Blum-Byrnes Accords. This agreement came as an unequal compromise in the face of France's concern over getting its own films shown on its own screens. The French public wanted American films. The Accords forced France to accept American films in an uneven ratio: it could show sixteen weeks of its own films, thirty-six weeks of anything else. The Accords changed the way the French made films because some filmmakers decided that the best way to meet the quota was to make high-quality films through the adaptation of literary works. Other French filmmakers hated these adaptations and started to experiment with new cinematic forms, resulting in a revolution of filmmaking in the late fifties that was called the French New Wave. The result, in turn, was a change in film form all over the world. French resentment over the influx of American film and other media surfaced again in the 1990s.

The business of film ripples through the economy, the policy, and the technology of the world at large to this very day. In the coming years, the mergers of enormous media powers—most especially America Online and Time-Warner—will bring wide-reaching changes not only in the economics of film but in what film actually means. They will create a confluence of various delivery systems—film, digital video, print, music, and the World Wide Web—that will make film as we now understand it a different form and kind of entertainment. All nations, our own included, understand the power of film and television to influence their people, to propagandize values and ideologies. Film may be a bargaining chip in foreign policy, always an economic commodity, sometimes the subject of the politician's wrath at home (as when candidates for office rail against the evil moral influence of Hollywood film) and consequently the subject of study of many different kinds of academic courses in which its power and complexity are acknowledged and analyzed. We will talk some about the politics and the business, because film is a big business and its creation, its form, and its content are about power, the core of politics. But mostly we will talk about the form (that is, the way films are put together so that we, as viewers, understand what they are attempting to tell us) and the content of film. We will come to all of this from the perspective of textuality—studying the film itself and how all its parts work—and find out how film, its production and reception, its place in our culture, makes up a large, coherent construction of meaningful and interrelated elements that we can analyze—a text that we can read.

Let's go back for a moment to our straw men, the film reviewers. The first thing almost any reviewer does is talk about (usually summarize) the film's plot. "Charlie Kane is an unhappy newspaper man. His wife leaves him, and he loses all his friends." "2001 opens with a number of shots of animals out on the desert. Then one tribe of apes attacks another until, in the middle of the night, one of the tribes discovers this strange monolith in the middle of their camp. There isn't much dialogue, but the apes look real enough."

What film reviews almost always evade is one of the few realities of film it-self, that it is an artificial construct, something made in a particular way for spe-cific purposes, and that plot or story of a film is a function of this construction, not its first principle. In other words, and as we'll see more in detail as we go along, the formal elements of film—the shot and the cut, for example—are unique to film. They are the basic forms of its construction—along with light-ing, camera movement, music, sound, acting—and they themselves were and are determined by things going on in the development of film throughout its history and the development of the culture that filmmaking is one part of. When I speak of film as "artificial," I don't mean it's false; I'm using the term in its root sense, made by art or, often in the case of film, by craft. Film is an arti-fice, and it becomes an artifact, made in specific ways, using specific tools, fash-ioned to produce and create specific effects (one of which is the plot, which we often do have to revert to for convenience and to make a point about a movie) with the aim of pleasing the audience who pays to see it. Film reviewers and most everyday discussions of film try to ignore the artificial, constructed aspect of film—its form—and instead talk about it as pure story. The characters of its story become, somehow, "realistic," as if they might "really" exist rather than result from the way the film itself puts meaning together.

There is no doubt that filmmakers and the development of film form over the last century play a role in this deception. Many filmmakers assume that most viewers are not interested in the construction principles of their work and have accomplished a remarkable feat, making the structure of their films invisible. In other words, one reason we don't pay attention to the form and structure of film is that the form and structure of film disappear behind the very story and char-acters they produce. This is a great act of prestidigitation and one of the main reasons film has become so popular. Movies have achieved a presence of being, an emotional immediacy that seems unmediated—simply there, without a his-tory, without apparatus, without anything actually between us except the story.

In the discussion that follows, we will explain, analyze, and demystify this apparent act of magic. As we come to understand that film has a complex and flexible form and that story and characters are created by that form, we will be-come more comfortable with the notion of film as something carefully and seri-ously *made*. From that point we will be able to move on and understand that the making has a history and the history has a number of parts and branches. One branch—the largest—is the commercial narrative cinema of Hollywood, the major subject of our study. There are a number of national cinemas, some of them, like India's, almost as large as America's, but without much influence outside the nation's borders. Still another is a more experimental cinema—often found in Europe, Asia, Africa, the Middle East, and Latin America but occa-sionally cropping up in the United States—which explores and experiments with the potentials of film form in the way a good novelist or poet or computer programmer explores her language in order to create new meanings, new struc-tures of thought and feeling.

Understanding film history will help us to understand the conventions of form and content. Clearly, films change over the course of time: they and their makers have a history, as we do, as the culture does. Visual structure, acting styles, story content, the way films *look*—all seem different now than ten or a hundred years ago. But, in many ways, these changes are only superficial. It would be only a small exaggeration to say that, with a few important exceptions, the structure of film and the stories and characters created by that structure have remained mostly unchanged, or have changed in only a gradual way, during the course of film history. Technical methods have indeed changed, and aspects of style (especially acting styles) have changed; but by and large the stories film tells and the ways it tells them follow a continuum almost from the very first images shown to the public. And yet film is always publicizing its uniqueness and originality. "For the first time on the screen…" was a popular publicity phrase in the forties and fifties. "The funniest," "most unique," "unlike anything you've ever seen," "the best film," and "you've never seen anything like it" remain useful nonsense phrases for film advertisements. In truth, every commercial, theatrical film is in one way or another like every other commercial, theatrical film, and all are consciously created to be that way! In order to get a film made in Hollywood, an agent or a producer or a studio head has to be convinced that the film you have in mind is "just like" some other film "only different." Watch the first half-hour of Robert Altman's *The Player* (1992) for a hilarious representation of what "pitching a story" to a Hollywood producer is like, and see Albert Brooks's *The Muse* (1999) for an ironic fantasy about the search for an original film idea.

"Just like . . . only different" is the engine that drives film. Hollywood cinema in particular (but all cinema in general) is based upon the conventions of genre, *kinds* of stories, told with styles and cinematic elements that are repeated with major and minor variations throughout the history of the genre. Through genres, films are influenced by history and, very rarely, influence history in return. Genres, as we will see in Chapter 5, are complex contractual events drawn between the filmmaker and the film viewer. We go to a horror film or a thriller, a romantic comedy or a science fiction movie, a Western or a melodrama with certain expectations that the film must meet. If it doesn't meet them, we will be disappointed and probably will not like the film. If a film masquerading as a genre turns out to attack or make fun of it, one of two things can happen. If other historical and cultural events are in sync with the attack or the parody, it is possible that the genre will wither and all but disappear. This happened to the Western in the late sixties and early seventies. Three moving and disturbing films that questioned the historical and formal elements of the Western—Sam Peckinpah's *The Wild Bunch* (1969), Arthur Penn's *Little Big Man* (1970), and Robert Altman's *McCabe and Mrs. Miller* (1971)—joined with the negative response to the Vietnam War and some profound questions about American imperial interests and the myths of manifest destiny to bring the Western down from its enormous popularity to a point from which it has barely recovered. These days, the Western is more likely to be a commentary on the genre rather than a repetition of it. Among the more interesting recent Westerns are those that use the genre as something like a cover for other investigations of character, history, and gender, such as Jim Jarmusch's *Dead Man* (1995) and Maggie Greenwald's *The Ballad of Little Jo* (1993).

The more likely response to a film that mocks its generic construction too forcefully is that no one will go to see it. This happened with Robert Altman's late seventies Western with Paul Newman, *Buffalo Bill and the Indians* (1976); the Bruce Willis action film *Hudson Hawk* (1991); and the Arnold Schwarzenegger film *The Last Action Hero* (1993). Of course, one ironic and self-mocking Bruce Willis action film, *Die Hard* (1988), was very popular (we will analyze it closely in Chapter 4). When Willis and then Schwarzenegger took the mockery too far, however, and the action hero stereotype was made too obviously like a cartoon and too self-conscious, viewers rebelled. Stereotypes, the expected character, the unsurprising story, the hoped-for conclusion, the invisible style are all part of our contract with the movies, what their makers believe we demand of them. Such demands are certainly not restricted to movies alone: in television, pop music, news reporting, and politics, we tend to be most comfortable with what we've most often heard. We are wary of the new. Our popular culture is, more often than not, an act of affirming already held ideas, of defining, delimiting, and limiting what we accept as the real.

The worst thing we can say about a film is that it is "unrealistic." "The characters weren't real." "The story didn't strike me as being real." Reality is always our last resort. If someone thinks we're not being serious, we're told to "face reality." If our ideas are half-baked, overly narcissistic, or even just silly, we're told to "get real!" If we are college teachers or teenagers, we're told we'll find things different "in the real world." Reality can be a threat, the thing we're not facing, or not in, or not dealing with. But it can also be a verbal gesture of approbation. "That was so real." And, of course, it's the greatest compliment we can give a film, even though—and this is the great paradox—in our media-wise world, we know deep down that what we are seeing has very, very little to do with reality.

The fact is that "reality," like all other aspects of culture, is not something out there, existing apart from us. Reality is an agreement we make with ourselves and between ourselves and the rest of the culture about what we will call real. Maybe, as some people have argued, the only dependable definition of reality is that it is something a lot of people agree upon. This is not to say that there aren't actual, "real" things in the world. Natural processes, states of matter (heat, cold, the relative solidity of physical things), the fact that, in temperate climates, plant life dies off in the fall and returns in the spring—these constitute a "reality," perhaps because they happen without our presence. But no matter what natural events and processes occur, they have little meaning without human interpretation, without our speaking about them within the contexts of our lives and our culture, without our giving them names and meanings.

We find films realistic because we have learned certain kinds of responses, gestures, attitudes from them; and when we see these gestures or feel these responses again in a film or a television show, we assume they are real, because we've felt them and seen them before. We've probably even imitated them. (Where do we learn the way to kiss someone? From the movies.) This is reality as an infinite loop, a recursion through various emotional and visual constructs, culturally approved, indeed culturally mandated, that we assume to be "real" because we see them over and over again, absorb them, and, for better or worse, live them. In an important sense, like films themselves, "reality" is made up of repetition and assent.

Here is where the reality factor is joined with genre, history, culture, convention, and the invisible structure of film that we talked about earlier. What we call "realistic" in film is, more often than not, only the familiar. The familiar is what we experience often, comfortably, clearly, as if it were always there. When we approve of the reality of a film, we are really affirming our comfort with it, our desire to accept what we see. Desire—simply wanting to see the familiar or a twist on the familiar and receive pleasure from the seeing—is an important idea, because filmgoers aren't fools. No one literally believes what they see on the screen; we all desire and in a certain sense covet, and in a greater sense *want*, what we see, despite what we know about its probability or, more likely, its improbability. We respond with a desire that things could be like this or, simply, that we might want to inhabit a world that looks and behaves like the one on the screen. We want to share, or just *have* the same feelings that the characters up there are having. We want to accept them uncritically, respond emotionally. Our culture keeps telling us over and over that emotions don't lie. If we feel it, it must be so.

In the discussion that follows, we will steer our way through the thickets of desire and try to find why we want so much from movies and how the movies deliver what they and we think we want. By examining form and the ways in which our responses are culturally determined, we will attempt to look at our responses in order to understand what we are really getting when we ask for realism, why we should be asking for it at all, and why our expectations keep changing. You may recall that the first film to win an Academy Award in the new millennium, *American Beauty* (Sam Mendes, 1999), was part fantasy, with many "unrealistic" touches, and full of fantasy that seemed to echo "real" desires. The film is proof that "reality" is not a given, but chosen.

Culture is another important idea in this book. Chapter 4 will cover in detail what cultural studies is and how our very ideas about culture, and popular culture in particular, keep changing, almost as much as the culture that's being studied. But since we will use the term before then, let me begin to introduce it here.

Culture is the sum total of the intricate ways we relate to ourselves, our peers, our community, our country, world, and universe. It is made up of the minutiae of our daily lives: the toothpaste we use—the fact that we use toothpaste—the music we like; the political ideas we hold; our sexual orientation; the image we have of ourselves; the models we want to emulate. Culture is more than ourselves, because our selves are formed by a variety of influences and agreements. So culture is also made up of the general ideological components, the web of beliefs and things we take for granted, in the society we live in. Politics, law, religion, art, entertainment are all part of our culture: they form its ideological engine, the forces of assent, the values, images, and ideas we agree to embrace and follow or struggle against.

We will use culture here in a broad sense, perhaps close to what the French think about when they worry about their culture being at stake because of the influx and popularity of American movies. In our definition, culture doesn't mean "high-toned" or refer only to works of high art that are supposed to be good for us. Rather, culture is the complex totality of our daily lives and acts. Culture is the form and content of our selves in relation to our community, our country, our social and economic class, our entertainments, our politics and economics. Culture is the way we act out ideology.

Ideology is the way we agree to see ourselves, to behave, and to create the values of our lives. As I suggested, ideology and culture are intertwined. When I decide to act calmly or angrily in a difficult situation, my reaction is determined by ideological and cultural demands of appropriate behavior. In this case it is determined by my gender, which culture forms in the course of my upbringing. Men are "supposed" to react strongly, if not violently, while women "should" be more passive, without an aggressiveness that would be perfectly acceptable in male behavior. Much of our culture nominates as "nerdy" behavior that is intellectually driven and outside the norm. But "norms" are not created naturally. They are made by the ideological assent we give to—in this instance—what kind of behavior or personality type is considered "normal." Who determines the norm? We all do to the extent to which we assent to ideological and cultural "givens." If we suddenly, as a culture, agreed that intellectual work was as meaningful and "manly" as physical work—athletics, for example—the ideological engine might shift gears and "nerds" would become as heroic as jocks. The givens of ideology are actually created over the course of time and are changeable. For example, in older films, women were seen as needing to be saved by a heroic male, a reflection of the ideologies of the time. Today, we often see in film and cheer a strong female character. Contemporary horror films are a good example of the newly seen power of women over destructive forces, while contemporary action films often question male heroics, even while celebrating them.

Of course, when we speak of culture, it might be more accurate to think of cultures. Neither culture nor ideology is singular or monolithic. Let's move from film for a moment and take popular music as an example of how complex culture can be and how it can move in many directions. Hip-hop and rap emerged from African American popular culture in the seventies and eighties. Rap moved from the streets to the recording studios and into the wider population by the mid-1990s, and then separated into a number of strands. One strand, Gangsta Rap, became a way for male African American teenagers to express anger at middle-class white society. But its language of violence and misogyny also disturbed parts of African American culture and signified class and economic divisions within that culture. It brought down the wrath of some of the white establishment as well. Rap as a whole quickly transcended the music world into the larger cultural arena where art, industry, politics, and promotion are intertwined. It became sound, fashion, aggression, record sales, movie deals, police busts, highway noise, and big business. Attraction for many and irritant to some, rap became a phenomenon of the culture, a practice of one subculture (a term used to define one active part of the entire culture) and a representation of all of the culture.

The point is that culture is made up of expressions and intersections, representations, images, sounds, and stories, almost always influences of or even formed by gender, race, and economics. It is local and global, moving and changing, depending upon the needs of individual and groups. It can be as peaceful as family churchgoing or as violent as Serbian weekend warriors, who dress up like the movie character Rambo and set out to kill those they believe are their ancient enemies.

In *Film, Form, and Culture*, we will look closely at all the contexts of film (and television and new media): where it fits in the culture, what constitutes its popularity, and why popularity is sometimes used to condemn it.

Finally, a word about the films we will discuss. We will be thinking about and analyzing theatrical, narrative, fiction film—films that tell stories that are meant to be seen by relatively large numbers of people. While we will refer to documentary and to some avant-garde practice, our concern here is with the kinds of film that most people see most of the time. We will talk a lot about American film, because that is the dominant cinema around the world. But there are other very important and very wonderful cinemas and individual filmmakers outside Hollywood, many of whom make their films in response to Hollywood. We will talk about world cinema, the roles it plays, its individual filmmakers and their films.

But doing all this raises a problem. What particular films should we discuss? Within the context of a book, it is impossible to mention (not to say analyze) everyone's favorites, or to deal with films that everyone has seen or wants to see. Adding to the problem is the fact that there is not really an established canon in film studies as there is in literature. Of course, there are great films. Everyone agrees that *Citizen Kane* (Orson Welles, 1941) is among the most important films ever made, and we will discuss it here. (In the first reference to a film, I've followed the convention of giving the title, director's name, and date of release.) But every film scholar and film teacher, like every filmgoer, has his or her favorites. I am no exception. The choice of films I discuss and analyze is therefore often very subjective. I've tried to follow the principle of part for whole. Rather than drown you in titles, my hope is that the analyses of the films I do discuss can provide tools for thinking, talking, and writing about other films; and that each discussion of film, genre, or larger theoretic principle will serve as a template for work on other films, other genres, and other related interests.

One more word on the selection of films. Because film has a history, I have included many older films, even (especially) black and white films. Black and white was the norm—the reality!—before the late sixties. My hope is that you will want to see the films referred to and get a sense of how wonderful they were and still are.

No matter what the film, you will be asked to connect things and to refuse to believe that the experience of any one thing exists in isolation from any other experience. This book therefore invites you to look at the movies (and, by extension and example, television and the computer screen) as one item in the enormous palette of your own experience and the wider experiences of the culture we all belong to. It invites you to think of a film narrative as seriously as a literary narrative and to understand that the array of images and stories, beliefs and prejudices, love and rejection, peace and violence that we learn about in literature we can learn in very different ways from film. In effect, this book is about the end of film innocence; it is an invitation to discover a world in which nothing is simple, nothing is "just there," and nothing can be dismissed without, at least, your being conscious that dismissal has consequences.

We end each chapter with a box that correlates the CD-ROM contents to the various material discussed in the text. The CD is a companion to the text: it covers many films, but not every film that's in the text, and it occasionally goes beyond the text to demonstrate what can only be shown with moving images. The films excerpted in the CD complement, rather than duplicate, the examples used in the text.

For a complete table of contents for the CD-ROM, see p. 257.

1

IMAGE AND REALITY

Oliver Stone's violent, hallucinatory film *Natural Born Killers* (1994) contains a scene in which the homicidal Mickey is caught by the police in front of a drugstore. The media are present; television is capturing Mickey's capture. The police get Mickey on the ground and viciously beat him with their clubs. The camera assumes a position at some distance from the action, observing it. Before our eyes, Stone re-created, in a fictional space, the infamous videotape of the beating of Rodney King by the Los Angeles police that took place in 1991. In that event—which, at the time, became a major controversial issue in our society that continues to this day—Rodney King, an African American, was stopped by the police for a traffic violation and brutally beaten. The videotape of the beating, which was shown over and over again on television news, seen by millions of people, was an eloquent example of how a simple image can communicate a violent truth. Or so everybody thought.

When the police who took part in the King beating were first brought to trial,

A still from the videotape of Rodney King being beaten by the police.

their lawyers used the videotape as evidence against the prosecution. The defense lawyers turned themselves into a parody of film scholars, teaching the jury how they should read the images in a way that was favorable to the defense. They showed the

Oliver Stone's re-creation of the beating in his film, Natural Born Killers *(1994).*

tape in slow motion, backwards and forwards, frame by frame. They instructed the jury in the methods of close visual analysis, and they used their analysis to prove to the members of the jury that they weren't seeing what they thought they were seeing. What was really on the videotape, the defense said, was an offender violently resisting arrest. What the police were doing was actually part of an "escalation of force." The jury, perhaps predisposed against the victim in the first place, believed it.

THE "TRUTH" OF THE IMAGE

There is a curious cultural cliché that says pictures don't lie. It's part of the greater cliché that seeing is believing. Somehow a thing seen directly—or through a visual representation like a painting, a photograph, or a film—brings us closer to some actual reality. Words are too obviously not things themselves; words are made-up sounds, represented by made-up letters, put together in a contrived grammar that everyone in a culture uses to communicate through a decision that the particular words will refer to particular things. Language is clearly cultural and not natural: it is human made and accepted with some variations throughout a particular culture. Every English speaker understands what the word "food" refers to, even though the particular kind of food that comes to mind to each individual may vary. More abstract words, like "cool," may have a range of meanings that keep changing. But vision, sight, seems to bring us the thing itself—to "reality." Things that are *seen* appear to be and even feel as if they are unmediated; that is, they seem to be conveyed directly to us, not conveyed indirectly. Nothing stands in their way. They are true.

But, in fact, the image, photographed, painted, or digitized, is not the thing itself. It is a representation of a composed, lit, hand, lens, or computer-mediated transmission onto paper film or binary code of the thing itself. But even when we acknowledge the intervention of optics, chemistry, computer science, and the photographer in the recording and developing of the photographic image, we still haven't considered all the mediation that goes on. An image of the thing is not the thing. The subject of a photograph is not neutral: the subject—a person or a thing—is first chosen to be a subject, and then poses or is posed for the camera, assumes a camera-ready attitude often dictated by the culture (smiling, for example). Even a subject caught unawares by the camera has been changed by the very act of having been caught unawares. By the event of being captured on film, a subject unaware of the presence of a camera is frozen in photographic time and space, turned into an image, made into something he wasn't when the camera snapped his picture. The natural object—a landscape, for example—is marked by the fact of its being chosen, as well as by the time of day during which it is photographed, the way the photographer composes it for shooting, chooses an appropriate lens, and manipulates the quality of light, first with the camera and then in the darkroom or in an image manipulation program on a computer.

Here is a core issue for everything discussed in this book. People wish to perceive "the thing itself," but it is a wish impossible to come true. Whether in a photograph, in a movie, or on television; whether on the page, from someone's own mouth, or from a teacher and her textbook; what we hear, see, read, and know is mediated by other things. Recall the way the Rodney King video, a videographed record of "the thing itself," a man being beaten, was made to mean what various people, in various contexts, decided it should mean.

But the artificiality of the image is a hard concept to accept, because evidence seems to go against it. "Seeing is believing." The image looks too much like the thing. Unlike words, which interpret or mediate experience ("let me describe what happened," we say, and then give a verbal interpretation of what we've seen, sort of like summarizing the plot of a movie), images appear to be present and immediate: there, whole, and real. Of course we know they are not exactly the thing itself. A picture of a cat is no more a cat than the word "cat." It just looks more like it. Even "in reality" when we look at something out in the world, we aren't seeing the thing itself either but an image of it, in fact two images, focused upside down by the lens of each of our eyes onto their retina, righted and merged in the brain to create the sensation of an object in space. The point is that everything we do is mediated, and everything we see is some kind of representation. We *choose* how close to reality—which is itself something built upon complex, often unconscious, but always learned agreements we have made with our culture—an image might be. Often, having made the choice, we revel in it, because the image seems to be delivering the thing itself to our eyes.

Images entrance us because they provide a powerful illusion of owning reality. If we can photograph reality or paint or copy it, we have exercised an important kind of power. This power is clear in the linguistic tracings of "image": "imagination," "imaginary," and "imagining" are all related to "image" and indicate how the taking, making, or thinking of a picture is an integral part of understanding. Through the image we can approach, understand, and play with the material of the external world in ways that both humanize it and make it our own. At the same time, the image allows us to maintain a real connection with the external world, a solid, visual connection.

We love to look and see. It's part of our curiosity about the world and our desire to know. There's even an erotic component to our desire to see, which films depend on so much that critics have adopted a term for it: scopophilia, the love of looking. The term is slightly more benign than voyeurism, the act of looking at a person who is unaware of our look, but it is still erotically charged. We love to look and we especially love to look at the pictures of things, and often we do it to satisfy a variety of desires. We take and look at photographs, make videos, and create digital images; we do it as amateurs, often allowing the camera to be our intermediary amidst the chaos of real events, or we enjoy the work of professionals. Images are our memory, the basis of our stories, our artistic expression, our advertising, and our journalism. Images have become an integral part of popular music since MTV, and they are, of course, the core of movies.

We so believe in the presence and reality of images that we may take them at face value. They are, we often think, exactly what they are (or what someone tells us they are). Journalism and politics are infamous for doing this: picking out some aspect of an event, editorializing on a public figure by choosing a particularly unflattering pose, and then manipulating and describing it to present only one part, one perspective of the event itself. Television news, by concentrating endlessly on murder and violence, uses images of a small part of what is in the world, which, in their selection and repetition, may convince some that this is what most of the world is about.

We invest images with emotion and meaning; we may forget that they are *images*—mediations—and create a kind of short circuit: if the image of a thing is close enough to the thing itself, perhaps we may be in some danger of neglecting the thing itself—those events actually going on in the world—and merely believe the image. The emotions we attach to an image can be simply set in motion by the images themselves, and we can ignore the origin as well the formal properties—the **composition,** what was chosen to be in the shot, the placement of the image in relation to others objects, the lighting, the angle—all the imaginative things that went into the making of the image itself. We can cut ourselves off from the events that made the image possible—the material of the external world—and make that short circuit, accepting the cliché that pictures never lie. If pictures never lie and are worth a thousand words, they must be dependable, true, and, if not the thing itself, at least a suitable substitute.

This is what Oliver Stone was thinking about when he imitates the Rodney King videotape in *Natural Born Killers*. The videotape contained an image of an event, taken without the knowledge of those who were participating in it, which is the closest thing image making can get to objective recording (an argument used by documentary filmmakers, who try to maintain the illusion that their images are closer to objective reality than those made by fiction filmmakers). But, as Stone shows, such footage is not "objective"; it exists because of the economics of video recording, the relative cheapness and ubiquity of amateur equipment; the willingness of an onlooker with a camera to turn it on as the beating was in progress, rather than do something to stop the beating; the willingness of television news programs to show over and over again any kind of novel, violent imagery they can find. The footage exists because of the desire of people to watch it. He re-creates the image, this time with all the expensive, professional apparatus available to Hollywood filmmaking, and turns it into an ironic commentary. Just like the original footage, where we feel sympathy for the victim of a vicious beating, we here feel sympathy for the trapped and beaten Mickey. But, in the fiction of *Natural Born Killers*, Mickey is a vicious, psychotic killer who needs capturing. He is, at the same time, something of a sympathetic figure. The reference to the "actual" Rodney King footage serves, therefore, to complicate our response and to make us wonder about how objective images can actually be. In many ways, Stone is expanding his experiment in *JFK* (1991), a film that is not only about a presidential assassination but also about how images and the history they try to create can be read in multiple ways.

What about the "objectivity" of the image itself? Anyone who took to heart the cliché "seeing is believing" saw, in the King video, a man being beaten by the police, in the fuzzy gray wash of an underexposed, amateur videotape taken at night. The trial lawyers, however, who analyzed the image from their own perspective in their desire to debunk the evidence in order to free their clients, proved to a jury—willing to believe them—that they didn't quite see a man being beaten but an aggressive person the police were trying to restrain. The evidence held in those images was a matter of political and racial conviction, not of any self-evident "truth." In Oliver Stone's re-creation, the police are brutally restraining a brutal, aggressive person, an unthinking, amoral killer. The image is a complete fabrication, done in the studio or in a carefully controlled location. Most likely the actor, Woody Harrelson, isn't even in the shot, replaced by a stunt man. There is, in a sense, nothing there, only a studio or location fabrication of an image within a narrative fiction, fully exaggerated as representatives from television news (including Japanese television, with an excited commentator whose remarks are translated through subtitles) look on, make their images, make comments, while the sound track is filled with the music of Carl Orff's *Carmina Burana*. The re-creation is, as I said, twisted with irony, begging us to provide a more complex reaction than we might have given to the original videotape or the trial lawyers' interpretation of it.

Stone has asked us to think about the construction of images, something that few films attempt to do because their value is built upon our desire not to ask what images are made of and what they might really mean. We love to look; movies love to show us things. Maybe we don't want to know what we're looking at and want to simply enjoy the illusion. In the case of *Natural Born Killers* Stone's ironies were lost on many people, who found the film too violent. Unwilling to decipher the complex visual structure of the film and understand what that structure was trying to say—that images of violence are manufactured to play upon our desire to see and enjoy violence at a safe distance—they took the images too literally and were repelled. They believed what they saw.

All of which leads us to the central question of this chapter: When we look at an image, and especially when we look at the images that make up a movie, what do we see? What's there, what do we think is there, and what do we want to be there? We can begin an answer by turning very briefly to the development of painting and photography, because film is so much an extension of the latter and borrows many effects from the former.

THE URGE TO REPRESENT "REALITY"

People painted before they wrote. Painting is among the earliest artifacts we have of prehistoric civilizations: a hand, a deer, images of the human figure and the naturalized world, things caught and seen and then, in the case of the deer, eaten. There's elemental magic in these early images, the kind of magic that says if you own a part of or representation of a thing, you have power over that thing. In this case, the "thing" is nature itself. These early cave paintings show that humans wanted imaginative control over the natural world and wanted to make permanent representations of it. The painted image came, in different ways in different cultures, to express not merely seeing but an interpretation, and a desire to own what is seen. Painting, along with story telling, grew from the same urge to interpret and control the world—to give a human and humanized shape. "Primitive" or "naive" art is simple and direct. Painting moved from the primitive in interesting ways.

Perspective and the Pleasures of Tricking the Eye

"Primitive" or "naive" art is never simple and direct, but seems that way because of the major changes that occurred as painting moved from a desire to capture the world through simple images to a scientific and technology-driven desire to remanufacture the world for the viewer's pleasure. We must understand that, no matter what a painting represents (or, in the case of abstract painting, doesn't represent), it is an interpretation of something seen that has been executed by the artist's hand. A painting is pigment on canvas articulated through a combination of color, shape, volume, and spatial organization. The way space is organized and the subject represented in a painting is very specific to a given culture and time, though it also bears traces of a particular artist's style and personality. Perspective, for example—the illusion of depth on a two-dimensional surface—is hardly a universal way of organizing space on canvas and did not always exist. Asian painting has never used it. Western painting didn't use it until the early fifteenth century. It was developed by the Florentine architect Filippo Brunelleschi (1377–1446) and the painter Masaccio (1401–1428). Perspective is based on mathematical principles of linear convergence, the way lines can be drawn so they appear to vanish at a single point in space.

People have theorized that perspective was invented for ideological and cultural reasons, because it allowed the wealthy patrons who sponsored artists to be given a privileged place in viewing the canvas. That is, perspective allowed the viewer a sense of ownership, a sense of standing before a space that was made for his gaze. He stood outside the painting, occupying a position that seemed to be at the convergence of an imaginary set of lines that opened into the canvas and then appeared to converge again behind the canvas. These "vanishing lines" created the illusion that the space of the painting completed the patron's gaze—indeed any viewer's gaze. The double convergence creates an important effect, for if sight lines converge toward the back of the image on the canvas, they also converge in the imaginary space in front of the canvas, a space that is filled by the controlling look of the spectator. This phenomenon would have tremendous repercussions in the development of film in the twentieth century.

By the neoclassical period (from the late seventeenth to the mid-eighteenth centuries in most of Europe) the ideological thrust of painting was to be as

Perspective was a mathematical invention that allowed a vanishing line to be created on a canvas and thus presented the illusion of depth on a two-dimensional surface. Photography and film adopted the principle. Photographers and cinematographers set up their cameras to show the vanishing line, and we can see it at work here, in one of the earliest films we have, the Lumière brothers' 1895 film of a train arriving at a station.

"true" to the natural world as possible. Interpretation and inspiration were, in theory at least, subordinated to imitation and to the capturing of the image, to reproducing it, proclaiming that nature could be taken and owned whole by the imagination. Many artists approached the imitation of nature through technology. The camera obscura came to prominence in the seventeenth century: a box with a pinhole through which light could pass, it projected an upside-down image on its opposite side. A painter would enter the box and trace the image of the outside world that was reflected through the pinhole. Another version of this contraption, called a "Claude Glass," after the admired French landscape painter Claude Lorrain (1600–1682), was also put to use by painters. It had a convex black mirror that concentrated an image of the landscape that could be painted over or copied. The Dutch painter Jan Vermeer (1632–1675) actually reproduced in his paintings the lighting effects that were created by the camera obscura.

Photography and Reality

The camera obscura was a sort of prephotographic device, designed to make possible the urge to capture the real world with as little apparent mediation as possible. Photography was invented in the nineteenth century out of experiments that, like those involving perspective, were both scientific and aesthetic. At its most basic, photography is a chemical process, during which a light-sensitive material is altered when exposed to light. When this altered material is chemically treated, the exposed particles wash away, creating transparent or translucent spaces where the light fell. The negative image (light for dark) is reversed during printing. The chemistry hasn't changed very much since the middle of the nineteenth century, though the optics have, and faster, more light-sensitive film stock was developed that made nighttime shooting possible. Within the past few years digital imaging has begun to render chemical processing obsolete. The aesthetics and ideology of photographic mediation are a different matter. Photography became a major factor in the ways we observed and perceived the world around us.

The great French film theorist André Bazin speaks about the inevitability of photography. What he means is that art has always been motivated to capture and maintain the reality of the world, to hold its images eternally. Photography is the climax of that desire because, Bazin believes, it is the first art in which, at the exact instant during which the image is transferred to film, the human hand is not involved. For Bazin, the taking of a photograph is a pure, objective act. He puns in French on the word *objectif*, which means both "objective" and "lens." Bazin was deeply committed to the concept of film and photography as the arts of the real, but he was also aware that the reality of film and photography was "artificial," made by art. He was intrigued by the paradox. He was well aware that in the seemingly automatic passing of a thing to its image, some human intervention always occurs. So, of course, even though the image passes through the lens to the film in the camera without the intervention of the human hand, that intervention has already occurred: in the crafting of the lens and the chemical manufacture of the light-sensitive film emulsion, by the photographer who chooses a particular lens and a particular film for a particular shot, in the way the photographer lights and composes the shot. Every photographer is a composer: think of the basic, practically universal gesture of an amateur picture taker, waving her arm to signal people in front of the lens to move closer together, to get in the frame. Think of the ramifications if this photographer purposively moved the camera slightly to the right to remove one member of the party from the frame. The professional photographer and the photographer as artist make more elaborate preparations for a shot and, after the shot is composed and taken, manipulate the image in the darkroom or on the computer screen. They reframe and crop, alter the exposure so the image is darker or lighter. They play with color. They make the image their own.

When photography came along in the nineteenth century, painting was put in crisis. The photograph, it seemed, did the work of imitating nature better than the painter ever could. Some painters made pragmatic use of the invention. There were Impressionist painters who used a photograph in place of the model or landscape they were painting. But, by and large, the photograph was a challenge to painting and was one cause of painting's move away from representation and reproduction of a direct kind to the abstract painting of the twentieth century. Since photographs did such a good job representing things as they existed in the world, painters were freed to look inward and represent things as they were in their imagination, rendering emotion in the color, volume, line, and spatial configurations native to the painter's art.

Photography was not wholly responsible for the development of abstract painting. Its development fit well with other movements both in the world and in the art of the late nineteenth and early twentieth century, movements that began to call attention to form and away from an apparently simple representation of "reality." The very inventions of the age—photography, movies, railroads, the telephone—along with the coming apart of old political alliances and traditional class and family connections pushed artists to embrace new forms that would speak to the changes in old concepts of space, time, and political allegiances. The important point here is that photography introduced to modern culture another form of image making, of visual representation, one apparently more "real" than painting because it seemed to capture an image of the world out there and bring it—framed, composed, and contained—before our eyes.

It's worth repeating again that the principle of representation (and mediation) is that an image is not the thing itself but a thing in itself with its own formal properties and methods of interpreting something else. This sounds perfectly obvious until we recall the phenomenon of short circuiting we discussed earlier. We tend to look at a representational painting or a photograph as something that uniquely represents another original object and that acts as a trigger mechanism for an appropriate emotional response. The surrealist painter René Magritte made a famous picture, *La Trahison des images (The Betrayal of Images)*. It's a very "realistic" picture of a pipe, the smoking kind. Magritte paints a title directly onto the canvas: "*Ceci n'est pas une pipe*" ("This is not a pipe"). Within his own painting, he creates a concise lesson about representation. The image is not the thing. But it remains a hard lesson, harder still when it comes to photography.

When we look at the family photo album, we don't ask how the images were constructed and what the construction is saying about the subject of the photograph. We don't wonder why the photographer chose to be outside the frame, behind the camera; we may not question why one aunt is not smiling, or why some relatives have been cut out of the composition, or why father is way in the back, barely visible. We desire to see and feel something through the image. So we look at the images and feel nostalgia or joy or pain about the family represented in the photographs.

However, when the transparency of the image is closed off, when the photograph is of something unrecognizable, or the painting is abstract, or an avant-garde film denies recognizable plot, our first question is, "What is this about?" We want our images to be transparent, to seem to relate some kind of story that we understand, to allow us to look through them to the meanings they seem to convey. They exist to transmit the real world and to trigger emotional response.

Manipulation of the Image

During its relatively brief existence, photography has taken on many culturally and economically determined forms. In the very early days, in order to overcome a perceived inferiority to painting, photographers adopted a painterly style. Some of them hand-colored their work, after composing a figure or land-scape in poses or compositions similar to those used by the Impressionist painters. As photography found its independent path, many other styles emerged, all of them depending upon some kind of manipulation of the image during the picture-making process. These included the creation of "abstract" photographs, images that reveal only patterns, shapes, and volume. This style flourished in the twenties at the same time that Dadaist and Surrealist artists in-corporated the photographic image into their work. During this period, the photographer Man Ray created abstract patterns by putting actual objects di-rectly onto photographic paper and exposing them to light. The resulting "pho-tograms" parody Bazin's notion of the objective lens. Here there is no lens and the "real" is turned into the abstract.

When, again in the1920s, photography became more common in journalism and advertising, manipulation of the image became extreme. Removed from the status of art—with all its implications of personal style, subjective vision, and revelation—the photograph became a tool for representing specific commercial and political points of view with the purpose of selling commodities and focus-ing opinions. Shifting from one cultural realm of style and ideological determi-nation in which individual expression counted strongly, photography became part of another, a corporate style in which the image of a politician making a speech, or a group of strikers in a menacing posture, or a woman assuming a conventional pose of seduction while wearing a particular brand of makeup or clothing has specific designs on the viewer and asks for specific responses, to make a political point or show a hamburger in the best light—even if the hamburger is painted, sprayed, lit, and in general "styled" to make it look the best it can.

Images like these are obviously determined by external, cultural, economic, and political needs. But the image in the cause of economics and politics is dif-ferent from the image in the cause of art only in its purpose. All images, all sto-ries, all creations made by people have designs, in all senses of the term. The particular designs of journalism and advertising photography are narrow and focused, wanting the viewer to respond with a political action, hatred for a dic-tator, putting money into circulation by purchasing a product, in a word, by buying into something—an attitude, idea, or ideology. This kind of photogra-phy does not primarily imitate, reveal, or show. Rather, it exhorts, cajoles, and manipulates. It exploits fully the one abiding reality of representation and me-diation: a call for some kind of response from the viewer. Something does in-deed come between the thing itself and the image. In the case of the work of art, that "something" is a form and structure that ask of us an emotional and intel-lectual response meant to help us understand the artist and the way she under-stands the world. In the case of the journalistic, advertising, or political image, that something is a form and structure that ask us to agree to the general values of our culture and the various commodities it creates, to form an opinion, to spend money or cast a vote. In the case of movies, form and structure ask us to respond to many of these same requests simultaneously.

Reality as Image

The argument of this book is that reality is always a mutually agreed upon social construct, a more or less common consensus about what is out there and what it all means to most people. Our shared ideas of truth, beauty, morality, sexuality, politics, and religion; the ways we interpret the world and make decisions on how we act in it are determined by a complex process of education, assimilation, acculturation, and assent that begins at birth. It is a cliché that human beings are out of touch with nature, and that more than a few of us are out of touch with reality. The fact is, even when we are in touch, it's not with some given natural world or some objective, existing reality. Being in touch with nature means acting upon a learned response to the natural world. In fact, responding with awe in the face of natural beauty dates back only to the eighteenth century and became a major cultural event only in the nineteenth. Before the late seventeenth century, people in Western Europe did not pay much attention to nature's grandeur; they were not moved by it nor did they care much to contemplate it. A mountain range was something in the way. A complex shift in sociological and aesthetic responses occurred in the early eighteenth century and can be traced in its development through travel literature and then in poetry, fiction, and philosophy. By the mid-eighteenth century, wild, mountainous landscapes became the site of grand, overwhelming emotional response. The mountains had not, themselves, changed; cultural response had. The "Sublime," the effect of being transported before nature's wildness and in front of representations of that wildness in painting and poetry, was born. With it came nineteenth-century romanticism and attitudes toward the natural world that remain with us still.

Reality is not an objective, geophysical phenomenon like a mountain. Reality is always something said or understood about the world. The physical world is "there," but reality is always a polymorphous, shifting complex of mediations, a kind of multifaceted lens, constructed by the changing attitudes and desires of a culture. Reality is a complex image of the world that many of us choose to agree to. The photographic and cinematic image is one of the ways we use this "lens" (here in a quite literal sense) to interpret the complexities of the world.

Reality becomes a kind of cultural baseline upon which we can build a variety of responses. One response is a feeling of security. We feel safe in front of something that strikes us as "real" or realistic. Another response is to dismiss someone who doesn't seem to be operating from this same base. We bless something (a film, a painting, a novel, a political program, a way of life) with the name of realism if it comforts us with something we desire or are familiar with, or have been told we should desire or be familiar with. We ask or are asked to face reality when we or someone else acts in unfamiliar ways. We say "that's not realistic" to dismiss someone or something that does not fit into our range of beliefs, hopes, or desires. "Get real," we say. "Get a life."

So, when the critic André Bazin said that the history of art is equal to the history of people's desire to save an image of the real world, he quickly modified this idea by saying that the desire to capture reality is in fact the desire "to give significant expression to the world." In that phrase "significant expression" lies the key. It's not the world we see in the image but its significant, mediated expression. For Bazin, such expression becomes very significant in photography and film because of the apparent lack of interference from a human agent. This is a peculiar paradox. The image is a significant expression of the real world; it almost is the real world because its image is formed without human interference. Recall Bazin's theory that, at the instant of transferring the image to the film, the photograph occurs without human intervention. As we have seen, this theory has a kernel of truth, but is deeply compromised by all the manipulation that goes on before and after the image is actually made (and even while the image is being made, because lenses are not neutral). Out of the paradox come many of our confusions over what the photographic and cinematic image actually is and actually does.

FROM THE PHOTOGRAPHIC TO THE CINEMATIC IMAGE

The alleged reality of the cinematic image is, in reality, a mechanical event. In a sense, film itself is a reality machine. Time and space—the coordinates of Western art, story, and life—are represented by the vertical strip of images that travels through the projector. Twenty-four photographs, or frames, go past the projector lens each second. A simple, very nineteenth century mechanical process pulls the filmstrip down, one frame at a time, while a shutter in the shape of a Maltese cross opens and closes the lens so that each frame is projected on the screen in its turn. The resulting illusion is extraordinary. Because

Before the moving picture, photographers began analyzing motion into its component parts through multiple exposure. One of the most important of these experimenters was Etienne-Jules Marey (1890).

of the operation of the shutter, the screen is actually dark for a total of almost thirty minutes during an average two-hour film. And because of a cognitive desire to attach the events of one image to the next, and thanks to perceptual optics that cause our eyes to see images fused together above a certain rate of flicker, the series of stills projected on the screen is interpreted by our brains as a continuous flow. Space and time appear unified and ongoing. Even on video or DVD (digital video disc) the images scan in sequence across the screen. Analogue mechanics have become transformed into digital electronics and will soon replace the filmstrip. But the result is still the illusion of a unified and ongoing space, not the thing itself, but its analogue representation. Remember the character in *The Matrix* (Andy Wachowski, Larry Wachowski, 1999) who could actually read the digital stream that made up the simulated world? He—in the fiction of that particular film—was getting close to "reality."

Moving Images

The search for "reality" in photographic images moved with some speed in the nineteenth century when it joined with the invention (or, more appropriately, the inventions) of cinema. Before the very late nineteenth century, the moving image and the photograph developed along separate lines. Projections of painted images, sometimes called magic lanterns, had been around since the seventeenth century. Various devices that created an illusion of figures in motion, or the sense of moving images in a large space surrounding the viewer—devices with wonderful names like zoetropes, phenakistoscopes, thaumatropes, cycloramas, and panoramic views—had been around since the eighteenth century and reached their apogee in the nineteenth. These were mostly toys or

Reading through the code to see the simulated digital world. The Matrix *by Andy Wachowski, Larry Wachowski (1999).*

sideshows that, in various ways, placed painted images in progressively different positions of movement on the inside of a revolving drum. By peering through slits in the side of the turning drum, or—in the case of cycloramas—standing in front of an unrolling canvas, the figures or painted landscapes seemed to elide into each other in a semblance of continuous motion.

Magic lanterns, zoetropes, and photography intersected in the late nineteenth century in a quasi-scientific way through the work of two photographers, Eadweard Muybridge and Etienne-Jules Marey. Muybridge was born in England and did much of his work in America. Marey was French. In their work, the nineteenth-century curiosity about mechanical invention, industry, and the ways in which both could overcome the limitations of time and space met and pointed to the development of movies—a time and space machine that rivaled the locomotive and the telegraph.

Muybridge and Marey photographed human and animal movements in ways that analyzed the motion into its component parts. Marey actually used a gunlike photographic mechanism to "shoot" his photographs (and the terms "shooting a picture" and a "shot" originate from that machine). With its aura of scientific investigation, their work situates one branch of photography in that tradition of Western culture that seeks to analyze and quantify nature. It very roughly duplicates the discovery and implementation of perspective in painting during the fourteenth century, which together form a part of the larger movement to comprehend, own, and control the natural world, to become the visual owner of the image, even enter it imaginatively. With the advent of film, science and technology and imagination merged to make the reality machine.

Leland Stanford, a former governor of California who liked both horses and science, invited Eadweard Muybridge to help him settle a wager concerning whether at one point in a horse's gallop all four hoofs leave the ground. Muybridge proved it by taking a series of photographs at high speeds. Muybridge and Stanford went on to publish photographs of animals in motion in *Scientific American*, and Muybridge parlayed this into a career of public lectures in which he demonstrated his analytic series of shots of animals—as well as naked people—in motion. He published a version of his work in 1887, the eleven-volume *Animal Locomotion*. (Marey had published his animal locomotion studies, called *La machine animale*, in France in 1873.) Muybridge further combined his analytic photographs with the old kinetoscope-zoetrope toy to create an illusion of movement of his animals and people and, by 1881, was projecting them on a wall to a large audience. Scientific investigation, commerce, and spectacle merged in the projected image.

The image was becoming a commodity. The rapidity of this event was accelerated during the last decade of the nineteenth century when Thomas Alva Edison's employee, William Dickson, developed a way to record moving images on a Kinetograph and show them on a Kinetoscope. Edison had wanted to make moving images as an accompaniment for his phonograph, but decided to concentrate on the image alone, thereby holding back the development of sound film for almost thirty years. The work of Edison's company in the late nineteenth century led to a slow but steady proliferation of moving images in peep shows, in which "flip cards" or a film loop was viewed through a viewer in a machine; in nickelodeons, where working-class people paid a nickel to go into a small room and see a short film projected on a sheet; and finally by the 1920s in the movie palaces built as part of the successful attempt of moviemakers to create a "respectable" middle-class audience for their images. By the late twenties, in an economic slump, the movie studios revived Edison's original notion of synchronizing image to sound and made "talking pictures" to the delight of audiences and a resulting rise in box office receipts.

The steady progression from the individual photographers, inventors, and entrepreneurs who developed the moving image to the film studios, which were actually large-scale factory operations that mass-produced these images, may seem, at first, a big leap, but it took less than twenty-five years.

The immediate and almost instantaneous emergence around the world of movies as a popular commercial art was just slightly in advance of the great boom of popular culture that would take place in the twenties. Film's invention came with the great nineteenth-century technologies that included telegraphy and the railroads. Its beginnings coincided with the growing influence of newspapers. It completed its growth as a mass medium in the twenties, at the same time as radio, and shared its popularity. In the end, film infiltrated the imagination more than any other nineteenth century invention because it told stories with images. It also made its story tellers rich.

The popularity of movies was so great that, shortly after the turn of the century, demand for films soon exceeded supply. Various theater owner-entrepreneurs on the East Coast—most of them first generation immigrants from Eastern Europe who had engaged in wholesale and retail selling before entering the business of film exhibition—decided that the best way to supply their theaters with product was to manufacture it themselves. They would make the images they needed to sell. They fought with Edison, who attempted to control the patents on his motion picture machines and who sometimes employed thugs to beat up the filmmakers and take their equipment away (constituting what film historians call the "patent wars" of 1910 to 1913). The filmmakers went to California to escape Edison's reach, settled in Los Angeles, and rather quickly established their own tightly knit companies that, by the late teens, evolved into the studios that centralized all facets of motion picture production and exist, if only in name, to this day.

In the history of film, the first quarter of the twentieth century was a particularly active period of creativity on all levels: the development of film's visual narrative structure; the creation, the buying, and the selling of studios and human talent; the invention of the star system; the integration of the entire production and distribution of images through theaters owned by the studios, which guaranteed that the studios had an automatic outlet for their products. This is—in very compressed form that we will open up in the next chapter—the history of production that moved from an individual, director-based activity into a huge industrial operation, headed by an executive who delegated individual films to producers and peopled by an enormous in-house staff of writers, directors, composers, designers, electricians, actors, and other craftspeople.

The speed of the process by which moviemaking developed into commerce was driven by the willingness of audiences to look and look and look and want to see more and more. Movies supplied a visual imagination and narrative flow for the culture at large. They extended basic stories of popular culture—stories of sexuality and romance, captivity and release, family and heroism, individualism and community—into visual worlds that were immediately comprehensible, almost tactile, *there*, in front of the viewers' eyes. In the movies, time and space appeared as if intact. Human figures moved and had emotions. Life seemed to be occurring. The moving image was a vibrant, story-generating, meaning-generating thing. More than literature, painting, or the photograph, moving images eloquently expressed what many, almost most, of the people across economic and social classes wanted to hear and see. The fact that what they were hearing and seeing was an illusion in every respect seemed not to matter. It might, in fact, have contributed to film's popularity. Seeing and feeling in the secure knowledge that no obvious consequences are involved is an important aspect of our response to any aesthetic experience. The moving image was a particular attraction to everyone who wanted to see more, feel more, and do it in the safe embrace of an irresistible story. It still is.

In the following chapters, we will analyze the endurance of the desire to see and what it's made up of. We will examine the elements of image, motion, story, creator, and creation, and the culture they and we inhabit. We will examine how and why moving images work and speculate about why we respond to them. In the course of that examination, we will try to account for a great number of kinds of films and filmmakers, and film viewers, too.

Film, Form, and Culture: The CD-ROM
The Introduction to the CD-ROM draws attention to the artificiality of the image and the ways in which we perceive as "real" the image, which is mostly made up in front of, inside of, or after the film is taken out of the camera.

NOTES AND REFERENCES

Image and Reality   Basic resources for information on the way we perceive image and reality are Rudolf Arnheim, *Art and Visual Perception* (Berkeley and Los Angeles: University of California Press, 1974) and E. H. Gombrich, *Art and Illusion* (Princeton: Princeton University Press, 1969).

Representation   In the 1970s and 1980s painters called photorealists took Polaroids of their subjects—a human face, a city street, a diner, a motorcycle. They placed a grid over the photograph and a corresponding grid over the canvas and then copied the photograph, square by corresponding square, onto the canvas. When you look at a photographic reproduction of a photorealist painting, you often can't tell that it's a painting.

Perspective and the Pleasures of Tricking the Eye   Professor Sharon Gerstel of the University of Maryland supplied information about the history of perspective. Erwin Panofsky's *Perspective as Symbolic Form,* trans. Christopher S. Wood (New York: Zone Books, 1991), is a good source for the theory of perspective. Professor Elizabeth Loizeaux of the University of Maryland offered ideas about the camera obscura. Michel Foucault's essay "Las Meninas" argues the theory of perspective as a means of owning the space of a painting. It is in *The Order of Things* (New York: Random House, 1970), pp.3–16.

Photograph and Reality   The references to and quotations from André Bazin are from *What Is Cinema?* vol. I, trans. Hugh Gray (Los Angeles and Berkeley: University of California Press, 1968), p.12. This is an invaluable book for understanding the theories of reality and the moving image. See also Bill Nichols, *Ideology and the Image* (Bloomington: Indiana University Press, 1981). For an emotional and theoretical discussion of photography, see Roland Barthes, *Camera Lucida : Reflections on Photography,* trans. Richard Howard (New York: Hill and Wang, 1981). A classic work on the Sublime in literature is M. S. Abrams, *The Mirror and the Lamp: Romantic Theory and the Critical Tradition* (New York: Norton, 1958).

Moving Images   Anne Friedberg, *Window Shopping: Cinema and the Postmodern* (Los Angeles and Berkeley: University of California Press, 1993), offers a good reading of nineteenth-century technology and the development of mass media.

The Intersection of Photography, Film, and Economic Processes   Material on early movie machines, Marey, Muybridge, and Edison can be found in Charles Musser, *The Emergence of Cinema: The American Screen to 1907* (New York: Charles Scribner's Sons, 1990), pp.15–132. For Etienne-Jules Marey, see Marta Braun, *Picturing Time: The Work of Etienne-Jules Marey (1830–1904)* (Chicago: University of Chicago Press, 1992). David A. Cook's *A History of Narrative Film* (New York: W. W. Norton & Company, 1996) and Kristin Thompson and David Bordwell's *Film History: An Introduction* (New York: McGraw-Hill, 1994) are excellent sources for information about the development of film as art and industry. See also Scott Bukatman, "Gibson's Typewriter," in *Flame Wars: The Discourse of Cyberculture,* ed. Mark Dery (Durham: North Carolina University Press, 1984), pp.73–74.

The Economics of Realism   Thomas Elsaesser's collection of essays, *Early Cinema: Space, Frame, Narrative* (London: British Film Institute, 1990), is a good source of information on the formation of the film industry. See especially pp.153–59.

2

FORMAL STRUCTURES: HOW FILMS TELL THEIR STORIES

THE IMAGE, THE WORLD, AND THE BEGINNING OF THE STUDIOS

The evolution of the photographic image into the moving narrative image is itself a narrative of the making and comprehension of illusions. It is a narrative that runs almost as smoothly as a good Hollywood film. And it is a narrative that is tightly linked to the economic history of filmmaking. Almost since the beginning, filmmaking and money making went hand in hand, one determining the other. Filmmakers, from very early on, understood on an intuitive level that images were profoundly manipulable. Even more, these filmmakers knew that by manipulating the image, the image in turn would manipulate how and what people saw and the way they responded to what they saw. This would in turn create the desire to see more images—to *pay* to see more. As sophisticated as the Renaissance painters, who plotted the sight lines in their paintings to create the illusion of depth and presence, filmmakers could plot all aspects of the image for very similar purposes. Sight lines, plot lines, character, spectator positioning—how an ideal viewer is literally created by the images and the narrative going on in the screen—are all planned to reduce the sense of distance between spectator and image and optimize an illusion of participation.

From Image to Narrative

Let us take a moment and stay with the early development of the moving image and its stories in order to more easily understand the structuring of illusions and the formation of conventions—those structures of form and content that, once invented, are used over and over again. This chapter will start with an examination of how image and narrative structure were formed and then move into a discussion of how that form and its variations were perpetuated throughout the history of film. We need to understand the formation of image and story and then go on to its meanings.

Moving-picture projection was developed almost at the same time in the United States, France, England, Germany, as well as other countries around the world. In 1888, Eadweard Muybridge,

The Lumière brothers filmed things happening in the world and also made things happen for the benefit of their cameras. From its earliest moments, film was attracted to slapstick comedy, based on physical interaction of people and objects. Louis Lumière, Watering the Gardener *(1895).*

the photographer, visited Thomas Alva Edison, the inventor. Muybridge urged Edison to combine Muybridge's image projector, the zoopraxiscope, with Edison's phonograph. In 1889, Edison met Etienne-Jules Marey, who had developed a moving-image filmstrip, in Paris. In 1891, Thomas Edison's assistant, W. K. L. Dickson, demonstrated a viewing machine in which could be seen a smoothly moving image of a man—Dickson himself. In France, in 1895, Auguste and Louis Lumière projected a short film they had made of workers leaving their factory. The French magician, Georges Méliés, who had watched the films of the Lumière brothers, projected his first film in 1896.

The Edison Company's early attempts at filmmaking were of single, staged events: a coworker sneezing, a couple kissing—the erotic image emerging in cinema at its very start. The Lumière brothers shot events going on in the world: their workers leaving their factory, a train arriving at a station. But they soon began staging incidents: a child squirting a gardener with a water hose, brother Auguste feeding his baby. The magician, Méliés, on the other hand, worked largely inside his studio, mocking up images, creating trick shots on film. He showed people disappearing in the middle of a scene, people underwater, men traveling to the moon. Before distributing the finished film, Méliés had his factory workers hand-paint each frame, creating an illusion of color.

This greatly reduced history may give a faulty impression. While we know the history of Edison's work, as well as what was happening in France and in other countries where similar inventions were occurring at the end of the nineteenth century, it grows increasingly difficult to develop a coherent history of film's very rapid early development after this point. It is especially hard to say who was the "first" to do anything for the simple reason that approximately three-quarters of all films made during the **silent era** (roughly 1895–1927) are lost. But the Lumière brothers, Méliés, and the Edison factory do provide us with models for certain lines of development in film, lines by no means straight or uncomplicated. What they developed leads to a notion—a theory, actually—that three

Film and the erotic are linked in some of the earliest images we have. Thomas Edison, The Kiss *(1896)*

fundamental conventions of filmmaking emerged from their work. From the Edison factory came both the Hollywood studio system, with its division of labor, and the Hollywood narrative style, based on character and action. The Lumières pointed the direction to the **documentary,** to film's power to record events that would occur anyway, even if the camera were not present (we will talk in some detail about documentary filmmaking in Chapter 5). From Georges Méliés' magic trick films came the cinema of fantasy, of science fiction and the wondrous voyage, which would, of course, become an important part of Hollywood filmmaking.

Another French filmmaker, Jean-Luc Godard, who, throughout his career as critic and director from the 1950s to the present, has been interrogating the nature of the film and television image, came to a different conclusion. He suggested (through a character in his 1967 film, *La Chinoise*) that the Lumière brothers, those presumed documentarians and makers of *actualitès*—events filmed as they were happening, events that *would* be happening even if the camera weren't there—did not in fact give us documentaries of late nineteenth-century Parisian life. From the prospect of a century, Godard suggested that what the Lumières really made constitutes our fantasy images of what Paris looked like in the late nineteenth century. Their images constitute the imaginary—the shared image fantasy—of the way things were, through the images of film. Méliés, Godard suggests, seems to be the documentarian of the fantasies of late nineteenth-century, middle-class France.

This is a neat turning of things on their heads. More than an intellectual puzzle, Godard's proposition gets to the root of the question of the image. Just because the Lumière brothers turned their cameras on events in the street does not make them recorders of things as they were. Indeed, we know that they set up many of their shots in advance. They composed their images carefully, often employing the fundamentals of perspective invented during the Renaissance. Because Méliès made trick shots in his studio does not make him a mere fantasist. Each was involved in different kinds of early cinematic mediation, of putting on the screen images that were not about reality but about different ways of constructing reality cinematically, different ways of seeing and interpreting the world. The same is true of the work of the Edison factory. Edison made moving images that moved people's imaginations, all the while working toward the commercial exploitation of his inventions. His work prefigures the Hollywood process in which commodities that demonstrate the imagination's ability to fashion images that are eloquent and moving can be manufactured for profit.

Ultimately, cinema did not evolve simply into two or three separate paths, but into various branches, growing out of basic impulses, almost never pure, to see, manipulate, and represent the world in images. "Documentary" and "fiction" intertwine in curious ways. Film sees the world from a variety of perspectives, which often intersect. Whatever the origin of the moving image—whether it is a recording of what is already there in the world or made up in the studio—imagination, culture, ideology, and economics intervene. They mediate and form what we finally see on the screen; we, as viewers, mediate in turn, interpreting the images to make them meaningful to us.

THE ECONOMICS OF THE IMAGE

As cinema developed, the impulses of the Lumières, Méliès, and Edison were joined in intriguing ways. From the Edison factory came the economic impulse, the urge to treat the image as commodity, to own it, rent it, sell it, profit from it. From the Lumière brothers came the urge to reveal, to present an image of what appears to be the world as it is, but always turns out to be the world as it is seen in a particular way on film and the other visual arts. They also sold and profited from their images. From Méliès came a sense of the image as the space of fantasy; he also developed a concept and methods of image fabrication that finally came to form the basis of American film production, part of its economy of manufacture. Méliès also sold his images and profited from them.

The work of Méliès was about control, crafting every element of the image, putting it together, element by element, for specific effect. Whereas Auguste and Louis Lumière allowed a certain serendipity to occur when they exposed motion picture film to the outside world, Méliès arranged and accounted for every element in the shot. Working in the studio, using stop action (shutting off the camera, removing or putting something in the scene, then starting the camera, so the person or object seemed to pop into or out of view), working with miniatures, painted backdrops, and then hand-coloring the film, he and his factory allowed nothing to occur by chance and little of the outside world to intrude. Even though legend has it that the first stop-action event in a Méliès film occurred by accident, in fact the elements of his image making were calculated, created and circulated by the filmmaker and seen by the viewer in a closed accounting system in which nothing appeared by chance. This was to prove to be the future of the Hollywood system of image making, where "reality" is a product manufactured in the studio, and economy means not only the calculation of profit and loss but the entire circulation of imagination, production, distribution, and exhibition, each calculated to create the maximum return of emotion and grosses at the box office.

The triumph of artifice. Human figures (on the right) are combined with drawings. Georges Méliés, A Trip to the Moon *(1902).*

The System Develops: Buster Keaton and Charlie Chaplin

As an example of the way these various threads became woven into the kinds of films we watch today, I want to remain in the early history of cinema and concentrate on two comic filmmakers, Buster Keaton and Charlie Chaplin, whose films and working methods remain a model for current film.

Before the **studio system,** filmmakers experimented with different attitudes toward the external world and the economics of the image. Many filmed outdoors, where light was available and backgrounds were ready-made. Much of the pleasure of watching the films of the silent comedian, Buster Keaton, for example, comes from seeing images go by of the world of early twentieth-century America. This world is not foregrounded, however. Keaton's images are not documentary, not about chance, but rather about his body in flight, running, falling, endangered, engineered into precarious situations. One of the great moments in silent film comedy comes in Keaton's *Steamboat Bill, Jr.* (1928). Keaton stands in the midst of a terrific storm and the facade of a house behind him suddenly falls. It is a full-sized house, or at least the front of one, towering over the still figure of Keaton. When it falls, the sense of his fragility is marked. He will be crushed. But the engineering of the trick is such that the facade of the house falls straight over him so that the cutout of the window in the middle of the top floor neatly falls around his body. He stands stock-still without a flinch, and then he runs away.

The essential physicality of this stunt is unthinkable in any other medium because none other, not even live theater, could create the illusion of the *thereness* of the actor's body and the house falling on him within a space that is so obviously in the world. Only film can make things look "real" by means of fabricating and composing reality out of a trick occurring in space. In the case of the Keaton gag, the two-dimensionality of the image (like all images, film has no depth, so things can be hidden, angles and points of view can trick our eye, depth and volume can be manufactured), the obvious weight of the building—which was, in fact, a set and probably extremely light—the presence of the body, that figure in a landscape that film depends upon like no other medium other than painting, make the stunt startling, funny, and in the peculiar manner of film, "real."

Manipulated, used, and also *there*, the human figure and the landscape are part of the mise-en-scène of a film by Keaton or any other great physical comedian, including the much maligned Jerry Lewis. **Mise-en-scène**—a French theatrical term that literally means "put in the scene"—is an element of any good film, comic or not, and refers to the way space is organized and perceived in a film, including the way figure and background are composed. Mise-en-scène also includes lighting and movement, the use of black and white or color, the distance between camera and figure—everything that happens within the frame, including the frame itself. In almost any Keaton film we see Buster and the streets, curbs, houses, cars, and people around him. Space is used generously; it is open and wide and many things occur in the frame other than the main action. Keaton himself becomes one of the many elements that occur within that space. At any time, any one of these elements may be called upon to become a prop for a gag or a stunt. As in the case of the house facade in *Steamboat Bill, Jr.*, parts of the world may be built specifically for the gag. But even the apparently spontaneous appearance of people and streets in a Keaton film are part of its preconceived presence, its mise-en-scène. Our response to Keaton's images is—as Jean-Luc Godard said of the Lumières—the response of our fantasy of what the world might have looked like. Even in Keaton, though, we do not see the world itself. We see its image. Its memory. And that remains strong enough, present enough to surprise and delight us.

Keaton's great rival in silent comedy, Charlie Chaplin, worked somewhat closer to Méliés' method of studio shooting. Chaplin had less use for the outside world than Keaton. He worked almost exclusively in the studio and reduced the mise-en-scène to himself. The main signifying element in a Chaplin film is Chaplin. He might indeed engineer a complex gag, as when he gets caught in the gears of an elaborate machine in *Modern Times*. (*Modern Times* is a post–silent film made in 1936, but Chaplin doesn't talk.) Constructed in the studio, the process of the gag highlights Chaplin and his combat with the guts of the machine rather than the mad confluence of physical structure and the body as in Keaton and the falling house.

Foregrounding his own persona, making that persona, the Tramp, a representation of character, attitude, and sentiment, a figure onto which the viewer could overlay his or her own desires, vulnerabilities, and feelings of social or economic inadequacy, Chaplin could demand that focus be kept on his body. Here he was quite unlike either the Lumière brothers or Méliés and closer,

Keaton loved to place himself within the physical world, allowing the camera to observe the body caught and triumphing. Buster Keaton and Clyde Bruckman, The General *(1926).*

The subject of his own mise-en-scène, Chaplin understood that viewers were interested in seeing him; and he obliged. Charles Chaplin, Modern Times *(1936).*

perhaps, to the tradition of Edison. The latter foregrounded characters and faces in his early films; Méliés and the Lumières worked with a larger mise-en-scène in which human figures were often only one element of many. For them, the moving image represented intersections between subject, foreground, and background. For Méliés, those intersections were crafted together in the studio, parts of them literally by hand, whereas Chaplin's studio work uses little of the potential sleight of hand (or eye) offered by the camera, by paintings, and by trick shots. His was the cinema of personality, of the star.

The different styles of Keaton and Chaplin represent, in a sense, the next level in the culture of the image, in the processes of cinematic representation and the transition from film as craft to film as commodity. Their work also puts another turn on our investigation of the reality of the image. As comedians, the images they made and the stories they told exaggerated the world and the place of the human figure in it. Though both filmmakers indulged in the comic movements of falls and chases, pursuits and being hit by blunt instruments, their styles were quite different. Keaton saw his cinematic world as a place for combat between his body and the physical things of the world. Chaplin saw it as a site of sentimental triumph, of the cleverness of the "little guy," conquering odds and winning the heart of a simple woman. Image making for him provided the vehicle to carry his character of the Tramp through misadventures to redemption and the triumph over class, from despair to a measure of self-possession. He wanted all this to take place in a world whose presence was immediate and apparently unmediated. He wanted his audience's hearts.

But we can find a delightful paradox when we compare Chaplin with Keaton that makes the parallels with Méliés even more interesting. As much as he liked to work his gags in the middle of the ongoing, outside world, Keaton, like

Méliés, also understood how he could manipulate the components of the shot to best effect. Keaton liked to make the artificiality of the image part of the joke of his films. In *The Playhouse* (1921), Keaton plays with multiple exposure, performing an entire vaudeville act by himself, with himself as every member of the audience. In *Sherlock, Jr.* (1924), Keaton is a movie projectionist who dreams himself into the screen, into the image, and is overcome by its conjuries. Scenes change; the weather changes; the flow of images confuses him and causes him to take pratfalls.

This sequence in *Sherlock, Jr.* is among the great statements and admissions of how artificial the film image actually is. Keaton, in all his films, is either doing or being undone by things that happen around him. Objects and people in the image conspire; Buster flees and then cleverly gets the better of them. In *Sherlock, Jr.*, he is conspired against by the very medium in which he works. The image itself turns against him. Chaplin, however, appears as the master of the image and intends to subdue it to his comic persona. He tends to battle people more than things, as Keaton does, or use things for simple, heart-tugging comic effect, as when he sticks a fork in two rolls and makes them perform a ballet or delicately eats his shoe in *The Gold Rush* (1925).

The Growth of Corporate Filmmaking

Together, Chaplin and Keaton indicate what is happening as filmmaking grows to industrial proportions and, in the course of that growth, reconciles or fudges the boundaries between illusion, realism, audience response, and corporate need. Both very independent filmmakers, their styles reflected and incorporated the complex, sometimes contradictory parts of art and commerce that would form filmmaking both in America and abroad. Even their professional careers pointed to the directions filmmaking moved in the twenties.

Late in the twenties, Keaton, who successfully operated his own production company, signed with MGM, already one of the giants among film studios. By doing so, by signing with a studio that developed and promoted the producer system in which the director had only a small role, Keaton lost much of his creative control and creative edge. Earlier, in 1919, Charlie Chaplin, together with two of the biggest stars of the silent period, Douglas Fairbanks and Mary Pickford, along with D. W. Griffith, the great film director, formed United Artists, a film finance and distribution company. Keaton did not have Chaplin's foresight to remain in control of his work.

Both were used by the Hollywood system in different ways. Chaplin's privileging of his own star presence, making his figure the sentimental focus of a studio-bound construction in which everything is made in order to foreground the star and his story, became, in fact, the dominant mode in American filmmaking. Becoming part owner—with two other big movie stars and a pioneering director—of a studio, Chaplin further helped the studio system to come into dominance. (Ironically, later in his life, during the U.S. government's and the film studios' anticommunist purges in the fifties, Chaplin's career and reputation were all but ruined.) Keaton's individual talent was swallowed by the studio system. (But, later in his life, after the old studio system collapsed, Keaton emerged from oblivion and reentered film and television, a rediscovered comic talent.) Within the studios, the image that represented the world outside was subdued to the image of the world made within the studio's confines. The image made in the studio became, in turn, subdued to the attractiveness of story, star, and, always, economics. Mediated by story and star, and by the viewer's willingness to see what the story asked her to see, the image became "realistic." That is, it became transparent, invisible. It became the classical Hollywood style.

THE CLASSICAL HOLLYWOOD STYLE

Fabricating the Image

Let's first repeat and then elaborate some basic principles. What you see when you look at a movie is not what you actually see. What you are actually seeing on the movie screen is the reflection of a strong beam of light sent through a moving ribbon of plastic. Embedded in this plastic are dark and clear areas formed by the chemical residue of a previous exposure to light. These make up the images. The screen reflects the projected images back to you, and you interpret them as objects and figures, still or in motion. This means of projecting and perceiving moving images has not changed much since the late nineteenth century when it was invented. Newer technologies, the ones employed when a film becomes a videotape or DVD, are more complicated. The original images have been transformed into analogue electromagnetic waves, which are then recorded onto tape or digitized and burned into the grooves of a DVD, which are then read and reconverted into electrons. When they bombard the red, green, and blue phosphors of a television screen, a representation of the original image is created on the reverse side of the tube: an electronic representation of what was originally a representation made from light and chemicals. Soon, "film" will be digitally recorded from the outset, and the old chemical process will disappear entirely.

Our perception of cinematic narratives is an illusion, made up of fragmentary elements of light and shadow, pieced together and then interpreted as coherent, ongoing wholes. The studios who make the films were pieced together from a number of small moviemaking and movie distributing businesses in the 1910s and 1920s. Self-contained filmmaking "factories"—with employees who included everyone from writers, directors, and actors to set decorators and electricians—the studios created an economy of the visible, an organized, rationalized, commodity-driven form of production that depended upon the manufacture of a film out of various pieces, each one made by different groups of people in the studio hierarchy. The finished product depended upon the audience's willingness to interpret and decode those pieces, reading and responding to the story they told.

In order to accomplish the manufacture of up to two films a week during the peak years of studio production, from the late twenties through the late forties, the studios had to streamline production processes. They followed essential manufacturing processes by dividing up the work. At the top, the studio boss in Hollywood communicated with his financial officers in New York, who, by controlling the money, actually held the reins of the studio. The studio head in Hollywood settled on the stars and properties (books, plays, scripts) that were handed along to the producers. The producers in turn assigned writers, a director, and other crew to the film. By the time shooting was begun, everyone's role was laid out: shots were sketched on storyboards, sets were built, the script, usually the product of many hands, was largely finished. The work of making the film was and remains largely a process of executing a plan in precise, piecemeal fashion, so determined as to allow as few mistakes, as few time and cost overruns, as possible. We will look at the various people involved in the process in Chapter 3.

Part of the planning involves creating the images themselves as a staged process. Very often, a **shot**—which is any length of an unedited, or uncut, piece of exposed film (a close-up, or a long tracking movement of the camera, for example)—is actually put together bit by bit over a course of time, with many different hands contributing to the construction process. In studio filmmaking, very few of the various elements of a shot—the human figures, the background, foreground, sky, scenery, buildings—need to be present at any one time in its creation. The economics of the image require that the studio break the shot elements into the smallest, most manageable units, just as they break the entire production process down into manageable units. Everything that can be done indoors is. Whole sets or parts of them are put together on a sound stage or on the back lot. It's not possible to put up tall buildings in a studio, but it is possible to build the lower part of a building facade and compose the shot so that the character is standing in front of a structure that appears to be large because we are inclined to want to imagine a whole even though we see only a part. In any given shot, if more of the building needs to appear, it can be added in the special effects lab, or painted on glass and put in front of the camera (recall our earlier discussion of the two-dimensional image; in this instance, a *background* placed in the *foreground* can, through the trick of perspective and our own expectations of how space should be arranged, appear in the background when we watch the movie). Swamps are difficult places to shoot in; but a mound of dirt, a pool of water, some vegetation strewn carefully about, combined with careful lighting and composition, will convey the appropriate image. The swamp sequence in the German director F. W. Murnau's American film, *Sunrise* (1927), with a spotlight standing in for the moon and the camera gracefully moving around the characters on a movie set, remains one of the most lyrical shots in the history of film, despite its utter artificiality.

Going to sea to shoot a film is an expensive and tactically difficult proposition. It is cheaper to send a second unit crew out to shoot some boats in the ocean and then do the rest in the studio. A large tank of water with a skillfully

built model boat can sub-
stitute for the full-scale
event out in the vagaries
of the natural world. A set
of the captain's deck constructed on hydraulic lifts
that rocks back and forth
will serve for the dialogue
shots in which the characters need to be seen talking. For added realism,
the set can be placed in
front of a large movie
screen with a projector behind it. On the screen, a
film of waves and stormy
sky shot by the second
unit or taken from the studio library of stock shots
can be projected while the
dialogue scene is being
shot. **Rear-screen projection** is the most common
means studios used—and

The lyricism of artificiality. Within the studio, filmmakers can pull resources together to create images that suggest more than they show. Here, the idea of a moon and some water, with the camera behind the man's back (in the film, the camera gently tracks behind the man as he walks), has a lyrical and foreboding effect. F. W. Murnau, Sunrise *(1927).*

still use—for scenes shot in moving cars. A cutout model of a car is put in front of the screen, the driver and passenger sit and deliver their dialogue, and the street is projected on the screen behind them. In older studio films, rear-screen projection would sometimes be used to show two people simply walking down a street. The actors would be put on a treadmill.

These are relatively straightforward image manipulations. More complicated are the paintings or models or mattes of backgrounds and foregrounds that, well executed and well lit and integrated with the human figures in the frame, give the illusion of a complex and articulated world. The paintings, the models, and the actors need not be in the same place at the same time, and the painting may have openings cut out for the human figures to be projected into. A process called a "blue screen matte" or "traveling matte" allows the various parts of the shot to be photographed in front of a blue screen. The various shots that will eventually make up one completed shot are projected one after the other through an optical printer, which is simply a projector and camera that can be carefully calibrated. The blue color is dropped out, the components of the shot merge, resulting in an image of illusory wholeness, even of illusory motion when the matte shot includes a figure in motion: Superman flying, Bruce Willis falling down an elevator shaft in *Die Hard* (1988), the SAC bomber flying over Arctic wastes in *Dr. Strangelove* (1964)—indeed almost any sequence in which a figure or object is foregrounded in front of a complicated background.

Indeed, we usually think of such highly wrought special effects in relation to action or science fiction films, and we take a special pleasure in seeing the results of "f/x." We enjoy the reality effect of such shots while acknowledging their artificiality. But the fact is that all Hollywood studio films, no matter what their genre, use special effects much of the time.

And it is an old tradition. In 1903, Edwin S. Porter made a short film called *The Great Train Robbery.* An early Western and among the first films in which the story shifts back and forth between narrative sequences, it contains a scene in a railroad car where the scenery going by out-

This railroad car is a set. The image of the outside rushing by is probably created by projecting the image on a screen just behind the cut out of the door in the railroad car. In reproducing this image, we have created a modern-day equivalent of Porter's illusion by enhancing the rear-screen projection. Edwin S. Porter, The Great Train Robbery *(1903).*

side is actually matted in— taken at another time and then matched with the set of the railroad car through either rear-screen projection or optical printing. The difference between this sequence and a film by Méliès is that the trickery is not supposed to be noticed. It is not meant to be part of the visible appeal of the film. This peculiar process shot—as rear-screen projections or matte shots are called—is a forerunner of all those shots of people driving their cars in front of movie screens showing images of passing roads and streets or people walking up roads whose surroundings have been painted and matted in long after the actors have gone on to other films.

Are there shots in films in which everything we see was present when the shot was made? Certainly. This is part of the appeal of documentary films, for example, in which the camera observes, with a minimum of intrusion, a sequence of events that might have occurred had the camera not been there. The documentarist looks for or tries to re-create a whole ongoing event, and we will examine this work in Chapter 5. The post–World War II Italian neorealist movement was based on making films in the street, observing people in their surroundings with an immediacy that was powerful and sometimes shocking. Hollywood took immediate notice. In the late forties and early fifties, American films used some exterior, on-location shooting, especially in low-budget gangster films. American theatrical films in the sixties and seventies, responding to yet another European innovation, the films of the French New Wave, tended to move away from the synthetic image, at least for a while. Sequences in cars were actually shot in cars moving along the street. Crews spent more time at locations, with actors and their surroundings present within the shot as the shot was taken. Historically, in European cinema, there has been as much dependence on constructing an image from component parts as there is in American filmmaking. But abroad and at home, there have been and continue to be individual filmmakers willing to go outside the studio and shoot in the world. When that happens—in the streets and countryside of Calcutta in Satyajit Ray's Apu trilogy (*Pather Panchali*, 1955; *Aparajito*, 1956; *The World of Apu*, 1959), or in the streets of New York in so

The gangster on the street. In Stanley Kubrick's The Killing *(1955), Johnny Clay gets a suitcase to pack the stolen cash. The move to on-location shooting in the fifties marked an important break with the studio tradition. Many independent filmmakers, like Kubrick, working on a small budget, took their cameras outside, away from the studios. The visual texture of the mise-en-scène began to change.*

many American gangster films of the 1950s, and in Martin Scorsese's best work—the image and our relationship to it change. The reality effect becomes even stronger, and the sense of seeing a world as it might actually exist makes the image stronger. Recently, a Scandinavian group of filmmakers, calling themselves "Dogma 95," have vowed, like the neorealists, to do away with studio fabrication of the shot—to do away with the studio altogether. In their work and that of other filmmakers, both European and American, the response to the closed and secure world generated by the studio offers the opportunity of opening into a more detailed, textured, less manageable image of the world outside.

In Hollywood today, the artificial construction of the image has made a major comeback. All the old practices of rear-screen projection, matte work, and other forms of image manufacture are now being done by computer. Through digital manipulation, the image is put together bit by bit. Characters are pasted into the middle of crowds, the members of which are digitally duplicated, or on mountaintops, or in outer space. Dinosaurs are graphically rendered and made to leap across a plain as humans look at them; a gigantic spaceship hovers over New York; a huge ocean liner hits an iceberg and sinks; incredible acts of transformation and destruction are possible with no location necessary other than a computer terminal. Anything and anyone can be placed anywhere and made to do anything. The same holds true for sound. Digital sound allows intricate sonic mixes to be made in which every single sound, from footsteps to the human voice, is built and processed to achieve the best effect. The purpose of digital image and sound manipulation is the same as old-fashioned optical work: to save the filmmakers money.

Paradoxically, major digital effects are very expensive and time-consuming, but they give the studios the greatest amount of control possible and engineer the viewer into the image and then beyond it into the story. With the digital,

Shot on location in Calcutta. Satyajit Ray's The World of Apu *(1959) is the last of a trilogy of films (including* Pather Panchali, *1955, and* Aparajito, *1956) in which a culture is explored by seeing characters in their landscape.*

there is a seemingly unlimited possibility to substitute spectacle for substance. There are times in the economy of filmmaking when expense is born for the sake of control. But this will soon change. The more common the use of digital composition, the cheaper it will become, and in a few years, the old filmmaking process will disappear altogether and digital cameras will directly transform the image into the abstractions of binary code, which will be delivered via digital tape or DVD to theaters or high definition television. The next installment of *Star Wars*, for example, will be made digitally, with actors inserted into a computer-generated mise-en-scène and recorded directly on digital tape.

The Whole and Its Parts

The construction of shots, including all the choices that go into how many elements will appear in the shot at any one time of its manufacture, and how the shots will be edited together, is a combination of economics and aesthetics. The economy of the image is entwined with the economy of production and the economy of perception. While the studios change, while production practices alter to incorporate new technologies, even while some experimentation in form and content is allowed to occur as the culture surrounding filmmaking changes, the basic structures of shot making tend to remain the same. The formal structures, the very substructure of film construction and film viewing, are largely unchanged, or changed so subtly that they are hardly noticeable. The production process is executed in bits and pieces, from the selection of a story to the writing of a screenplay—often by many hands—to the creation of sets, the direction of scenes, and the **editing** of the scenes into a whole. Film is made in bits and pieces. And that is what we see on the screen: bits and pieces of image and story so cunningly put together that they appear as if they were an ongoing whole. Film acting, for example, is built shot by shot. A performance in a film is not a continuous process as it is on the stage but is put together out of many parts. A film is not shot in sequence, nor is a sequence made completely in one **take.** (For convenience, we use the term "scene" as the unit of action or a segment of a story, while a "sequence" is a related series of related scenes or shots. In many cases, scene and sequence are used interchangeably.) To do so would be time-consuming and a waste of money. Therefore, an actor has to perform in spurts, in short spasms of emotion, guided by the director and a staff member called the continuity person (or, in older Hollywood parlance, the script girl), whose job is to keep tabs on everything from the position of a necktie to a half-completed gesture, to a facial expression or the direction of a gaze that must be held from shot to shot.

Any given part of a film can be made at any time. The middle may be shot first, the third sequence last, the end at the beginning, the next-to-last sequence just before the middle. For example, if a number of scenes throughout a film take place in the same room, it is more economical to shoot all of those shots at the same time, rather than leave the set unused and then return to relight or re-build it. If a high-priced, in-demand actor is involved in a film, it is more economical to shoot all the scenes in which that actor is involved rather than recall the actor to the set again to shoot a scene that will occur later in the narrative. If a location—that is, a site, usually out of doors, at a distance from the studio—is involved, all the scenes that take place at that location will be shot together, no matter where or when they appear in the film. There is a story about the making of the film *Blow-Up* (1966), directed by the Italian filmmaker Michelangelo Antonioni. He wished to make his film in chronological order. Two major parts of the film, one early, the other at the end, took place a day or two apart in the story, in a London park. Actual filming began in spring and concluded in the fall. When director and crew returned to the park for the last sequence, the leaves had changed color. They had to spray them green to re-create the earlier effect. An American filmmaker would have shot all the sequences in the park at one time and worked out the temporal arrangements during the editing process. Or, instead of shooting outside at all, the American filmmaker might have had a tree and some grass put up in the studio, matting in the rest of the environment in the effects lab or, these days, on a computer.

Making the Parts Invisible

Creation through bits and pieces is a production procedure, not a reception problem. In other words, as viewers we are not so supposed to see the fragmentary, stop and start process that filmmaking is. With relatively few and important exceptions, films from all over the world are constructed on a principle of radical self-effacement—of rendering their form invisible while causing few economic difficulties during the creative and manufacturing process and *no* obstacle at all for the viewers during the process of reception. This is made possible through a set of conventions and assumptions by means of which the viewer will accept the illusion of transparency and see the film as an unmediated, ongoing whole, a story played out in front of her eyes. Form and structure, the artifice of the image, and the fragmentary nature of screen acting will all melt away and merge together in apparent wholeness.

This effect is not unique to movies. Recall our discussion of perspective. Although perspective is based on carefully calculated mathematical structures, the result of perspective in painting was to naturalize the image, to give the illusion of three dimensions on a two-dimensional surface and, by so doing, provide a window through which the viewer's gaze could own the contents of the image. Painting presented "content," represented things in the outside world, until late in the nineteenth century. When photography and film took over this job, painting began to represent its own form, to speak about surface, color, form, and texture. When it did, it created obstacles. Looking at abstract art, people keep wanting to know "what it is trying to show."

Music depends upon its ability to link itself effortlessly to emotional response. Few people understand the mathematical complexities of harmony and counterpoint, know what a hemi demisemiquaver is, or can explain the sonata form. In the early twentieth century, a group of composers rebelled against the transparency of musical form and wrote atonal music based on the mathematical principles of the twelve-tone scale. They sought less a pathway to emotion than an expression of musical form. Their work demanded knowledge of how music works and attention to something other than the emotions of the sounds. This music was not very easy to listen to or very popular.

Prose writing also has its version of an invisible form. Reading some books requires little attention to the structure of language. The structure of the book may ask the reader to concentrate instead on what the writer is saying and what his characters are doing, which correlates with our desire to see what the painting is about or feel the emotions of the music. Those writers who concentrate on form, who foreground the structure of their prose and how it makes meaning—Henry James, James Joyce, Samuel Beckett, Jorge Luis Borges, Toni Morrison—become the focus of academic study. In ordinary reading, though, the greatest compliment many will give to a book is that it is a "page turner." The phrase implies the reader moves past page, prose, form, and style into the movement of story and character.

There is no equivalent phrase for film, probably because there are relatively few films that are *not* the equivalent of "page turners" and because, while we are watching, the "pages," the images, are turned for us. The assumption is that the structure and style of any film will be invisible, allowing the viewer to enter and move into the story and the emotions of the characters. The point is for us to be carried away by plot and the motivations of the characters. Image structure and editing, the way the story is put together, are subservient to the story and the characters' lives.

Story, Plot and Narration

Our task, now that we have an inkling of how a film is put together and its parts made invisible, is to bring the form and structure of film—its means of production, construction, and comprehension—back into consciousness and make them visible again. To start, let's redefine "story." This is what the film tells us, the process of events the characters go through and enact. Plot is the abstract scheme of that story, what we summarize after we've seen the film, what film reviewers on TV and in newspapers give us. Narrative is the actual telling of the story, the way the story is put together, formed, and articulated.

Narrative is the structure of the story. Take Steven Spielberg's *Jaws* (1975). Here's some plot: a great white shark terrorizes a beach town, kills people, and is finally hunted down by three men in a boat. I could elaborate that into something closer to the story, although it would be more description than story and in any case would be *my* story, derived from the film, because I am giving it narrative structure: Sheriff Brody is pulled from a peaceful domestic life by the intrusion of the terrible creature into the town he has been hired to protect. The shark attacks people, but the elders of the town want it kept quiet so as not to ruin holiday tourist business. There is tension between Brody and the elders, and also uncertainty. Brody has been hired to do the bidding of the town, but he has a moral responsibility to protect the innocent. And so forth.

I could also elaborate this in a way that comes closer to the film's narrative: the presence of the shark is indicated by music—low, almost staccato chords played on bass fiddles, a mirror of the high staccato strings used in *Psycho*. When the shark is ready to attack, the film allows us to look as if through the shark's eyes, moving in the water toward its prey. Suspense is further created by playing with the gaze of Sheriff Brody on the beach. He looks and looks at the water. People move in front of him, and he has to bend and rise to see. There are false alarms, and our tension keeps rising. The intercutting of **shot/reverse shot** from Brody (the shot) to what he sees (the **reverse shot**) reaches a climax when Brody finally does see something in the water. At this point, Spielberg uses a device that Alfred Hitchcock developed. By combining two movements of the camera—a tracking shot in one direction and a zoom in the opposite—he shows Brody as if space were collapsing around him, thereby heightening our awareness of some exciting and terrifying event.

In this brief analysis, I began by recounting plot and then moved from plot to structure, that is, from content to form, describing some of the ways the narrative is put together to tell us its story. This analysis also puts the structure into a context by revealing that Spielberg didn't invent everything but borrowed and developed some stylistic devices from another filmmaker. The point is that all aspects of a film are based on formal, structural principles, and meaning as well as emotion is always communicated by structure. We see, understand, and feel by the way we are manipulated by the shot and the arrangement of shots by editing into a narrative structure that tells a story. Meaning or emotion does not exist without a form to communicate it. We never simply "know" something, or

On the level of plot, Brody is looking out for the shark. But the structure of this sequence does more than tell us that: it draws our gaze to the character's and, by alternately looking at him and assuming his own point of view, creates expectation and excitement—especially when that point of view is blocked. Steven Spielberg, Jaws *(1975).*

see something, or are told something. When we respond to a film, there is always a formal structure driving that response.

THE SHOT

Film form can be reduced to two basic elements, each of which can be used in a great variety of ways. They are the shot and the cut. A shot is any unbroken, unedited length of film. That length can be the entire magazine of film in a 35 mm camera (twenty minutes or more) or the length of tape in a video camera. A shot can also be brought into existence in the editing room when an otherwise unedited length of film has some unwanted material trimmed from either end. In its purest form, a shot may not have anything cut or edited into it. If it does, it becomes two shots, one shot broken by another that has been spliced into it. The shot is determined by its physical existence as an unbroken entity—or its appearance as such.

In film, the shot remains cinema's unit of internal continuity. It allows film to represent space and time as connected and ongoing: it composes space and either guides the viewer's eye within its space or offers a reflective, meditative gaze at that space. What happens in a shot can be as simple as the camera gazing at a character or as complex as a movement in which the camera follows a character across a long and articulated space. In Welles's *The Magnificent Ambersons* (1942), the camera watches for many minutes as a character standing in a darkly lit, turn-of-the-century kitchen falls into hysteria while talking about the decline of her family and her home. The intensity of the sequence grows from the camera's unflinching gaze and the power of the actress's performance. This is a rare moment in film in which a performance—in the usual sense of an ongoing and developing process—is allowed to develop on its own, and Welles's unwillingness to give us any other view, to cut into or away from the action, gives us no option but to watch it unfold. In *Weekend* (1967), Jean-Luc Godard creates an intricate, long, circular track and pan of a farmyard, to the accompaniment of a Mozart sonata. (When the camera **tracks,** it moves on its base, linearly or diagonally through the scene; when it **pans,** it pivots on its base from side to side or tilts up and down.) Godard moves around the circle, one way and then the other, four and a half times; people move in and out of the shot; we see the piano player, who is playing the concert in the farmyard itself; people listen and move on; a man walks past. The result of this complicated shot is to provide a kind of visual analogue to the form of the music. Martin Scorsese creates a four-minute tracking shot in *GoodFellas* (1990), during which the camera follows the main character and his fiancée as they walk from the street into a nightclub, down the steps, through an enormous and busy kitchen, onto the main floor, over to a table, which is set up for them as they approach, and sit down and talk as a comedian begins his act on stage. The shot is an extreme expression of cinematic energy; an affirmation of the camera's ability to create and traverse space and time.

But, as we know, nothing is what it appears in a film. Sometimes, the filmmaker creates the illusion of a single continuous shot when in fact it has been

A still image from the four-minute take and the zoom/track in GoodFellas *by Martin Scorsese (1990).*

broken. At the end of the infamous shower sequence in Alfred Hitchcock's *Psycho* (1960), Marion Crane's lifeless body is slumped over the side of the bathtub. The camera moves from a close-up of her eye, past the bathroom door, to the adjoining bedroom, coming to rest on her pocketbook on the night table, where she had put the stolen money she planned to return the following day. The movement is deeply ironic, for Marion's dead eye sees nothing, and we are left with the emptiness of her murder and its disconnection from the robbery she committed. The movement from eye to purse seems to be one shot. However, close examination reveals a trick. As the camera passes by the bathroom door, there is a very quick dissolve (a dissolve occurs when the end of one shot fades out as the beginning of another fades in). What apparently looks like one shot is actually two.

The first sequence in which the reporter, Thompson, goes to visit Susan Alexander in Orson Welles's *Citizen Kane* (1941) begins with a dramatic boom shot, in which the camera arcs over the roof of the nightclub where Susan is performing. (A boom shot occurs when the camera moves on a **crane** and covers a great amount of space.) A storm rages, the camera moves through the nightclub's rooftop neon sign, heads down and through the skylight into the room where Susan sits at a table. The effect is powerful, but it's a big illusion. The rooftop is a model in miniature. If you look closely at the sequence on a DVD, this becomes apparent, and you can even make out the separation in the construction of the model of the neon sign, which would have been pulled away by technicians as the camera approached. Obviously it would have been impossible (or impractical) to send that camera through a skylight on an actual roof. As Hitchcock does in *Psycho*, Welles uses a dissolve, here hidden by flashing lightning and the sound of thunder and pelting rain, to connect two shots. The first part begins on the model rooftop; the second starts at the top of the studio set and booms down to the characters below. These shots create the illusion of one continuous shot.

THE CUT

Like the shot, editing also addresses time and space by building the temporal structure—the movement of characters and events across the narrative of a film—and directing our gaze, and that of the characters, to those things and events the filmmakers deem important. Editing also creates transitions, movements from one place or time to another. A dissolve, for example, in which one shot fades out while another fades in, is an editing effect, as is the fade to black of a sequence to mark the end of a narrative moment. The formal expression of editing is the cut, a literal severing of the shot. If a shot is an actual or apparent unbroken length of film, editing is what breaks it. But editing joins together as well as cuts apart. Through editing, filmmakers build the structure of a movie by arranging its shots. At its simplest, editing is what is done to a shot. Editing is cutting; but *an* edit usually refers to the joining together of two shots. There are a number of editing styles, the most dominant of which is the classic **continuity style** of American filmmaking—a major component of the classical style—the main purpose of which is to link shots in such a way that the act of linking vanishes and the illusion of coherence and unity is foregrounded.

A reasonable question would be, Why edit at all? Why not just create the sequences of film each in one shot, so the unity of time and space would be maintained without having to trick the viewer's eye into believing that parts are wholes? The answer to the question lies deep within the history and culture of Hollywood studio filmmaking and speaks to the development of the classical style. Very early in film history—at the time of Edison, the Lumière brothers, and Georges Méliés, and lasting until just after the turn of the twentieth century—films were short and usually made in one or a few shots. There was not much camera movement, and the space defined by the composition of the shot was often frontal and static. People have theorized that this frontal, static gaze was an attempt to represent the view of a stage from the point of view of the auditorium, a perspective most early filmgoers would have understood and found comforting. Over the course of a relatively few years, as spectators became more comfortable with the spatial arrangement of the shot and the composition of the image, filmmakers began experimenting with the construction of story—the narrative—of films. The single shot seemed not to provide enough flexibility. Flexibility is the key answer to the question: filmmakers began cutting to alter points of view, keep the viewer's eyes engaged, and find ways of creating a narrative that could be more easily achieved by cutting scenes and sequences together.

The Development of Continuity Cutting

Imagine this problem: A film calls for two events to happen simultaneously. A woman is held captive by a man of evil intent. Her fiancé knows where she is and is coming to rescue her. How can this information be structured for maximum effect? One method might be to show each action in a single shot, each complete in itself, one after the other. This method would extend the single-shot construction that was the mainstay of early cinema, but it would not provide temporal control. In other words, the action of the story would be at the mercy of the linearity of the shots, not the rhythm of the action: the heroine is held captive; the hero rides to her rescue; the hero arrives and saves the heroine.

The successful solution of the problem created an illusion of simultaneity by editing the sequences together so that a shot of the woman in captivity and a shot of the fiancé coming to her rescue were intercut in an alternating sequence. Intercutting two sequences, often called parallel editing or cross cutting, provides a means to integrate story parts with finesse and flexibility. Early filmmakers discovered that suspense could be created by changing the lengths of these alternating shots, perhaps shortening them as the hero approached the captive heroine. Audiences accepted this structure with ease, and it became one of the foundations of the classical American style.

Edwin S. Porter's *The Great Train Robbery*, made in 1903, is an early example of a film that intercuts sequences—of the robbery itself, of the townspeople at a dance—and it pointed the way to great flexibility in narrative construction. For a short time in the early part of the twentieth century, the control of this flexibility extended to film exhibitors—the owners of the movie houses! *The Great Train Robbery* includes a famous shot of one of the robbers pointing a gun toward the camera and firing as if at the audience. Exhibitors were at liberty to put this shot at the beginning or at the end of the film.

Other elements of cutting were developed during the period between 1905 and the early 1910s, all of them crucial to the continuity style and to a cinema being created to entice and hold the viewer's gaze. One element was a solution to a seemingly simple problem. A filmmaker might need to get a character up from a chair and out of a room, catching her again from the outside of the room as she passes through the door. With a mobile camera, it would be quite possible, and very dramatic, to do a backward track, **dollying** the camera (moving it on tracks or another device) away from the person as she gets up and moves through the door. During the early period, however, cameras were not very mobile. Since they needed to be hand-cranked, they couldn't be moved easily, unless apparatus and operator were placed in a moving vehicle, not useful for the closed space of a room. Beyond the physical limitations, there was also, I think, a desire for a rhythmical structure in film that could only be attained by cutting, a rhythm that would keep the viewer's attention through changing shots as opposed to continuous unbroken shots. Narrative rhythm became an important driving force in the development of editing.

Cinema, early and late, is full of shots of people getting up from seated positions, leaving a room, getting into a car, going to their destinations. These are essential narrative transitions. During the pre-1910 period, however, these movements were not always cut together in consistent ways. In an early film, it is quite possible to see a person rising from a chair in the first shot and, in the second, the person rising from the same position she had already occupied before the cut. The effect is seeing the person getting up from the chair twice. This is not incompetence but rather the sign of a cinematic grammar incompletely standardized, as if one didn't know (or care) that the clause on either side of a coordinate conjunction should be different and instead said, "She got up out of the chair and she got up out of the chair." There were no conventions of continuity cutting, no rules; they had to be invented and used over and over again before they became conventions. But, as we noted earlier, "invented" is not quite accurate. The individuals who developed the grammar of continuity cutting were not theorists and were certainly not scientific. The process was an intuitive one, and you can see it developing across the period and especially in the short films D. W. Griffith made for the Biograph company between 1908 and 1913. He made almost 500 of them, a number of which have survived to supply us with a textbook of the emerging classical style.

Griffith and others learned how to match shots, so that the analysis of a single movement—the person getting out of a chair and leaving the room—would appear not to be the fragments of an action that they actually are but the illusion of one continuous action. Even the hard part, synchronizing the cut of the woman leaving the room to the shot of her exiting the door on the other side, becomes smoothed and timed to achieve the right sense of forward, purposive motion, not only of the character but of her story as well. Coordinates become, in effect, commas. Hiding the cut by editing on a continuous movement, distracting the viewer with something else going on in the frame, and, from 1930 on, using dialogue or sound as a cover became a major function of the continuity style.

Shot/Reverse Shot

One element of continuity cutting is, in many ways, its most important, because it establishes a basic structural principle for the way narrative is created in film. This involves the concept of the gaze, the way characters look at one another and the way we look at, and get caught up in, the looks of the characters on screen. We are connected to a filmic story largely through the orchestration of looks, and the prime conductor of the process is the shot/reverse shot: one character looks (shot) and we cut to what the character is looking at (reverse shot). Making the fragments of the editing structure invisible and creating the illusion of an ongoing action depend upon building the gaze of the spectator into the story telling or narrative space of the film. Our glance is directed, woven, sewn into the visual structure so that we forget the act of cutting and become involved in what each cut reveals. In fact, critics often use a surgical metaphor, calling the process in which our gaze is stitched into the narrative the "suture effect."

Perhaps the most insistent, unvarying version of the shot/reverse pattern occurs in the presentation of a simple dialogue sequence between two characters. This structure has been so common for so many years (the pattern was developed *before* the coming of sound) that if you watch any movie or dramatic or news interview television program, you are guaranteed to see the following: two people begin a conversation with the camera framing them together in a **two-shot.** This shot will last perhaps ten or twelve seconds. The sequence will then cut to a shot over the shoulder of one of the participants looking at the other. After a very few seconds, the sequence will cut to a reverse shot of this, over the shoulder of the second participant, looking at the first. These reverses, each one lasting perhaps three to six seconds, will continue, perhaps punctuated with one-shots, that is shots of one of the participants alone in the frame, for as long as it takes the dialogue to conclude. And it will conclude with the original two-shot of both figures.

Because this cutting pattern is so universal, rather than take an example from a film, I will create an abstract example that can be applied as a template to any movie that you are likely to see. Imagine the following scene: a man walks into a room, sits down across the table from a woman, and starts a conversation. A third person in the room is standing and listening. The editing structure might be as follows. Each item indicates a shot you might see on the screen:

1 The woman looks up toward the door.
2 Shot of the door opening as man enters.
3 The woman looks up, surprised.
4 The man approaches and sits down at the table.
5 Shot of the third person in the room, who raises his eyebrows.
6 The man and the woman talk in two-shot (both are together in the frame).
7 Cut to an over-the-shoulder shot from the woman to the man.
8 Reverse shot over the shoulder from the man to the woman.
9 Repeat this pattern three times, then return to
10 The two-shot of the two people talking.
11 A shot of the third person smiling.

The core of this sequence might actually have been constructed out of six separate shots. For example, the woman looking toward the door, registering surprise, and then smiling might have been filmed in one shot. The man entering the room, approaching the table, and sitting down might constitute the second. The two-shot of the man and woman talking at the table would make up a third, and the change in camera position from over the shoulder of one of the participants to the other would make up the fourth and fifth shots. All of the onlooker's reactions would be shot together, as would the two-shots of the couple at the table and the over-the-shoulder shots. Although six shots are used to construct the sequence, many more than six would actually have been taken (and would be called "takes" of the same shot). Each of the shots actually used would be chosen from a number of takes, in which the same setup, dialogue, and action were repeated, over and over, until the director feels she has enough good ones to choose from. (Bear in mind that, traditionally, only one camera is used in filmmaking, so that each wide shot, one-shot, two-shot, or close-up is done separately.) Out of all these takes, the shots are cut together to create the continuity of the sequence.

Some of these shots may not require all the participants to be present. The shot of the man entering the room might include all three people, as would the initial two-shot of the conversation. But the shot of the woman looking up would not necessarily require the presence of the other two actors, nor would the shot of the onlooker responding to the conversation (especially if these shots were done in **medium** or full **close-up**). In the over-the-shoulder shots that make up the dialogue at the table, it may not be necessary to have present the actor over whose shoulder the camera is gazing. If the shot shows only a little bit of one actor's face, a stand-in performer will do. In television interview programs, it is common practice to shoot reaction shots of the interviewer after the person interviewed has left. These are then cut in to give the impression that the interviewer is responding to the answers given by his subject.

In the editing of a sequence, as in the composition of a single shot from different elements, the filmmakers create and we read what we need in order to understand the forward momentum of the story. In our made-up sequence, it is easy to imagine that a look of anticipation from the woman toward the door makes us anticipate something, and our anticipation is fulfilled by the cut to the man entering. The looks from the bystander serve to seal the participants and the viewer into the content of the sequence and create a dramatic context for what is going on. If the bystander smiles warmly, we believe everything is fine; if the bystander sneers or grimaces, we might suspect an evil deed is about to occur.

Sight Lines

Remember that each of the shots for such a dialogue sequence, or any sequence in a film, is made independently and then cut together during the editing process to create the sequence. It is important for the purposes of constructing the sequence, and for maintaining continuity when the sequence is viewed by an audience, that the sight lines maintained by the characters remain constant. The characters must look in the same direction in each shot, for fear of breaking the rhythm of the viewer's own gaze at the scene. This is called an **eye-line match,** and it is another constituent of the continuity style. If a character is looking to the left in one shot, that eye line must be maintained in the succeeding shots of the sequence, and the other character must be continually looking to the right. What's more, as the cutting moves our gaze from one character to the other, the position of the camera must remain along the same plane in front of the characters. This is the critical and, like everything else in this process, absolutely arbitrary **180-degree rule.** At no point in the dialogue sequence, or in any other sequence in any film that chooses to follow the rules, is the camera allowed to cross a 180-degree line imagined to stretch from left to right across the scene. You can visualize this by imagining that you can look straight down at a scene of two people and see a line drawn directly behind, or even through, them. The camera may be placed at any point on one side of that line, never behind it (and never exactly 90 degrees in front of it because the space would appear too two dimensional). Such rules came into being out of fear that, if the characters were looking in different directions from shot to shot, if the camera moved to the other side of the 180-degree line or was positioned at a direct 90 degrees to the figures, audiences would be confused and the artificial structure of cinematic space would be revealed.

When such conventions are followed with such regularity in film after film, we begin to take them for granted. Our gaze is so woven that a two- or three-way pattern is formed in which we, like the viewer of a perspective painting, are given pride of place and the illusion of ownership of the narrative space. Things happen for our eyes, and as our eyes are entangled with the gazes of the characters in the film, we feel a part of events, an element of the narrative. Like every other aspect of continuity cutting, the shot/reverse shot sequence achieves complex results from quite simple means. The shot/reverse shot is, of course, not restricted to dialogue sequences, and it can be fodder for unexpected results. Near the end of *Psycho*, Lila Crane, the sister of Marion, who was brutally murdered in the shower, goes into Norman's mother's old, dark house to visit with the old lady. From the moment she starts up the stairway leading to the house, Hitchcock constructs the sequence from a series of shot/reverse shots during which we look at Lila as she registers a response of fear or curiosity and then cut to the object of her gaze: the house, a room, a fixture, a bed. Through this construction, Hitchcock so synchronizes our expectations and fears with Lila's that he can play two jokes. The first one is on both the character and us. Lila enters Mrs. Bates's room and approaches the bureau, her eyes caught by—as the camera, in reverse shot, zooms in on—a bronze sculpture of two folded, smothering hands. As she stands by the bureau, her reflection in the mirror is bounced back from another mirror behind the one she is looking at, so that there are actually three Lilas. We look from behind and see Lila's back. In the mirror before her, we see her reflection and, in the second reflection, we see her back. These images occur very quickly, so that before we can actually make out her reflections, she is startled by them, shrieks, turns, and we shriek with her. As she turns, Hitchcock cuts to the mirror behind her, now object of her gaze and ours; she sees that the figure who startled her was her, so do we, and we both relax.

The joke that's played on us alone occurs when Lila examines Norman's room. Again, Hitchcock cuts from Lila looking to what Lila sees: Norman's bed, a stuffed doll, a record of Beethoven's *Eroica* Symphony on Norman's phonograph. Lila takes a book off the shelf and registers the fact, which we see in the reverse shot, that it has no title on its spine. She looks at the pages and registers surprise tinged with a bit of horror in the reaction shot that follows. But Hitchcock refuses a final reverse shot. He does not show us what Lila has just seen in the book. For a moment, the suture is cut, and we are left on our own.

The shot/reverse shot convention is such a powerfully established part of the institution of making and watching cinema that a clever filmmaker can tinker with it to provoke a specific reaction. But the tinkering is rare enough, especially in Hollywood cinema. Its normalization is what allows filmmakers to work quickly and within budget and us to understand the narrative easily and quickly without our attention's being diverted by the way the narrative is formed.

Using the shot/reverse shot sequence to play a joke. Lila Crane examines Norman Bates's room. Her gaze is caught by something.

She goes to the bookcase, pulls out a book, and looks at it. As she is about to turn the page...

There is a reaction shot—a shot of her reacting to what she sees.

But, instead of cutting to the point-of-view shot that would show us what Lila is seeing, Hitchcock cuts to an action occurring elsewhere in the motel, where Sam is confronting Norman. We never get to see what's in the book. Alfred Hitchcock, Psycho *(1960).*

RESISTANCE TO CONVENTION

It is important to note that ideology is at work in the construction of the classical style. Most film viewers have assented, across our culture and, increasingly, across the world, to what film is supposed to be and not supposed to be—what it should look like and, to a large extent, what it should say. They have agreed that film is the transparent communication of story: no work should be involved in getting access to that story, and no conscious process of reading and interpreting that story should be required. Film should give all and demand little. It should not—we mentioned earlier—be serious, demanding, or "deep." There are many levels of assumptions here, and they need to be unpacked.

As we have said, the work of imagination, no matter what its face—painting, music, novel, or film—is not a simple mirror image of reality, pure emotion, or pure story. Imagination requires mediation, of color and shape, of sound (carefully, even mathematically determined, in the case of music), of words, of moving images. In all cases content—story, characters, emotions—is never simply there, waiting for us to see it. Content is generated by the form and structure of the imagination's work and is specific to the kind of work being done. The form and structure of painting are different from that of novel writing or filmmaking. In all cases, some kind of interpretive work is involved on the part of the viewer or listener. On some level, reading is involved, reading in its most general sense of engaging the form of a work, comprehending it, interpreting it, comparing it with other, similar examples of its kind, contextualizing it, in short, making sense of it. Sense is not a given. It must be made.

Making sense out of film is not automatic. We have to learn how to read narrative images, a job that is easily and quickly accomplished at an early age. Around the turn of the century, early filmmakers had to begin learning how to make images legible, how to structure them so that they would be easy to read and the stories they told immediately comprehensible. "Learning," however, is not quite precise, because early filmmakers did not have a body of knowledge to absorb. "Intuiting" is a better word, because these filmmakers were really guessing, in a haphazard manner, how image and narrative structure would work best. By the late 1910s, their guesswork was largely done. They accomplished a task they did not even know they were beginning: the creation of a universal, legible structure of image, movement, and narrative that would dissolve into pure story in front of its viewers. The components of that structure, as I've noted, have not changed very much. They are, with rare exceptions, routine and repeated in film after film. As with any routine, the more we do it, the less we are aware of it, and the more automatic our responses to it become.

When we watch a film, we are part of a great process of assent to its presence and wholeness, even though it is absent and made up of fragments. The assent is an ideological event: what we *want* to see and what we are *asked* to see are mutually agreed upon and takes precedence over the "reality" of what we are actually seeing so that we usually do not question it. Earlier, we defined ideology as the way we agree to see ourselves, to behave, and to create the values of our lives. Here we can expand that definition of ideology to include the idea of—as one writer put it—assenting to the "obviousness" of things. We take the conventions of cinematic form as "obvious" and, therefore—as we are doing here—have to work through their obviousness to the structures that create the effect of that "obviousness" in order to understand how they work and how we respond to them.

Shot/reverse shot structures and over-the-shoulder dialogue sequences have to be parsed like a sentence in order to see their artificiality and understand how they work their "obvious" forms on us, without our even being aware. With this in mind, we can understand that under the ideological banner of pleasure without toil, of leisure activity that demands only a positive emotional response, filmmakers and filmgoers have been joined in the process of making images and stories that are immediately understood and enjoyed, so immediately that they appear there, ready-made and unique—obvious—even though they are not there and are made with a great deal of artifice, put together in bits and pieces, and so far from unique that they have been repeating themselves, form and content, for over a century. No other dramatic, visual, or narrative form uses these conventions (although they have been modified for use in comic strips and have been varied for television), nor does anything like them exist in ordinary experience. (No one leaps from one side to the other when watching two people talking.) They have lasted almost 100 years and are ubiquitous, so much so that the first thing a filmmaker usually does when he wishes to explore alternatives to the Hollywood continuity style is refuse to do over-the-shoulder shots or obey the 180- and 90-degree rules.

Continuity cutting is an industrial standard, like a driver and passenger side door on a car, like the exact tolerances that enable a screw and bolt to fit together. Like any standard, it creates functionality and universality and becomes the means that permit filmmaker and audience to ignore the details of structure while they go about the work of communicating emotions and advancing a story. From the principles of continuity cutting, narrative is generated and a story is told. The key element is that the story is told with the least interference from the structure that creates it. Creative energies and viewer comprehension need not be absorbed with formal complexity because the form—as complex as it is—is so conventionalized that viewers look through it, as if observing a story unfolding on its own. As we saw in the example from *Psycho,* an innovative director may exploit these techniques and make them yield different responses. Most filmmakers do them by rote. As viewers, we are so acculturated to these compositional and cutting techniques that we don't know they are happening—which is exactly the point. To film a dialogue sequence is to create an **over-the-shoulder cutting pattern**. Therefore, to watch a dialogue sequence is to watch the over-the-shoulder, shot/reverse shot cutting pattern. We take it as a given and, essentially, don't notice it—we see right through it. More precisely, we don't respond to the cutting except to move within its secure and comforting pattern, imagining ourselves between the glances of the participants on screen.

The classical Hollywood continuity style is incredibly economical. Since every filmmaker must know how to shoot a dialogue sequence, or a suspense sequence, or a sequence in which a woman looks at a man and knows she's in love, the setups (lighting, camera position, marks on the floor where the actors need to stand) are relatively easy to make. They are shot simply and inexpressively in a shallow space, with bright, even high-key lighting, the camera set quite still at eye level to the characters. Much of the burden of narrative is carried by the dialogue. The rest is carried by facial gestures, body language, props, mise-en-scène—all of which are fit to make a sequence and entire film.

Almost always, they are determined by a thousand such sequences made in other films. Fragmenting a sequence into many different shots makes it possible, as we've seen, not to have all the actors present at the same time or the entire set built at once. If an intense confrontation between a good guy and a bad guy in a warehouse calls for individual shots (one-shots) of each character threatening the other, only the character in the particular shot need be present. Someone out of camera range (usually the person responsible for keeping track of the continuity from one shot to another) can read the lines of the good guy while a shot is made of the bad guy yelling threats and brandishing his gun. The two parts of the sequence can be cut together in the editing room, where a better reaction from one of the actors, taken at a different time and from a different scene, can be cut in if needed. Coverage, shooting the sequence from different angles and making numerous takes of those angles, ensures that the film can be put together to the producer's liking, in line with conventional cutting procedures in the inexpensive confines of the editing suite. As long as attention was paid to where the eyes of each of the antagonists were looking, as long as the lighting was consistent and nothing changed in the background—a clock, for example, which must not be permitted to indicate the passage of shooting time but only the passage of narrative time—the editor can match movement, dialogue, and sound so that the intercutting between the two characters will be subordinated to what they are saying.

As we've seen, the economy of the continuity style operates on the side of reception as well as production. As viewers, we have been so acculturated to the style's nuances that a mere exchange of glances, edited across the gaze of two characters, can tell us volumes. Suspense and horror films, for example, depend absolutely on a character's look of surprise or fright that prepares us to expect to see the object of this agitated gaze. That object can be shown in the following shot or a few shots later. But shown it must be to close the circulation of the look, the expectation, and to satisfy that expectation. Even new cinematic ideas quickly become conventionalized when they prove popular. Contemporary thrillers and horror or science fiction films made in the classical style may use an expressive dark-blue, smoke-filled lighting for nighttime. Some horror films use exaggerated point-of-view shots to allow us to "see with" the eyes of the monster. But these have all become conventions; we expect to see them and we know what they mean when we do. These elements of the classical style have become, like all the others, invisible and, at the same time, heavily coded. Especially in the horror film, we are wise enough about these codes to laugh at their obviousness, even while enjoying them: the recent *Scream* and *I Know What You Did Last Summer* series, as well as *The Blair Witch Project* (Daniel Myrick, Eduardo Sánchez, 1999), depend upon our understanding of the codes and our continued willingness to be taken in by them.

On one level, we take no notice of them, but on another level, these conventions communicate to us, succinctly, economically, what we need to know to understand the story being told and to feel the emotions that must be felt. When the camera dollies in to a close-up of a character whose eyes are slightly raised and, after the dolly in, there is a dissolve with wavy lines from one shot to another, we know what's coming: a dream, a daydream, a memory, or a fantasy sequence. Someone steals into an apartment or underground parking garage and hides in the shadows. A woman follows, going about her business as if nothing has happened. Our gaze is privileged by so many other sequences just like this that we see and know more than the woman does. Trained to move across the cuts, we know that women in dark spaces inhabited by a villain unseen by them are vulnerable. We experience unease and fright in anticipation of what might happen. No matter what is going on in the rest of the story, this combination of shots tells a story of its own. The characters' point of view doesn't matter, only ours. Whenever a camera moves around in an arc or rapidly dollies forward toward an object, our emotions surge (perhaps because the camera is otherwise so often still). Facial expressions or body movements, edited in counterpoint to each other, tell volumes. A nod of a head, a stiff smile, parted lips, narrowing eyes, hands held up to a wide-eyed face with mouth agape; a shot of a hand moving down toward a pocket; shoulders hunched or hands held away from the body; a head buried in open hands or a hand cupping a chin—these and dozens of other stock movements and gestures make up a rhetoric of narrative codes used by film.

Gender drives many cinematic conventions. Gender-specific stereotypes of the strong man saving the weak and passive woman informed the early development of cross cutting—the editing of captivity/rescue sequences by intercutting shots of the woman in peril with shots of her approaching rescuer. In general, the structure of the gaze in film is really the structure of the male character and of the male viewer, gazing at the female character who is built into the narrative as the object of desire. The exchange of looks in film is very often erotic, and so the structure of the gaze drives the narrative, drives our emotions, and propels the characters across the cutting and into each other's arms. Even small gestures are gender-marked, and much narrative material is expressed through the gender of the person who uses it. Only women put their hands up to their faces to express horror, fear, sadness. Men may jerk their shoulders back or put an arm out—often a protective arm if a woman is with him. A man will allow his head to fall on his forearm in a moment of stress or pull it down between his shoulders to express anger. Women cast eyes upward for a variety of sexually related reasons; men work their mouths, usually in a self-contained smile or smirk. Men may raise their eyes, but usually as a look of annoyance. In almost every instance, from the editing structure to the slightest movement of an actor's arm or face, form dictates content and sexual desire dictates both.

Directed by the looks of the characters and, on a higher level, by the structure of looks and cuts that are used uniformly over all of cinema, the viewer need be shown and told quite little. Events, responses, emotions, narrative movements become coded. Having seen films and television, we know how to read the structure. Like a computer code, it runs our responses and, within given limits, can be assigned variables. So, it would be absurd to say that *all* films are alike, that they all communicate the same meanings and garner from us exactly the same response. But the ways they order our responses, code them, and communicate them are indeed quite uniform—so much so that radical variations from the established patterns become visible to us and are accepted or rejected to the extent that they disturb us with their visibility.

Viewers and reviewers remarked how director Quentin Tarantino played with narrative chronology in his 1994 film *Pulp Fiction*. Chronology is an important aspect of the classical style, and it has not advanced very far from Aristotle's classic notion that dramatic narrative construction should consist of a beginning, middle, and end. (Jean Luc Godard once commented that Aristotle was quite right; narrative should have a beginning, middle, and end, but not necessarily in that order.) A film narrative must proceed along a recognizable path of development and must come to closure. Any dissonance, any disruption to the lives of the characters generated at the beginning and worsened toward the middle, must be resolved by film's end. *Pulp Fiction* seems to disrupt this movement. The end of the very first sequence of the film, in which the two gunmen are caught in the middle of a holdup in a diner, takes place at the end of the film. In the middle of the film, one of the gunmen, John Travolta's Vincent, is shot to death, coming out of a toilet—meaningless, violent death being a main narrative anchor of Tarantino's movies. There he is, alive again, at the end of the film in a sequence the beginning of which we have already seen.

The structure is less radical than jokey and actually helps Tarantino tie up his film and leave audience members less queasy than they might have been. It gives Vincent a reprise, while also sending him back to the toilet in an attempt at ironic counterpoint to the event that occurred earlier and to further emphasize the anal references throughout the film. It also offers a mock redemption to Samuel L. Jackson's Jules, who decides to leave his life of crime and take up religious work. The minor break in narrative continuity is amusing, only provocative enough to make an audience curious. More serious efforts are found in the work of other filmmakers, most often from outside the United States, where experiments began early and still continue. There is, for example, a British film called *Betrayal* (David Jones, 1983), written by the playwright Harold Pinter, whose narrative runs backwards, starting at the end and ending at the beginning. An episode of *Seinfeld* parodied this narrative trick. Mike Figgis's *Timecode* (2000) breaks its narrative into four quadrants on the screen, using sound to focus the viewer's attention on one or the other of the four interlocking events taking place. In the classic *Last Year at Marienbad* (1961), by the French director Alain Resnais, normal continuity cutting is made non-continuous, and the entire convention of linear chronology in film narrative is called into question. Any reverse shot, in this film about the uncertainty of memory, could possibly take place at another time than the shot that preceded it and therefore not be a reverse shot in the normal sense at all. Other alternatives to the classical style, classical continuity, and conventional narrative development have occurred throughout the history of film. They were occurring, even as the classical style was in the process of inventing itself.

Eisensteinian Montage

There was an important moment in the history of film when continuity cutting was challenged as the way to make the perfect film. It arose out of political turmoil. The Russian Revolution of 1917 unleashed enormous creative energies across the arts in the new U.S.S.R. Revolutionary artists were driven by a desire to make aesthetics, culture, ideology, and politics interact on a visible, formal level and make them accessible to as many people as possible. In filmmaking, artists such as Lev Kuleshov, Alexander Dovzhenko, Vsevolod Pudovkin, Sergei Eisenstein, Dziga Vertov, and Esther Shub looked to editing—or **montage**, as it is more accurately called when applied to their work—as the means by which the raw material of film, the shot, could be turned into a statement charged with revolutionary energy. They looked closely at Hollywood films, particularly at D. W. Griffith's work, to find out how they worked. What they discovered was that the continuity cutting being developed in the West was a form that led to reconciliation or redemption: men rescued endangered women, bad guys were overtaken by good. There was always climax and closure, in which "good" prevailed. In *Intolerance* (1916), Griffith was not averse to having Christ and the angels descend over the scene to close the narrative and unify it for eternity. The revolutionary Soviet filmmakers had something else in mind. They were looking for perception, not redemption; they wanted to pass on the charge of history to their viewers, not the calm of eternity. They found the way through montage.

Eisenstein in particular was fascinated by the ways in which montage could be used as an aesthetic and an ideological tool. In his films (*Strike*, 1925; *The Battleship Potemkin*, 1925; *October*, aka *Ten Days That Shook the World*, 1928; *Old and New*, 1929; *Alexander Nevsky*, 1938; *Ivan the Terrible*, 1943, 1946) and the essays he wrote about them he formulated a structure of filmmaking that was more than montage; it was an attempt to generate the pulse of revolutionary history in his viewers. Eisenstein believed that the basic unit of film structure was not the shot but at least two shots cut together. The process of cutting shots together was not to be an operation that repressed the visibility of what was happening in the name of continuity. Rather, montage was form hurled at the viewer. It was to be visible, legible, and powerful, a way of making the viewer sit up and take notice. Eisenstein's filmmaking colleague, Dziga Vertov—who, among many other films, made twenty-three issues of a newsreel called *Kino Pravda* between 1922 and 1925 and *Man with a Movie Camera* in 1929—referred to his own method of filming and editing as the "kino eye"—the cinematic eye. Dziga Vertov believes in the kino eye, said Eisenstein. I believe in the kino fist!

For Eisenstein, the shot was raw material and montage the film artist's tool that allowed him to cut images together in ways that would cause conflict and visual dissonance. Eisenstein would play shots off one another in order to make the viewer see something greater than the individual shots alone. A montage sequence might be built from the rhythmic or dynamic elements of the individual shots: conflicting diagonal lines, the movement of figures in one shot placed against an opposite movement in another; conflicting *ideas*, a woman calling for peace and calm cut against the chaos of advancing soldiers and hysterical crowds. This interaction makes up part of the montage pattern of the great "Odessa Steps" sequence in *The Battleship Potemkin,* in which the Czarist navy attacks civilians on shore in retaliation for a mutiny aboard one of their ships. The sequence builds from shots of the people of Odessa demonstrating support for the mutiny to the attack itself, which is rendered in rapid, often shocking cuts of gunfire, the crowd, a lone woman carrying her dead child down the steps as soldiers marching with their rifles at the ready move up to her in the opposite direction. Masses of people, soldiers, civilians, seen collectively, in groups, one, a few, or many, moving in opposite directions and cut together in a montage that defines the outrage of the attack and its brutality. In the most famous montage in the film, which has been parodied by Woody Allen in *Bananas* (1971) and Brian De Palma in *The Untouchables* (1987), not to mention the crazy *Naked Gun 33⅓: The Final Insult* (1994), a woman with a baby carriage at the top of the Odessa steps is shot by the troops. As the sequence proceeds, and the montage returns to her every few seconds, she sinks lower to the ground. But these successive shots are not in continuity with one another. That is, each time we see a shot of her falling, she is not in exactly the same position as she was in the previous shot. Usually, she is in a more upright position than she was at the end of the last shot. The suspense and agony of her fall are therefore discontinuous, stretched out, repeated.

Working against the codes of continuity cutting being developed in Hollywood, Eisenstein refused to indulge in an illusion of linear time, replacing it instead with an emotional time, the time of suspense and of thought, extending the woman's fall so that the viewer understands the enormity of the crime against her (echoed elsewhere in the Odessa sequence by a brief and stunning shot of an old woman in close-up, who, having exhorted the crowd to reason with their attackers, is shot in the eye). As the woman finally falls, she loses her grip on the baby carriage, which, finally, is released to roll down the steps, against the tide of the oncoming troops and the fleeing crowds, in a montage of accelerated speed toward destruction.

Eisenstein's was a cinema of ideas and huge political emotion, in which the conflicting patterns of images attempt to represent the conflict of history itself— a Marxist history of class struggle, the overturning of oppression, and the victory of the proletariat. Eisenstein wanted nothing less than to give cinema the form of dialectical materialism, that philosophy of history which sees events and ideas churning in conflict with each other, negating one another, creating new syntheses, constructing the new out of conflicting elements of the old. Nothing suited Eisenstein better than to create Soviet montage as the dialectic to Hollywood editing.

His ambitions outstripped political reality. Eisenstein visited America in the late twenties, shot footage in Mexico, and negotiated with Paramount Pictures to make a film of Theodore Dreiser's novel *An American Tragedy.* He lost ownership of the Mexican footage, and his ideas and politics were too radical for Paramount, which reneged on the deal. He returned to a Soviet Union in the throes of a violent retrenchment. The arts were undergoing the revisions of socialist realism, a state-ordered aesthetic that cut back formal experimentation and promoted a transparent representation of worker and peasant heroes. Eisenstein had already run afoul of Stalin, who was partially responsible for stopping his Mexican film. This gay, Jewish, avant-garde communist filmmaker was permitted to make fewer and fewer films, and he spent much of the rest of his life writing and teaching.

Eisenstein's films have left only the most sporadic influence in Russian cinema or any other. His style can be recognized in some of the documentary films of the thirties, including those financed by the American government, films like Pare Lorentz's *The Plow That Broke the Plains* (1936) and *The River* (1937). In Hollywood, Eisensteinian montage was mostly turned into another variety of special effects and then largely forgotten. But his films and his theories of montage remain an important force in the history of cinema as a response to the Hollywood style. Flashes of Eisenstein are suddenly breaking out in cutting styles of MTV music videos (hardly a revolutionary form) and, in a more interesting ways, in the work of Oliver Stone, especially in *JFK*, *Natural Born Killers*, and *Nixon* (1995). Here, as Eisenstein did, Stone will cut against temporal expectations. He will repeat a motion or a character's comment. Like Eisenstein, he turns time into an emotional and political force, a way to express an idea rather than a simple trajectory for the story to follow.

Depending on the Shot

Although there continue to be experiments in the assembling of shots that make up the narrative, it is not in the area of cutting or montage that the most important responses to the Hollywood style have occurred. Many filmmakers who wish to make films that go counter to the Hollywood style concentrate their attention on the shot rather than the cut. First, they locate continuity cutting as the main badge of the Hollywood style they do not wish to wear. But, unlike Eisenstein, their interest is not in the effects achieved by juxtaposing shots. Rather, they examine the expressive

"*…where the streets were dark with something more than night*" *(Raymond Chandler).* The Big Sleep, *by Howard Hawks (1946).*

opportunities of the shot itself. These filmmakers look to camera movement, lighting, and the complexities that can be achieved in composing an image to achieve their effects. When they do cut, it is usually to move from scene to scene or to break down a sequence into its most important parts, rather than use the conventional patterns of editing a sequence. They will often flagrantly disobey continuity rules, cutting to the opposite side of the imaginary 180-degree line, cutting rhythmically, not attempting to hide cuts by editing on similar actions, and not using over-the-shoulder cutting at all. Often they will use **long shots**— much longer than the average nine seconds of the classical style.

Films as diverse as Murnau's *Sunrise* (1927), Welles's *The Magnificent Ambersons* (1942), Howard Hawks's *The Big Sleep* (1946), Bernardo Bertolucci's *Before the Revolution* (1964), Chantal Akerman's *Jeanne Dielman, 23 Quai du Commerce, 1080 Bruxelles* (1975, discussed in detail in Chapter 3), and Terence Davies's *The Long Day Closes* (1992)—to name only a very few—illustrate the ways filmmakers can work against the rules of continuity, using long takes, alternative cutting patterns, and unusual visual and dramatic rhythms to achieve results that differ from those of standard Hollywood practice. In films such as these, the viewer's gaze is, in a sense, unlocked, cut away from the story and made instead to look at how story is being created. In a sequence in Bertolucci's *Before the Revolution* (1964), two men converse on a park bench. The sequence is constructed out of cuts that break the 180-degree rule. Each cut places the camera 180 degrees on either side of the two men. A dialogue sequence in *The Spider's Stratagem* (1970) is punctuated by fades to black. The fade to black is a convention of the Hollywood

Breaking the 180-degree rule. In setting up the shot/reverse shot pattern for this dialogue sequence in Before the Revolution *(1964), Bernardo Bertolucci places his camera on the other side of the 180-degree line.*

style that signifies the end not only of a scene but of a particular narrative moment. But here, when the scene fades back in, the characters are in the same place and their dialogue is continuing. *The Spider's Stratagem* is about a young man caught in history, tricked by politics, betrayed by his father, and lost in time. The strange fades to black in the sequence communicate the character's dilemma, his inability to know where his own story begins and ends.

There are often breaks in the rules like these, even in American films. Tarantino loves the **long take**—the unbroken shot. It indicates the cardinal rule about rules: they are there to be broken.

Mise-en-Scène

Directors who depend on the shot more than the cut are called mise-en-scène directors. We have already examined mise-en-scène, and it is important to summarize the concept. Recall that, in cinema, mise-en-scène applies to almost everything that goes into the composition of the shot, including the composition of the shot itself: framing, movement of the camera and characters, lighting, set design and general visual environment, even sound as it helps elaborate the composition. Mise-en-scène can be defined as the articulation of cinematic space, and it is precisely space that it is about. Cutting is about time; the shot is about what occurs in a defined area of space, bordered by the frame of the movie screen and determined by what the camera has been made to record. That space, the mise-en-scène, can be unique, closed off by the frame, or open, providing the illusion of more space—and also more time—around it. In *Traveling Players* (1975), a film by the Greek director Theo Angelopoulos, for whom cutting is a cardinal sin, a group of people move into the past by taking a long walk down a street in one long shot. Time moves backward as they walk while the shot remains uninterrupted. There is a sequence in the film *Grand Illusion* (1937) by the director (and son of the Impressionist painter) Jean Renoir in which a group of World War I POWs receive a carton of gifts. Among the gifts is, unaccountably, some women's clothing. One of the soldiers puts the clothing on, and the rest stare at him in stunned silence. Renoir creates their response by gently, slowly, panning across the men staring. The movement within the shot yields up the space the men inhabit, suggests that it extends beyond the frame, and delicately emphasizes their confused sexual response to this sudden appearance of a man in women's clothes. Had Renoir cut from face to face, the effect would have been quite different, suggesting the isolation of one man and his emotional response from the next person in the group. If he had offered only a wide shot of all the men together, their individual expressions would have been lost. The pan joins individual to group, making the revelation of space not only physical but emotional and communal, and the response more generally and genuinely human. It allows us to understand the response and not lose our perspective. Closeness and comfortable distance remain.

Editing is a way to form a narrative temporally, in both the making and the viewing of a film. Editing speeds up the shooting by creating a rhythm of forward action. Even the over-the-shoulder cutting of a dialogue sequence, which creates an event that takes place in one space over a short period of time, is moved along by the rapid shifts of point of view between the participants. Editing also takes the power of choice from the viewer, selecting what the filmmaker believes is important to see. Mise-en-scène filmmaking directs our attention to the space of the shot itself. It slows things down—especially on the production side, where care must be taken in performance, lighting, and composition. If a long take is involved—like the shot in Scorsese's *Goodfellas* that lasts almost four minutes—careful planning is required to make sure that actors and camera move synchronously. In a long take, actors must act. There's no chance to save a performance by cutting away to someone or something else in the scene. If a mistake is made, the entire shot has to be made again. The economics of Hollywood production frown on such methods.

For the viewer, a film that depends upon mise-en-scène and long shots makes special demands. Without editing to analyze what's important in a scene by cutting to a **close-up** of a face or an object, the viewer is required to do the looking around in the shot, to be sensitive to changes in spatial relationships and the movements of camera and actor. Even a film that uses a lot of cutting may still depend on the mise-en-scène to articulate meaning as each cut reveals a different spatial relationship. Perhaps a general rule is that films made in the classical continuity style point to and usher the viewer through the progress of the narrative. Films that depend on mise-en-scène ask the viewer to pause and examine the compositional spaces of the narrative. The classical continuity style is directive; the mise-en-scène style contemplative.

The Long Take in *Citizen Kane*

There is a sequence in *Citizen Kane* that tells us about Kane's childhood, concentrating on the moment when his mother signs over his care to the rich Mr. Thatcher. The sequence concerns the shifting relationships between mother, son, father, and a new patriarchal figure, who will take the son from his parents and introduce him to the world of wealth and personal isolation. Welles describes these relational changes not so much through what the characters say to each other as through the way the camera and characters move through the space of the sequence. The sequence begins with Mrs. Kane looking out the window and calling to her son, who is playing with his sled in the snow (the sled that, at the end of the film, will be revealed as "Rosebud," Kane's dying memory). The camera pulls up and back as Mrs. Kane turns around, and as the camera moves, it reveals a figure to her right. This is the new guardian, Mr. Thatcher. The camera tracks backward in front of them as they move to the other side of the room, talking about signing the papers that will give Thatcher custody of Kane. Through all of this, the child outside in the snow remains visible and audible through the window even as the camera moves back. Welles employs a technique known as **deep focus,** by means of which everything in the frame, from front to rear, remains equally sharp. As a result of the deep focus and the long backward track of the camera, space expands to the rear of the frame. The small cabin in which all of this takes place is expanded into a larger area of psychological change and uprooting, which is underscored by the appearance of the father in the shot.

As Mrs. Kane and Thatcher continue to move toward the opposite end of the room, Mr. Kane is revealed on the left side of the frame. Throughout the shot, he remains always slightly behind his wife as she and Mr. Thatcher approach the table where the papers are. In their movement to the table, the child, still playing outside the window, is sometimes blocked out by the figure of his mother or father, but throughout the shot a triangulated dynamic is maintained between the three adults and between the adults and the child. After withdrawing her gaze from Kane out in the snow, the mother looks straight ahead and then down at the table. Thatcher's and Mr. Kane's gazes remain fixed on Mrs. Kane. She is the pivotal figure, the one making the choice. The two men are dependent upon her actions while the child is separated from her, almost literally pulled away by the visual effect created as the camera moves from the window to the table.

After Mrs. Kane and Thatcher sit down at the table and Mr. Kane comes closer to the two of them, the camera tilts up, causing the father to appear for a moment as a slightly threatening figure—threatening, at least, to those ready to sign away his child. Note that an unusually low camera position often has the effect of making a character loom over the frame in a threatening manner. However, Welles will sometimes use this position ironically to indicate that the imposing figure is about to fall from power. An unusually high camera position diminishes a character. Hitchcock will often use a disorienting high angle shot to show a character in physical or moral jeopardy. In our sequence from *Kane*, the father's power is weak and diminishing. He's about to lose his son to a man who is practically buying him from his mother. The three adults talk about their business deal while young Kane remains clearly visible through the window, on the other side, far behind them, now forming the apex of the triangle. Mr. Kane relents in his opposition to the deal the moment he understands how much money is at stake. He then goes to the back of the room and shuts the window—as if shutting his son out of his life. Mrs. Kane and Thatcher follow; she opens the window again, and, finally, after about two minutes and thirty seconds, there is a 180-degree reverse shot of Mrs. Kane from outside the window.

This complex arrangement and rearrangement of space and figures create a kind of Oedipal ballet in a small room, a dance of shifting parental relationships and authority that results in both gain and loss for the child. The ballet of camera and character in their dynamic spatial confines is more eloquent than the spoken dialogue and much more descriptive of narrative events.

Another less complex long take in *Citizen Kane* occurs right after Kane's electoral defeat. It is a long dialogue between Kane and his friend Jed Leland. The camera is set below the level of the floor and looks up at these two figures, one a giant just cut down to size by his election loss, the other an obsequious friend who is beginning to find his own power. The camera moves with them, but there is no cutting. The power lies in our observation of these two figures whose place in their world is changing before our eyes.

Other Resisters

Very few filmmakers depend solely upon shot length and shot content to articulate the narrative space of their films. Many directors combine the shot and the cut together to create a mise-en-scène of space and time that enables them to develop narrative subtleties. This, in turn, permits the viewer to comprehend a range of meaning and emotion in the frame and across the cut. Alfred Hitchcock's films invite us into threatening spaces, but at the same time they allow us ways to look at the characters and the things they do with some detachment, even irony. John Ford, the master of the Western landscape, places his figures in open, outdoor spaces, bounded by the rocks of Monument Valley as a symbol of a mythical West both overwhelming and able to be mastered. He constructs frontier towns on the edge of this landscape and carefully renders, visually and in the stories he tells, how difficult it is to build the borders of civilization, and the cost to the people who build them. Ford's editing is fairly conventional, but in films like *Stagecoach* (1939), *Fort Apache* (1948), and *The Searchers* (1956)—to name a very few—his shot construction creates images of a frontier past always diminishing, always on the edge of historical imagination.

The mise-en-scène of Robert Altman's films—such as *MASH* (1970), *McCabe and Mrs. Miller* (1971), *The Long Goodbye* (1973), *Nashville* (1975), *Buffalo Bill and the Indians* (1976), and *Short Cuts* (1993)—is made up of peripheral spaces and offhand conversations. The camera restlessly zooms in and out among many faces of many people doing and saying many different things, often at cross purposes to one another. (A zoom shot is created when the lenses change focal length—from wide angle to telephoto, for example—while the camera remains stationary.) What we see in these films is a visually and aurally busy world of people always moving together in opposite directions, whose lives meet and cross in peculiar and often shattering ways. The space of the shots is often compressed through the use of a telephoto lens, and Altman will cut from one zoom shot to another using that long lens. Within the busy movement and compressed spaces of the shots and the sometimes unexpected and ironic cuts, conventional continuity is often left behind. We are asked to validate the connections between the shots and comprehend more than the characters, in their fragmentary existence, can see. Altman's style puts more burden on the viewer than conventional films to see how its pieces and its spaces fit together.

The burden can be considerable. Consider the "Dawn of Man" sequence in *2001: A Space Odyssey* (Stanley Kubrick, 1968). The sequence is built of long shots of an imaginary prehistoric landscape (filmed entirely in a studio using *front screen* projection), in which apes on the brink of humanity discover a weapon and with it the use of deadly violence. At the end of the sequence, one ape, in a delirium at having learned how to use a bone to kill, hurls it into the air. The camera tracks the bone rising and rising. As it begins to fall back to

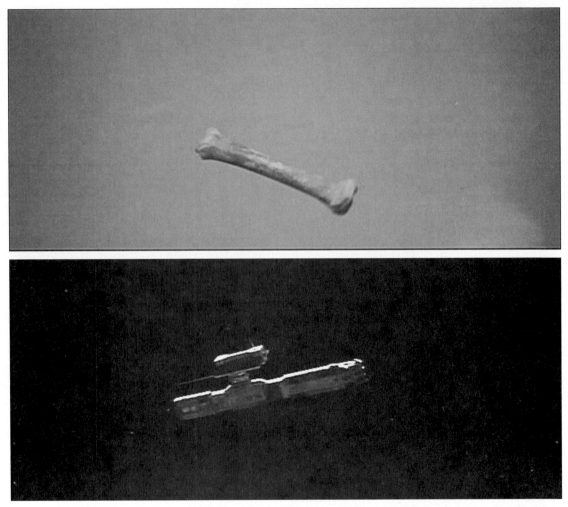

Cinema's view of the twentieth century: Stanley Kubrick's ironic view of weapons, technology, and the future: the cut from bone to spaceship in 2001: A Space Odyssey (1968)

earth, there is a cut to an image of a spaceship—thousands of years in the future and looking somewhat like a bleached-white bone—floating through space to the music of "The Blue Danube Waltz."

Eisenstein could not have imagined a more audacious montage in which past and future are sealed in the invisible fracture of the cut, linking together the birth of human violence and the future reawakening of human experience. In this moment, Kubrick turns editing into something akin to a statement about history, philosophy, politics, and metaphysics. Clearly, deciding to use editing for a particularly rich statement was important for a filmmaker who ordinarily depends upon the construction of the shot and camera movement to communicate his ideas.

Kubrick is a rare filmmaker who puts so much thought and concentration into a structural event in his films. Alfred Hitchcock is another. Hitchcock carefully planned every formal move in his work well before filming actually began. Cinematic form and structure, Hitchcock understood, are the means by which narrative is made and emotion generated. Nothing must be left to chance in the structure, and no one must interfere with the finished plan when shooting begins. Hitchcock was pleased to say that by the time he went to filming, he never had to look through the camera, because his plan for the film and his instructions on how to execute it were complete. As a result, Hitchcock's best films are made of complex structures in which each composition and cut relate a great deal of information. The space of the Hitchcockian world is created by positioning characters and camera to produce a composition that often ironically comments upon the characters' situation. He will relate figures and objects through a subtle cutting between gazes, creating an interplay between a character looking at something or someone and a shot in motion of the person or object being looked at, so carefully measured that the cutting back and forth builds a sense of threat or vulnerability.

Consider the sequence in *Psycho* when Norman invites Marion into his parlor, just before the shower murder. By cutting between the characters in their isolated worlds—their own little islands, as Marion says—and slowly increasing the visual association of Norman and his stuffed birds, including a terribly threatening, low-angle shot in which a stuffed owl looms over Norman's head, the sequence reveals much of the mystery of the plot. With its emphasis on dark and threatening spaces, fear and withdrawal, its association of Norman first with passivity and anxiety and then, in a shot in which he bends forward in the frame, with a threatening look toward Marion and the viewer, the mise-en-scène of this sequence forms the nucleus of the film. Its visual structure, along with the dialogue, lets us know everything that is going on and will go on—if we care to watch and listen.

Early in *Vertigo* (a film we'll talk about in some detail in Chapter 4), Scottie goes to visit Gavin Elster, the man who will set in motion an enormous ruse that will ruin Scottie's life. Scottie is already reduced and weakened. His fear of heights has resulted in the death of a fellow police officer and his own retirement from the police force. In Gavin's offices—large, ornate, overlooking the San Francisco waterfront, with a huge construction crane moving outside the window—Scottie is made to look small, sometimes almost cowering. Throughout much of the scene, Hitchcock has him sit, scrunched down in a chair composed in one corner of a frame, as Gavin, standing on a raised portion of the floor in his office, dominates him and the viewer. Through the spatial arrangement developed by the construction of the set and the camera, whose placement and movement keep diminishing Scottie's presence, we are allowed to comprehend undercurrents that are not articulated in the dialogue. Gavin tells Scottie a story about how Gavin's wife is possessed by a spirit from the past. In fact, Gavin is using Scottie in a plot to kill his wife, a plot that will eventually lead to Scottie's total breakdown. Scottie will become the diminished figure we see in this sequence. Like the parlor sequence in *Psycho,* this sequence in *Vertigo* gives away a lot of the film through the ways in which Hitchcock has us see his characters as part of his eloquent mise-en-scène.

Mise-en-scène can be more quietly articulate, often operating on an emotive level. In *The Conformist* (1971), the Italian filmmaker Bernardo Bertolucci created an enormously eloquent mise-en-scène in which characters, surroundings, and camera movement were created with almost operatic grandeur. The simple act of a character walking along a windy street is turned into an eloquent statement when a moving camera is placed at the level of the swirling leaves on the sidewalk, as the character walks by and the music helps sweep the movement along. In *Last Tango in Paris* (1972), Bertolucci goes even further and re-creates his mise-en-scène after the great British painter of contorted and wounded figures, Francis Bacon. Through color, character placement, and within the film's theme of male anxiety and self-destructive sexuality, Bertolucci makes a painter's mise-en-scène his own, and the result is an astonishing cross-disciplinary exercise in the evocative power of the shot. This is a kind of filmmaking in which, partly because of the creative eloquence of the shooting style, the viewer is asked to shift point of view, to look at things from many perspectives, to examine the spaces within the frame, to interpret character and feelings by means of color and composition.

In American film, we find this happening in some of Spike Lee's best work. *Jungle Fever* (1991), *Malcolm X* (1992), *Clockers* (1995), and *Summer of Sam* (1999) combine complex cutting, a rich and full mise-en-scène, and strongly expressed ideas that result in a swirl of often conflicting reactions—all of them inflected by the culture's own conflicts over race and gender. Like Bertolucci, though in the context of black, working, middle-class America, Lee's films are often created in huge emotions expressed in huge cinematic gestures that direct us to look and attend to political and racial meaning. Yet, they maintain a subtlety that allows room for thought as well as immediate reaction.

MISE-EN-SCÈNE AND POINT OF VIEW

Commonly, **point of view** in cinema means the representation of a what a character sees, and it is built out of the basic cinematic units of shot and cut. If a shot of a character looking at something is followed by a shot of an object or another person, we assume (because film almost never gives us reason to assume otherwise) that what we are now seeing is what the character is seeing. This is the closest film ever gets to the first-person effect in written fiction. The "I" in cinema becomes, almost literally, the "eye." We are asked to believe that we are seeing through the eyes of the gazing character. There have been very few experiments in creating film that is structured entirely in the first person. Welles wanted to make his first film—an adaptation of Joseph Conrad's novella *Heart of Darkness*—a first-person narrative, but couldn't make it work. The actor Robert Montgomery attempted to mimic the detective novelist Raymond Chandler's first-person style in his film adaptation *Lady in the Lake* (1946). The result was a wooden, silly-looking film in which the camera gets punched in the nose and coffee cups are lifted up to the lens to mimic the character drinking. The only time the main character is seen is when he looks into a mirror.

The first-person effect in film is best achieved by means of the interplay of gazes created through the intercutting of characters who look and the people or things they're looking at. Film, therefore, is mostly narrated by a mute third-person voice, the overseeing eye of the camera and the controlling movements of the cutting. First-person point of view is built into this general third-person structure, articulating it with the intensity of the individual gaze. Hitchcock's films, as we've noted, achieve this by cross cutting a character looking with what the character is looking at, most often with the camera in motion. For example, when Marion's sister, Lila Crane, approaches the old, dark house in *Psycho*, Hitchcock shows her climbing up the stairs with the camera moving back at a slightly high angle. (Breaking compositional symmetry by putting a character in an odd position, too low, too high, or just off center in the frame is a function of mise-en-scène, a method of communicating disorientation and unease, even a sense of dread.) In *Psycho*, the images of Lila's climb intercut with images of the house moving closer almost suggest the point of view of the house itself, gazing back at the approaching figure. The sense of expectation and menace is extreme.

In *Taxi Driver* (1976), these effects are embroidered upon in interesting ways. *Taxi Driver* is a film whose essential theme is about point of view: how a character sees and interprets his world. In this case, the point of view is restricted to the consciousness of a psychotic cabdriver. The film achieves this effect by creating an exclusive point of view in which the world articulated on the screen is a reflection of what Robert De Niro's Travis Bickle, the crazy cabbie, sees. The mise-en-scène of *Taxi Driver* is expressionist; that is, it is the exterior representation of a disturbed mind. We see the world as Travis experiences it: the nighttime streets of Manhattan filled with hookers and gangs, pushers and crazy people yelling as they walk by, a homicidal lunatic (played by the film's director) sitting in the back of the cab, people beaten up on the street. Scorsese will emphasize Travis's disorientation and madness even when the camera is looking at him. As Travis walks down the street, there will suddenly be a dissolve—an optical effect that is conventionally used as a narrative device to create a transition in time and place—though here nothing changes. Travis continues to walk down the street. The dissolve is suddenly given new meaning as an indication of the slippages in Travis's own mind. The famous "Are you talking to me?" sequence, with its jump cuts (removing little bits of the sequence, creating a skipping effect, as if the character's own attention was sparking on and off) and mirror shots, continues the perception of a narrow, obsessive, decaying mind.

THE NARRATIVE OF THE CLASSICAL STYLE

The construction of mise-en-scène is one of the most complicated things a film and its makers can undertake. It takes thought, an almost painterly sense of how space can be used to define character and create response from the viewer, and it takes time. Therefore, a film with a complex mise-en-scène costs money, which may account for the reason that coherent, complex mise-en-scène is rarely seen.

Mise-en-scène also often demands viewer attention. A film with a complex spatial design may have much more going on in it than a film that directs the viewer where to look by means of its cutting. This is at odds with the Hollywood style, which depends upon our having seen films in which the same formal devices of framing and cutting, of character action and reaction, and narrative structure are used over and over again so that we know what they mean as soon as we see them. They speed narrative along and place us squarely in the story. But, in a curious way, they are telling another story. In many ways the classical style constitutes its own narrative. It tells its own story of stimulus and effect, action and reaction, our desire to see and respond to the continuous stream of images and movements, characters, and stories that satisfy our seemingly endless desire. The formal devices of the classical style communicate meanings, transitions, elements of story that are the same from film to film. Facial expression, hands and body movements, props, camera movement, lighting, and cutting patterns are used over and over again to ensure that we understand perfectly what is going on. The curious and fascinating thing about all of this is that these repetitions of style and gesture are not taken as a joke when they are seen in context, unless they are self-conscious, stilted, their timing is off, or some other ineptitude is committed by the filmmaker; or they are being used to parody their own conventionality, as in those recent horror films. The reason, in part at least, is that we are not about to laugh at something that helps us so easily to understand what's going on in the scene and in the film. We are not about to laugh when these stock gestures and movements are carrying us forward through a story that has captured our attention to itself and away from the ways it is being created.

The classical style is therefore invisible and highly visible at the same time. Its visibility and invisibility can play counterpoint. A film dependent on ordinary structures of shot/reverse shot, eye-line matches, conventionally expressive gestures may suddenly indulge in a surprising camera movement or an unusual spatial composition. A filmmaker may wrench the invisible into the foreground by exaggerating a movement or a gesture, as Hitchcock does with the cross-tracking effect discussed earlier, or with the leap to a high-angle shot that he so often uses to express the diminished, vulnerable state of a character who has just made a terrible discovery or is in terrible danger. As we've seen, some filmmakers, in and out of the Hollywood system, make up new codes, give new meanings to movement and gestures, shots and cuts, or turn the old ones on their heads. Orson Welles and Stanley Kubrick use tracking shots to turn space into expressive containers of their characters' loss of power and diminishment. Oliver Stone revived Eisensteinian montage to mold time, character, narrative, and culture into alternative views of history. Mary Harron in *American Psycho* (2000) and Julie Dash in *Daughters of the Dust* (1991) turn mise-en-scène into a reflection of misogyny, in the first instance, and the shifting moments of family memory in the second. Both films will be discussed in detail in Chapter 3. All show that though the classical style remains triumphant, it is not invulnerable.

CONVENTION AND CONSCIOUSNESS

Perhaps the complexities of the classical continuity style and the responses to it can be summed up by a notion of unconsciousness and consciousness. The classical style asks that we be unconscious of form and structure but conscious of their effects. That is, most films want us to understand them immediately, directly, without mediation. Filmmakers who wish to explore the language of cinema and make its form and structure expressive in their own right—the way some painters and novelists use the language of their art to draw attention to its own devices—want us to be conscious at all levels. They want us to know when they are cutting and to ask how the editing pattern is creating narrative meaning; to be aware of a camera movement and think about its purpose; to look *at* the way people and objects are arranged in the frame and not look *through* that frame as if it were some kind of open window or mirror.

In the end, we have to be conscious of everything in every film. To be lulled by the classical continuity style into a trance of identification with light and shadow on a white screen is not useful. Assenting to the ideology of the invisible may be relaxing, but, in an important way, it is not safe. To look through form and structure does not mean that form and structure are actually invisible. They *are* present, working to create the meaning and generate the feelings you experience during a movie. To ignore them means that they and the corporate communities that created them are given permission to continue on their way doing what they want, telling stories that may or may not be beneficial to us in our dealings with the world. But to *read* them, consciously, analytically, with as much attention as we read those films that do not use the classical style, means that we not only are entertained, but understand why and how we are entertained.

Analyzing the illusory nature of film does not discredit it or diminish the pleasure of watching. Quite the contrary. The more you know about what you are and are not seeing, the richer the experience is, and the more reflective. It's exciting to respond emotionally and intellectually to film; to feel the story and understand how that story is being constructed; to see through the images to the characters and their turmoil and at the same time observe and understand what the images themselves are doing. It's possible and important to feel and understand, to synthesize and analyze.

We can extend this process of analysis and synthesis beyond the individual film to the individuals who are responsible for making them and then to a wider context and consider the role of film and other popular forms of entertainment in the culture at large. How do films reflect larger cultural events? Why does the culture support the conventions of story telling in film and other forms of mass entertainment? Why do films keep telling us the same stories? Who is doing the telling?

Film, Form, and Culture: The CD-ROM

Introduction: The CD contains a complete sequence of the house falling on Buster Keaton in *Steamboat Bill, Jr.*

Continuity: The CD supplies visual examples and an animation of the shot/ reverse shot style of dialogue shooting and the 180-degree style, as well as general principles of continuity of shooting.

Sound: Examples of how sound and dialogue work with the film image.

Montage: A complete visual study of Eisenstein's theory of montage, as well as examples from Pare Lorenz, who echoed Eisenstein in his documentaries of the 1930s.

The long take: A close examination of how Orson Welles used the long take in *Citizen Kane,* including an animated version of a shot from *Kane,* demonstrating the dynamics of the shot.

Point of view: This segment of the CD-ROM demonstrates how the viewer is situated in a film. Using a variety of films from various periods of film history, an explanation is offered of how we are asked to "see" the spaces and characters of a film.

Mise-en-scène: The dynamics of cinematic space in film are visually analyzed through the work of Griffith and Hitchcock.

Camera movement: The varieties of camera movement are defined and examples provided.

NOTES AND REFERENCES

From Image to Narrative   The story of Muybridge and Edison, and the information about early projection is from Charles Musser, *The Emergence of Cinema: The American Screen to 1907* (New York: Charles Scribner's Sons, 1990), pp. 62–68, 91. Linda Williams discusses the early development of the image and its relationship to the body in *Hard Core* (Berkeley & Los Angeles: University of California, 1989), pp. 34–57.

The Cut   In addition to Thomas Elsaesser's collection of essays, *Early Cinema,* cited in the previous chapter, two other books present a broad and stimulating examination of the early developments of the classical Hollywood style, concentrating on the development of cutting and narrative patterns: Noël Burch, *Life to Those Shadows,* trans. and ed., Ben Brewster (Berkeley and Los Angeles: University of California Press, 1990); and Tom Gunning, *D. W. Griffith and the Origins of American Narrative Film* (Urbana and Chicago: University of Illinois Press, 1991). Porter's 1903 film *The Life of an American Fireman* used to be considered the "first" film to intercut sequences. In fact, a more reliable print of the film was discovered in which the scenes were linked in a linear fashion, leading to the conclusion that the intercut version was a *later* edition, made by someone after intercutting had become the norm. See Stephen Bottomore's essay "Shots in the Dark—The Real Origins of Film Editing" and André Gaudreault's "Detours in Film Narrative: The Development of Cross-Cutting" in Elsaesser's *Early Cinema.* The standard work on the concept of the "suture," the stitching of the viewer's gaze into the narrative, is Daniel Dayan's "The Tudor-Code of Classical Cinema" in *Film Theory and Criticism.*

The Cut: Dialogue Cutting   The notion that cutting on a look to the thing looked at will create the appropriate emotional response is an old one. The story of the "Kuleshov effect" has it that, in the early 1920s, the Russian filmmaker Lev Kuleshov took a strip of film showing a neutral close-up of an actor. He then intercut that shot with one of a plate of food, a coffin, and children playing. When the film was shown, people were amazed at the versatility of the actor, who showed hunger at the food, sadness at the coffin, pleasure at the children.

The Cut: The Hollywood Economical Style   For the male gaze, read Laura Mulvey, "Visual Pleasure and Narrative Cinema," in *Film Theory and Criticism,* widely reprinted.

Convention, Ideology, Economics, and Resistance   There are a number of essays and books that discuss the ideology of the classical Hollywood style. Two excellent and accessible essays are Robin Wood's "Ideology, Genre, Auteur" and Colin McCabe's "Theory and Film: Principles of Realism and Pleasure" in Gerald Mast, Marshall Cohen, and Leo Braudy, eds., *Film Theory and Criticism* (New York: Oxford University Press, 1992). Bill Nichols, *Ideology and the Image,* cited in the previous chapter, is another good resource. The concept of "obviousness" is from Louis Althusser, "Ideology and Ideological State Apparatuses," *Lenin and Philosophy,* trans. Ben Brewster (New York and London: Monthly Review Press, 1971), pp. 172–73. For a detailed history of the classical Hollywood Style, see David Bordwell, Janet Staiger, and Kristin Thompson, *The Classical Hollywood Cinema: Film Style & Mode of Production to 1960* (New York: Columbia University Press, 1985).

Eisensteinian Montage   Eisenstein's essays are collected in two volumes, *The Film Form: Essays in Film Theory,* ed. and trans., Jay Leyda (San Diego: Harcourt Brace Jovanovich, 1977); and *The Film Sense,* ed. and trans., Jay Leyda (New York: Harcourt Brace Jovanovich, 1975).

Mise-en-Scène   An excellent discussion of composition and the construction of open and closed worlds occurs in Leo Braudy's *The World in a Frame* (Garden City, NY: Anchor Press/Doubleday, 1976). Andrè Bazin addresses the contemplative nature of the long shot throughout his essays in *What Is Cinema?* cited in the previous chapter.

The Long Take in *Citizen Kane*   Deep focus, or "depth of field," is a result of camera optics. A lot of light and a very small aperture opening (which translates as a high f-stop) create the effect. It is hard to do, expensive, and tends to call attention to itself, three reasons why it is rarely used in filmmaking. There are examples of faked depth of field, in which a special lens is used to focus two spatial planes. You can see it in Martin Scorsese's *Cape Fear* (1991).

3

THE STORY TELLERS
OF FILM

Who makes movies? We've looked at the structural stuff of which film is made, at the economics that are part and parcel of the structure, and we've looked at the work of a few filmmakers. But it remains very difficult to pin a precise creative entity to a film, like we can to a poem, painting, or piece of music. In the world of criticism, the very concept of the individual creator has come under examination in recent years. Some theorists hold that the notion of human individuality in general is just that, a notion: individuality isn't a thing that every person automatically has, hard-wired into the brain, but an idea that a culture creates and maintains about itself and its members. An ideology. One of the dominant fictions of movies and the culture at large is the importance of the individual and "individual freedom." Films are always telling us stories about the process of discovering and "being true" to ourselves, to the individuality we each have. But recent thinking holds that this is just part of a story we have been telling ourselves over the past six centuries. What we think of as individuality is really a complicated set of social relationships, in which "I" and "you," "we," "them," and "it" are continually shifting arrangements or positions that we all take up from moment to moment according to where we are, to whom we're speaking, or about whom we're speaking. The self, in other words, is neither innate nor permanent. The individual really is a shifting thing. The "I" writing this book is not exactly the same "I" watching a Rodney Dangerfield movie, teaching a class, or being silly with a friend. In fact, all the "I's" I am are constructed over a long life of being in the world, a "you" to the person talking to me, "he" to someone talking about me. Individuality is a function of the moment and the place.

If this is true about individuality in general, what can we then say about individual creativity? The theories that tell us that individuality and subjectivity are cultural formations rather than objective realities are powerful and persuasive precisely because they take culture and history into consideration. They counter individuality with larger forces in which the individual is one particle, always being altered. But even if all of this is true and individuality in the abstract is a cultural and ideological construction, we still believe in its existence and have proof of it whenever we or others act. After all, we do feel, think, and create. Therefore, we can consider various ideas about the individual: individuality is a shared, cultural belief. Acts, including creative acts, performed by an individual are always also formed by many forces, internal and external. A creative work—including and especially the creative work of filmmaking—has in fact many authors, including the audience and the culture that surrounds and infiltrates it. Individual contributions are finally determined when they are discovered in the work, rather than beforehand. The author is, in a sense, created backward from the work to the person.

With this in mind, we can work backward to discover what some individuals do in making a film possible on the production side. This will be useful because, if we understand the individual contributions to a film, we can continue to understand that a film does not come out of nothing but is the result of craft, calculation, and—sometimes—art, all of which are the result of human activity. We can understand as well that creative imagination need not be thought of in the romantic sense, as the unique working of an inspired individual, creating alone and calling upon the forces of solitary emotions. We can understand imagination as a collective event, the result of a collaborative project.

COLLABORATION AS CREATIVITY

Collaboration is the core of cinematic creativity. From the most independent filmmaker to the largest studio production, people work together, divide the labor, contribute their particular expertise. There may be one single, guiding intelligence that integrates or orchestrates all the collaborations, or there may be many. There may even be an external, abstract force that is doing the orchestration on the economic level: the force of the box office, which is the representative of the audience and its willingness to pay. We must understand, once again, that the Hollywood imagination is an economic system, an economics of the imagination. And this system now works across the world, infiltrating the filmmaking of other countries where individual creativity used to be more easily identified.

Filmmaking began as the work of rugged individualists. We discussed how the Edison factory in the United States and the Lumiére brothers and Georges Méliès in France worked to invent the apparatus of filmmaking and film exhibition and develop some of the basic narrative structures that survive to this day. Early in the twentieth century, other individuals battled (sometimes physically) with the goons that Edison sent out to protect his equipment patents and finally set up shop in Los Angeles. For a while, production in Hollywood and

New York was the work of individual filmmakers working with small companies, developing, helping to invent, their craft. D. W. Griffith was one of them. In collaboration with his cinematographer, Billy Bitzer, and working for five years for the Biograph Company, he made major contributions to the development of the continuity style. He then struck out on his own in the mid-1910s to create *Birth of a Nation* and *Intolerance,* two films that solidified the position of film as a social and cultural form.

But such independence was short-lived. Even Griffith understood the economic advantage of incorporation, of joining his work to that of a larger economic entity. In 1919, along with Charlie Chaplin and two other enormously popular actors, Douglas Fairbanks and Mary Pickford, he formed United Artists, a studio whose main purpose was to distribute the independent productions of various filmmakers. The arrangement never worked to Griffith's economic advantage, but it is indicative of what was happening to filmmaking at the time. The economics of production absorbed the imagination of individuals. The studio system evolved as a means of industrializing the imagination—making it economically viable—and turning individual activity into collaborative effort.

As in any manufacturing effort, speed and efficiency, established with the least cost, are essential in the mass production of film. We've spoken about how these efficiencies work in the previous chapter. The studios became self-contained entities, with facilities, technical staff, producers, actors, writers, composers, directors, all working within the physical bounds of the studio, all of them under contract. Some of these workers, from electricians to writers, formed unions, and as a result, clear divisions of labor were marked out. In short, every job had on-site personnel to carry it out, and every staff member knew his or her job. There is a temptation to reduce the outcome of this work—the films that the studios produced—to the anonymity of its mass production. Indeed, in the 1950s, and as we'll see in more detail in Chapter 4, criticism of popular culture did just that, implying that work of the imagination produced in a factory, for mass consumption and economic gain, could not attain the complexity and status of art. But an opposing argument would be more valid, that a new kind of art, created out of collaboration, emerged from the studio system. We can also argue that there are indeed important individuals involved in cinema's creative process, individuals who develop and use their talents in a collaborative effort in which individual skill becomes absorbed in group effort and assumes anonymity in the resulting films.

CRAFTSPEOPLE

On the level of the physical apparatus itself, a number of people plied their skills and talent in the studios (and still do, though more often as independent suppliers): electricians, camera operators, sound recorders, set designers, painters, greens people, film lab technicians, assistant editors. These people rig the lights; set up the camera (as well as turn it on and off and keep it focused on the scene being shot); dress and paint the sets; put up greenery; create the special effects that synthesize actors, backdrops, painted scenery, and models into a single image; develop the film; mix the sound; assist in the complex process of editing the shots; and then match the edits on the master negative that will be used to strike exhibition prints.

PRODUCTION DESIGNER

Others work on a more conceptual level, closer to our conventional notions of artists, developing the words, the design, and the images that make the film. The **production designer** (usually called "art director" during the studio period), for example, conceives and elaborates the settings, rooms, and exteriors that together help to give a film its physical texture, its spatial and temporal orientation, and that mark its setting in the past or present as recognizable, even authentic. If the film takes place in a particular historical era, the work of the production designer—along with that of the costume designer—takes on a special importance. During the studio period, each company had a head production designer—Cedric Gibbons at MGM, Lyle Wheeler at Twentieth-Century Fox, Hans Dreier (who began his career in the late 1910s at Germany's UFA studios) at Paramount—who had great responsibility for creating the general style of a particular studio.

In the post-studio period, production designers have developed individual styles and can sometimes be linked with the work of certain directors. There is the careful re-creation of thirties and fifties spaces and objects that Dean Tavoularis develops in Arthur Penn's *Bonnie and Clyde* (1967) and Francis Ford Coppola's *Godfather* films. Cars and dusty Midwestern towns in the former film; tables, chairs, carpets, wall hangings in the latter films are chosen and placed to evoke and represent the domestic space of a certain class and time. In *Godfather I*, a newsstand on the street is arrayed with period papers and magazines, which are laid out as they might have been in the fifties. A room in *Godfather II* is laid out to reflect the decorative style of the fifties and sixties. In *Apocalypse Now* (1979), Tavoularis creates for Coppola the nightmare jungle of Vietnam (in the Philippines).

Recall the dark, fantastic urban future designed by the late Anton Furst for *Batman*. Those sets—consisting mostly of hand-painted mattes that were processed into the shots of the film to give them a physical presence—help create the atmosphere of despair and unspoken terror that supplies much of the subtext for director Tim Burton's film. In Europe, the production designer Alexandre Trauner began work in the twenties and helped develop the "look" of French cinema, especially the thirties school of "poetic realism" that climaxed with Marcel Carné's *Children of Paradise* (1945). He went on to work with Orson Welles on his film of *Othello* (1952) and, in Hollywood, with the German émigré Billy Wilder. Like the work of any good production designer, his design can be detailed and crafted to catch the viewer's attention or made invisible—depending upon how the film's director crafts his mise-en-scène, which is based partly on the production design.

In this deceptively simple image from Coppola's The Godfather, Part II *(1974), we can see the art of the production designer and cinematographer (Dean Tavoularis and Gordon Willis for this film). Every item—telephone, books, chair—is precisely placed to evoke a well-to-do interior of the late fifties. Lighting emanates from the lamp and dominates the scene, which is composed to emphasize the figure on the right looking into the empty spaces of the room.*

Production designers combine the talents of graphic artist—which today includes computer-generated design—interior decorator, architect, art historian, or futurist to create ideas that—once executed in wood, paint, and organized by the set designer, matte painter, carpenter, greens person, and special effects people—fashion a world that the camera can photograph, or the computer generate, and the editor can assemble into a coherent representation of time and place. The production designer readies the space for the actors to inhabit and for the cinematographer, or director of photography, to film.

CINEMATOGRAPHER

The **cinematographer** is among the most important creative people in the production of a film. He (in a notoriously male-centric industry, there have been few women cinematographers, though recently their numbers are growing, however slowly) handles the lighting, chooses the appropriate lenses and film stock, decides on all the elements that determine the size of the image, its spatial qualities, density, color values or gray scale that will result in an image appearing, first on the film stock and finally on the screen, when the light of the projector is focused through it.

At his best, the cinematographer is a close collaborator with, and an adviser and consultant to, the film's director. In the days of the studios, some major stars had their own cinematographers assigned to them in film after film.

William H. Daniels, for example, worked consistently with Greta Garbo, MGM's glamorous and mysterious star of the thirties, because Garbo and the studio felt he could light her to best advantage. This was not an act of mere vanity but of the studio's and the audience's desire to have a consistent image of its star, which the cinematographer could best provide.

In some instances, a cinematographer exercises extraordinary creative license, expanding upon what the producer or director wants to see on film. This was the case in Gregg Toland's collaboration with Orson Welles on *Citizen Kane*. Toland signed on to the project because he felt that working with a new, young, imaginative director would give him the opportunity to experiment, which it did. He ground and coated new lenses, experimented with lighting, and figured out ways to create the deep field compositions and expressionist style that both he and Welles envisioned. The way *Citizen Kane* looks—its dynamic articulation of space, light, and composition—had more influence on filmmaking than anything else since *Birth of a Nation*. That articulation is the result of the Welles and Toland collaboration, which Welles credited. *Citizen Kane* is perhaps the only American studio film in which the names of both the cinematographer and the director appear together at the end of the film. Some would argue that on many films the cinematographer should get similar or even greater credit as the originator and developer of a film's visual style.

In many instances, directors and cinematographers remain together as a team. This is more usual in Europe and in the post-studio period in American filmmaking, where it is less likely that individuals will be assigned to a film and more likely that writer, director, and producer will choose whom they want to work with. Among the most famous director-cinematographer teams in film history was that of Swedish director Ingmar Bergman and cinematographer Sven Nykvist. When Bergman quit his filmmaking career—after he had become the most widely known European director of the sixties and seventies—Nykvist began working in the United States. He lends his rich style, in which he sculpts fine details of interiors in carefully modulated light and shadow, to an unlikely film, the popular *Sleepless in Seattle*.

Alfred Hitchcock worked with one cinematographer, Robert Burks, on twelve films. Hitchcock, who predetermined the structure of every shot before filming ever began, needed a cinematographer he could depend upon to accurately interpret his instructions. Carlo Di Palma, who photographed two of the Italian director Michelangelo Antonioni's extraordinary color films, *Red Desert* (1964) and *Blow-Up* (1966), has worked with Woody Allen on most of his films since the late eighties. In Hollywood today, some directors and cinematographers remain close collaborators: Steven Spielberg and Allen Daviau or Janusz Kaminski, Oliver Stone and Robert Richardson, for example.

EDITOR

The cinematographer is the individual with great responsibility for the overall character of a film's visual style, working closely with the production designer and director. He is present throughout preproduction and shooting. After shooting, the editor assembles the pieces of footage into a coherent whole. Editing has been one of the few major roles in filmmaking open to women, a fact that is all the more significant because the **editor** is the person who gives a film its final shape, makes it conform to the will of the producer (during the studio period) or the director (who, in the post-studio period, oversees the editing process). A cynical view might hold that, because the editor takes orders, producers felt quite comfortable having a woman in a passive role. But the primary talents of an editor are far more important than passivity and patience. A film editor needs great dexterity, a sharp eye for detail and rhythm, a prodigious visual memory. In the studio days, the editor was the one who managed to structure pieces of exposed film into the patterns of the continuity style. Under the producer's eye, she made the film the audience would see—and often remade it if previews went badly. Few directors shot with the precision and economy that could dictate and control the final shape of their material. Many directors shot and still shoot a great deal of footage, thereby giving the editor much to work with, much to put into comprehensible shape, and much to throw away.

Many films are still saved in the editing process. Bad acting can be covered up by cutting away from a talentless actor to something or someone else in the scene, with newly recorded lines dubbed in to create a better performance. Many films are invented during editing. The violent stunts of action films are constructed by editing. Sequences in which people knock each other down, fall off buildings, bash their cars into each other are constructed out of shots—themselves manufactured out of various image elements—carefully cut together to create the illusion of fists meeting faces and bodies falling through glass doors. But this needs to be put in the larger perspective of the continuity style, in which all motion, progression, movement, and unity are illusions built out of the ways small fragments of exposed film are cut together—and that is the editor's task.

In American cinema especially, editors have had major responsibilities for executing the cutting style of the studio, and some important editorial names are attached to their respective companies: Viola Lawrence at Columbia, George Amy at Warner Brothers. Dorothy Spencer worked at a number of studios on films as different as *Stagecoach* (1939), *The Snake Pit* (1948), *Cleopatra* (1963), and *Earthquake* (1974). Like cinematographers, some editors have worked consistently with particular directors, George Tomasini with Hitchcock, Dede Allen with Arthur Penn, Thelma Schoonmaker with Martin Scorsese, Michael Kahn with Steven Spielberg. Some of these are creative collaborations. In others, the editor helps the director keep his film coherent, and in all cases they provide the structure the audience sees.

COMPOSER

The composer of a film's musical **sound track** is only peripherally involved with the actual production of the film. He may not necessarily spend a great deal of time on the set. He is not directly connected with the construction of the film's visual elements, as are the production designer and cinematographer. Like the editor, he is more involved with fragments than wholes. The composer may confer with a film's producer and director, read the script, and make some melodies in advance. But his main work occurs during the editing process, when producer, director, and editor get a sense of the film's shape and begin organizing its final narrative and emotional direction.

Only the title score and music for the final credits are written as complete, if miniature, musical compositions. The rest of the music is written as "music cues," brief snatches of melody, sometimes only seconds long, that are composed to fit sequences or transitions between sequences, to distract from editing effects (or even bad acting the editing can't hide), and in general to create emotional responses from the audience, sometimes greater than the narrative, the mise-en-scène, or the acting can.

The history of music in film marks some of the major trends in moviemaking and the cultural forces that influence it. During the studio period, composers, like all creative people and craftspersons, were under contract to individual studios. They—like writers, cinematographers, editors, production designers, and directors—were paid labor, who worked under orders from the producer of the film, who, in turn, worked under the studio bosses. Many composers like Erich Wolfgang Korngold, Max Steiner, and Miklos Rozsa had distinguished composing and conducting careers in Europe before moving to Hollywood and becoming contract composers with various studios. Along with others, like Franz Waxman and Dimitri Tiomkin, they made their fame and fortune writing for movies. Some worked closely with a single director. Bernard Herrmann, who started his broadcast and theatrical work in New York with Orson Welles's Mercury Players, came to Hollywood with Welles and composed the score for *Citizen Kane*. He continued working with various directors and in 1956 began an eight-year collaboration with Alfred Hitchcock. His music for Hitchcock is so intensely involved with the narrative images Hitchcock creates that you can listen to a recording of Bernard Herrmann's music and experience the emotions of the film it comes from.

Herrmann's work with Hitchcock coincided with the end of the first era of the symphonic score and a period of change in the constitution of the studios. As movie attendance fell during the late forties and throughout the following decades, and as contracts with staff and players ran out, the studios changed from complete in-house manufacturers of narratives, with a ready, salaried staff always on hand, to less centralized production facilities and distributors. These days, the studios may assist in initiating a project, provide financing, and distribute the completed product to theaters, but leave the details and the staffing to the individual production group formed for the particular film. By the 1960s, an in-house composer and a studio orchestra were among those dependable, off-the-shelf services studios could no longer afford. The same period saw a rise in popular music—rock and roll especially—and a change in film marketing procedures.

Movie audiences had always been segmented to some degree. Studios produced "women's pictures," more accurately known as domestic melodramas, to appeal to the female audience and action films and Westerns to appeal to women or men. But, at least until 1946, the studios had an audience they could depend upon—an audience eager for their products. By the sixties, the studios had to seek out their audience and discovered that the most attractive group was those between their late teens and mid-thirties. Since this group proved to be a lucrative market, and because pop and rock music were very popular among this group, the symphonic score lost favor. Many films since the sixties use existing pop or rock music as background. Robert Altman's great Western, *McCabe and Mrs. Miller,* uses the music of Leonard Cohen in ways that make it so integral to the images that it might as well have been written for the film. Martin Scorsese creates such complex scores out of old rock and roll (especially for *Mean Streets* and *Goodfellas*) that some have referred to the films as visual jukeboxes. At the same time, Scorsese is sensitive to the power of the symphonic score. He commissioned Bernard Herrmann to create the music for *Taxi Driver.* It turned out to be that composer's last and, except for the music he wrote for Welles and Hitchcock, his greatest score. Unsatisfied that Herrmann was no longer available, Scorsese commissioned another old Hollywood composer, Elmer Bernstein, to redo Herrmann's score for his remake of *Cape Fear.*

By the sixties, more and more American films began using some version of rock or pop music, and the large studio symphony orchestra all but disappeared, as did the great names of film music composition. In Europe during the same period, some directors still collaborated with individual composers and carried on a sense of textual coherence between image, narrative, and score. Federico Fellini and Nino Rota, Michelangelo Antonioni and Giovanni Fusco, Sergio Leone and Ennio Morricone are some examples from Italy. Ennio Morricone, who wrote the scores for Sergio Leone's great spaghetti Westerns, such as *The Good, the Bad, and the Ugly* (1966), also composes for American film.

One film score convention remained. Almost from the introduction of sound, music associated with a film was turned into a commodity that could be marketed separately from the film. A song or score might become popular and be sold as a record, or a film's producer might specifically commission a song for a film with plans to sell it as a single after the film's release. Fifties songs like "The Tender Trap" and "Three Coins in the Fountain" are examples of this practice, which is now extended to various tie-ins like MTV videos. The video will plug the song and show sequences from the film. If a film score is made up of a collection of songs, the producers will certainly have them packaged as a CD for separate sale and extra income and advertise the music on the trailers—the coming attractions—for the film.

In America, the cycle shifted back to the symphonic score in the late seventies, partly because of nostalgia, partly because young filmmakers, who had been studying film history, were intrigued by the use of music during the studio period, and mainly because of the successful collaboration of Steven Spielberg and John Williams in *Jaws, Close Encounters of the Third Kind* (1977), *E.T.*

(1982), and *Raiders of the Lost Ark*. Today, whether an elaborate score is prepared specifically for a film or a series of rock tunes is selected for the sound track, music remains an important part of a film's narrative flow, part of its emotional dynamic and, in clever hands, an integral part of the film's structure. A film composer can become known for work in many fields, like Henry Mancini, and can also do wildly different kinds of scoring in different media. Danny Elfman wrote the music for the two *Batman* films and others by Tim Burton as well as the theme for television's *The Simpsons*. John Williams continues to compose for Spielberg and spent time as conductor of the Boston Pops. The end of the studio period seems to have released the composer into activity in many fields.

The role of the composer is oddly secure, because he can remain somewhat aloof from the production. The composer knows his role, knows that he must write to order. Little is left to speculation or temperament. (There is a funny, perhaps apocryphal, story of a conference held many years ago between the famous Russian émigré composer Igor Stravinsky and the studio executive Samuel Goldwyn about the composer's working for films. There was some mutual accord until the studio executive asked Stravinsky how long it would take him to deliver a score. "A year," he responded. The meeting and the collaboration were over.) For the composer, like the cinematographer, "individual genius" is subordinated to collaborative imagination. Art is put into the service of the manufactured narrative.

SCREENWRITER

It has not been so clear or easy for the screenwriter. He (and sometimes she) is the one figure in the talent pool of filmmaking who, certainly in the thirties and forties, was wracked with doubts, ambiguities, uncertainties, self-hatred, and mistrust. There is no great mystery as to why the screenwriter has been such a tormented figure or why we, as viewers, can have so little confidence about how much the person we see listed in the credits as writer was actually responsible for the film. American and European culture maintain the nineteenth-century image of the writer working in splendid isolation, with complete control over his or her work. Even when subsidiary myths are bracketed off—the Hemingway myth of the brawling, hard-drinking, adventurous writer—we still think of the process of writing itself as being carried out in a sacred isolation, where the creator is the controller of his or her production. Most writers believe this story, too, even though, like all cultural myths, it is only somewhat true. While much writing is, indeed, done alone, not all of it is (think of coauthorship, even in fiction). And there are few writers who are free of editorial intervention—few whose work gets into the bookstores exactly as was written, almost as few as there are film directors who see their own version of a film on the screen. There is, finally, nothing very romantic about writing: only people attempting to put good words on paper. If writers and their culture needed to maintain their myths of isolated inviolability, film executives knew better.

Writers had always worked in film, but in the late twenties and early thirties, when actors began speaking dialogue, the studios needed writers to do more than create a story and write intertitles between scenes, or written versions of what the actors were supposed to be saying, and instead write the actual dialogue the actors would speak. Studios had few places to turn. Hollywood, at that moment, was not a great literary Mecca, and the studios began importing often well-known writers from New York—novelists, playwrights, essayists—at high salaries. When these writers arrived in L.A., the studio bosses put them in offices and told them to make words from nine to five. The writers found themselves used as common labor. The studio executives loved it, because, semiliterate as some of them were, they felt delighted to have intellectuals under their control. Besides, they were offering a lot of money and expected their control to be heeded. To add insult to injury, the executives rarely allowed one writer to produce all the words for a given film. The studio bosses enforced the collaborative nature of film on all levels, whether the writers were willing or not. Studio executives put scripts through many hands, some of them specializing in very particular kinds of writing: comedy dialogue, romantic interludes, dramatic exchanges, midscript plot and character complications ("back stories" in current Hollywood parlance). Some scriptwriters, then and now, are known to be good "script doctors." They don't originate material: they fix the words others have written that a producer or director thinks aren't working or won't transfer well when filmed. The names of any of these writers may or may not appear in the credits. In fact, the writing credits are the least dependable of all, because so many hands may go into the creating of a shootable script.

Some major authors, like F. Scott Fitzgerald, couldn't quite manage it. The few who could, did it on a grand scale. William Faulkner contracted with Warner Brothers and worked with director Howard Hawks on such fine films as *Air Force* (1943), for which he did not receive screen credit, and *The Big Sleep* (1946), for which he did. He asked Jack Warner, head of the studio, if he could receive a special dispensation and work at home. Warner agreed, and Faulkner promptly left Hollywood for his home in Oxford, Mississippi. He wrote scripts for "them"; he wrote novels for himself and his public, and everyone, including himself, profited in many ways from both. This was a rare freedom, but it was not based on Faulkner's fame alone. Rather, it was a demonstration of a rare amount of good faith, understanding, and self-possession on everyone's part.

Moviemaking, like any large business enterprise, is not usually based on self-possession and understanding. Power is the motivating force, and power depends upon generating insecurity, resentment, and fear in order to work. That's why writers often felt miserable under the studio system. In the studio days, executives took all of this for granted, but the writers did not. An unpleasant culture was created for them, and many felt they were working in bad faith. But two good events emerged from this. One was the Screen Writers Guild, a powerful and, in its early days, a left-of-center union that the writers formed in the thirties to help protect their interests, as best they could be protected. In many instances, the job of the SWG was and is to arbitrate what writer gets credit on a film. During the thirties, it provided a base where writers could discuss the political and intellectual matters they couldn't deal with in their films.

The other, long lasting, series of events were the great studio films created between the early thirties and the mid-fifties, films that prove the old cultural myths wrong, that it is possible to get good writing and strong narrative structure through a group effort. While few films have shining, imaginative dialogue, many of them have good dialogue. Some of it captures the rhythms of the language of the day (even though, because of the Production Code and a general fear of offense, profanity was not heard in film until the sixties). Much of it delineates character and propels story and expresses emotions. Like the continuity style of which it is an essential part, dialogue becomes integrated within the seamless web of story and action. If a film coheres, the viewer cannot recognize the fragments of writing that come from various hands. Like the editing, like the music, it becomes unified and coherent, part of the story's presence.

There is somewhat less resentment and self-hatred among screenwriters these days. One reason is that there is little innocence left about the process. Most writers who go into the business know that it will be a collaborative event and that egos and romantic myths about independence and control won't work. Perhaps more important, a screenwriter stands to make a great deal of money. A quarter-million dollars is not unheard of for a first effort, millions for an established screenwriter, someone like Robert Towne (the writer of *Chinatown*) or Joe Eszterhas, who was paid three million dollars for his script for *Basic Instinct*.

The cynical view would be that sanctimony disappears in the face of profit; a kinder view is that more and more writers, who consciously choose screenwriting as their profession, understand what movie writing is all about and are able to join in the collaborative mix we've been discussing, doing their jobs with few fantasies about individual creativity. They *are* creative, but in ways that don't usually fit in with our preconceptions.

ACTORS

Early in the history of film, both filmmakers and audiences found a way to evade the entire issue of the creative individual behind the camera by focusing on the visible figures in front of them, the movie actors. Actors are, after all, the most recognizable, most promotable, sometimes the most memorable elements of a film. They create an illusion of embodiment, of giving story flesh and bone. They are turned into simulacra of our desire—representations of what we think we want to be and know we want to see. They are our collective imaginary, the cultural repository of images of beauty, sexuality, romance, strength, and power. Filmmakers, who at first (long ago, at the turn of the century) tried to keep their players anonymous so they wouldn't have to pay them a lot of money, soon had to yield to public curiosity—public *desire*—and actively promote the people who turned out to be their most valuable commodity.

A strong argument can be made that film as we know it—with all its attendant apparatus of publicity, fandom, expectation, identification, and desire—was born when public recognition and admiration of stars forced filmmakers to acknowledge that they could extend their profits by extending the stories they told about the people in front of the camera beyond the films themselves. The film narrative became only one in a larger constellation of stories. The star system became a great attraction and convenience for everyone. Audiences could live out fantasy and desire through their favorite players both on and off the screen. Sexual promise, so much at the core of what movies are about, could be expanded from film narrative to publicity narrative, and journalism became one more extension of the studio system. They could all feed one another. A studio's filmmaking and publicity machines meshed gears with newspapers, magazines, radio, and television to author a supernarrative of sex, wealth, and fantastic irresponsibility. This narrative continues today through radio and television movie reviews, through *Entertainment Tonight, People Magazine, Access Hollywood,* the tabloids, and the tourists' drive through Bel Air.

But what is the reality of the actor's role as creative individual? Film acting, and the very bodies who do the acting, should be understood as part of a film's mise-en-scène. A player is one element of the film's narrative space. How an actor looks, gestures, talks, moves, gazes can be understood in relation to everything else that's going on in the shot or from one shot to another, and becomes an important element of the film's total design. If the actor is well known and his or her gestures are part of a career-long development from film to film, an interplay of recollection is added to this mix. Coherence and continuity are the keys. A good actor can maintain, within one film and across a number of films, an intensity of style. She can create a performance that grows out of the particular film and is marked by a style that can be recognized from one film to another. Gesture, response, and delivery of dialogue propel the narrative of any one film and propel the actor through a number of films.

This may seem obvious, until one considers exactly what film acting is, which is precisely the reverse of stage acting or any other idea we hold about a performance. Acting in film doesn't involve a coherent, ongoing, developing representation of narrative-driven emotion, at least not on the actor's part. A performance is created *by* the film's structure, its mise-en-scène and editing. The actor actually "performs" in short spurts and in multiple takes of relatively short pieces of business, usually shot out of sequence. (Stanley Kubrick demanded his actors deliver take after take until, all inhibition and resistance gone, they produced the effects the director found useful.) The actual process of film acting is part of the continuity style, composed out of fragments in the editing room. In reality, the producer, the director, and the editor create the performance, if we define performance as a process in which a character and situation are developed. They emphasize what they want and hide what they don't, sometimes by no more complicated means than cutting away to something or someone else when a particular character is talking, or mixing parts of various takes of a scene, or cutting a reaction shot into one scene that might have been filmed for another. The filmmaker can provide accents to a scene by lighting, camera angle, and movement when the scene is being filmed and by music and editing rhythm when the film is being assembled. The actor must be able to call upon his or her tricks or talents for emotional delivery on demand and without a real sense of connection to what was going on before or may go on after, when the final cut is assembled. Like the writer and composer, the actor creates on demand and in disconnected bits—a look, a gesture, a piece of dialogue. The continuity style creates the illusion of physical and emotional presence and continuity. The actor's body is given, if not flesh, the immediacy of appearance, and it expresses the illusion of emotions deeply felt.

I noted that very good film actors and actresses have the talent to create a role within a film and a style that is carried from one film to another. These are the ones whose presence and style may either transcend the subservience to directorial and editorial manipulation or allow it to be used to everyone's best advantage. Some screen players create personae, versions of themselves that are made up of attitudes, gestures, facial expressions so coherent and maintainable that they become instantly recognizable and sometimes more interesting than the particular film they are in. When this is combined with the elaboration of a cultural myth about the actor's persona, a story built up in the collective popular consciousness from the actor's roles and publicity, a figure is created that transcends his or her individual films. John Wayne is more than the character in this or that film; he is, even dead, an evolving idea of a hero. Marilyn Monroe transcends *The Seven Year Itch* (1955) or *Some Like it Hot* (1959, both directed by Billy Wilder), becoming part of the culture's collective sexual insecurity and its mythologies of the sexually active, self-destructive woman. Others take up somewhat less cultural space, but demand our attention in and out of their films nonetheless: Humphrey Bogart, Henry Fonda, Katharine Hepburn, Robert De Niro, Kevin Spacey, Julia Roberts are actors with a reputation for intensity, grace, a peculiarity of gesture and gaze that draws us to them from film to film. So also the great comedians, old and recent: Chaplin, Keaton, the Marx Brothers, Laurel and Hardy, Jerry Lewis, Alan Arkin, Rodney Dangerfield, John Candy, Joan Cusack, Cameron Diaz.

Some actors can both transcend and inhabit a role. Marlon Brando has a recognizable class of attributes, subtle ways in which he moves a hand, tilts his head, inflects his despair. In *A Streetcar Named Desire* (Elia Kazan, 1951), *On the Waterfront* (Elia Kazan, 1954), *The Wild One, Godfather I,* and *Last Tango in Paris,* Brando has a camera-riveting presence. The way he is able to focus the viewer's gaze on the character he is making and the processes he's using to make the character foreground his presence as the central point of the film's mise-en-scène. The cliché about "taking up a lot of space" is quite appropriate to Brando. He is, with the help of a good director, able to put his resources in the service of the narrative. He can develop a role and allow the viewer to observe how he develops it. He anchors the narrative and then moves with it. But, while doing all of this, he focuses every action within the film and every perception of the viewer on his presence.

Some current film actors—Billy Bob Thornton, Bridget Fonda, Samuel L. Jackson, William H. Macy, Glenn Close, Parker Posey, John Cusack, Edward Norton, for example—can change their styles, shifting, chameleonlike, into different personae in different films. And there has always been a huge store of character and bit players, anonymous people with instantly recognizable faces who populate television and film and act as anchors. They are like human props, filling out the scene, transmitting important narrative information, securing our gaze. They give us comfort.

A talented player, who can sustain an illusion of performance and build a coherent character across the film's narrative, can be thought of as a creative figure *in* a film rather than a creator *of* the film. The actor whose persona transcends a film can be considered the cocreator of another narrative: her or his mythic life, articulated in films by the studio's public relations people, newspapers, and television. The strong supporting or bit player works for hire, does her job, helps fill the screen and the narrative, and moves quietly on to the next role. All of this demands an act of recognition by another creative figure, the viewer who enjoys the actor's work in a film and who observes and responds to celebrity, taking part in a story of desire, fulfillment, eventual loss, and sometimes pathetic death of the figure who is partly real human being and mostly illusory construct, the imaginary figure of the movie star.

Let's take stock. There is the group of creative people involved in various stages of film production, from writers to composer, from production designer to cinematographer. There is the creative presence of the actor in front of the camera. It is clear that filmmaking is collaborative work in which each individual contributes a part of the imaginative component that goes to construct the whole. Collaborative, however, is not quite the same as communal. Decisions about how the imaginative pieces are going to fit are rarely made by committee and never through full consensus among the participants. Someone is always in charge during a film's production, pulling things together, giving orders, keeping the hierarchy working—exercising power. We are left with two figures who might still be counted as the major creative forces of a film, and who fit the roles of head of the hierarchy: the producer and the director. Between these two figures, the power, creativity, and the myths of creativity are held in contention.

PRODUCER

Orson Welles once said that no one can figure out exactly what a producer does. At the Academy Awards, the "Best Film" award is given in the name of the winning film's producer. In the credits of a film, the producer's title is prominent, though often subdivided among many individuals: executive producer, coproducer, associate producer, line producer. What do these people actually do? Depending upon a number of factors, a **producer** is an initiator of projects, a fund-raiser, a deal maker, an administrator. The producer is also a cajoler, a protector of egos, sometimes a tyrant. The producer and her associates get the money and represent it. She oversees the writing, casting, design, and direction.

More often than not, the producer is on the set during shooting and in the editing room when the film is being assembled. All this control bestows a right on the producer to leave an aesthetic mark on the film itself. Even if it's just suggesting a camera angle or an actor's reading, or cutting a few frames or entire sequences during editing, the producer likes to think that administrative creativity should also extend to the artistic.

The amount of power that a producer has cannot be underestimated and never is in Hollywood. From the time that Irving Thalberg was appointed executive producer at MGM by Louis B. Mayer in 1923 and reorganized the film production process, the producer has been the focal point of the American filmmaking system. Mayer and Thalberg were the ones who established the film studio as an artistic version of the factory assembly line. The studio head, through his executive in charge of production, oversaw production in Hollywood. In New York, the studio owners (sometimes relatives of the studio head) controlled the finances. At the studio, the executive producer worked with the studio head in choosing stories and stars and assigning producers to individual films. Staffing for each production was done according to which writers, stars, director, and cinematographer best suited the project, were available, or whose contracts and schedules indicated that they were in line for some work. The executive producer assigned a producer to each film, and that producer oversaw the day-to-day operations of the film, ran interference for the cast and crew to and from the executive producer and the studio head. His word was law. His creativity lay in marshaling the forces, getting them to work according to plan and schedule, and conforming the film to the studio's style and standards.

The producer system created a perfect hierarchy for order and control. It put someone in charge whose main obligation was to get things done the way management wanted them done. The system mediated and moderated creativity, because the studio's representative was always there to make sure the film was made the studio's way. If this system repressed great flights of imagination, it permitted small ones and, by creating something of a uniform style for each studio, allowed room for variations. From volume came much mediocrity, but also a certain leeway for experimentation. When Orson Welles was invited to Hollywood by RKO in 1939, he was offered a multipicture deal with the right to final cut. The film he made would be the film RKO released. It was the kind of contract few directors have received before or since. It was one of the things that made Welles disliked in Hollywood from the start. But, as a recent biography of Welles has pointed out, the studio never gave up its control. They insisted on consultation at all times and held the right to cut the films for censorship purposes. Though Welles produced and directed *Citizen Kane*, RKO never gave up anything. The fact that RKO threw Welles out when management changed and promoted a new slogan for the studio, "Showmanship in place of genius at RKO," indicates that experimentation was never safe in the studio system; it only had its moments. Welles was fired after beginning work on a documentary, *It's All True*, that he was filming in Brazil for the U.S. government. The editing of his second film for RKO, *The Magnificent Ambersons*, along with the reshooting of its final sequence, was returned to the studio.

In the **post-studio period,** the producer's role has changed only slightly. While some producers still work for studios and sometimes run them, many are freelancers (women, like the action-film producer Gale Ann Hurd, are finally taking the chair). The studios themselves are no longer self-contained factories but part of large, often multinational corporations that have nothing to do with filmmaking, except that one of their holdings happens to be a film studio. Although a producer may no longer have one boss to whom she must answer, she still remains the mediator between the money and the production, which the producer often puts together (though not always: a film can now be organized by an agent, a director, or a star, who will then hire a producer). Unlike the old studio days, few things are "off the shelf" and few personnel are available down the hall. An array of service businesses has grown around the filmmaking process: equipment renters, sound recording studios, casting agencies, special effects people, caterers, and powerful talent agencies who represent all those people—writers, cinematographers, composers, production designers, and the like—who used to be under contract. The business of putting together the pieces has become complex, and the producer has to work her way through the complexity and turn out a product that will turn a profit.

In the end as in the beginning, the producer's creativity is that of a manager. He has to know how to initiate, negotiate, mediate. He must believe that he possesses an excellent intuition of what constitutes popular success and impose that intuition upon the entire production, with the control of a stern administrator. He has to believe that he knows "what the public wants" and get a film made that delivers it along with what the studio or the distributor wants, in the only form his bosses understand: box office receipts, cable deals, and videotape rentals. If not, Sony, or Rupert Murdoch, or AOL Time-Warner, or Viacom (owners of Columbia Pictures, Twentieth-Century Fox, Warner Bros, and Paramount, respectively) may not want him to produce any more films for them.

We have not quite yet answered the question, Who makes movies? We haven't answered it if we are still looking for filmmaking to fit the tradition of the creative individual. Even if we can comprehend the idea of collective creativity, that ideological relay switch almost always trips on, forcing us to say that anything made by a group can't be very creative. So we keep looking for answers even though the answers that come along never quite satisfy our longing for the romantic myths of creativity. Still, the cultural desire to find the creative person dwelling inside of and existing as an aura around a work of imagination is very strong, so strong that, without it, a work is in danger of getting no respect. As long as film remains a product of "them," instead of her or him, it is unmanageable by the critical mind; a handle can't be put on it. For film and the study of film to be taken seriously, a single, identifiable author (who is not a manager, a figure held in little respect in intellectual and academic circles) has to be identified. And, indeed, such a person has been identified, or perhaps imagined, in a curious, roundabout fashion.

THE AUTEUR

European Origins

European cinema had always been more individualized than American cinema. Production never occurred on the scale of the Hollywood studios, even though major outfits existed, such as Shepperton and Ealing Studios in England, Gaumont and Pathé in France, and UFA (largely supported by American studios) in pre-World War II Germany. In Europe, small crews and independence were much the style. A film's director often wrote or cowrote the script and guided the editing process. The producer was just another functionary, rarely the overriding force he is in American production. Films made abroad—especially those made for an international audience—were often more intimate and sometimes less dependent on the master narratives and stereotypes beloved of American filmmakers. It is important not to fall into a romantic overvaluation of European cinema. Some of it was different, a few filmmakers took chances, a number of its films are more intense and complex than all but a few American films. The prewar work of Jean Renoir and Marcel Carné in France, Fritz Lang and F. W. Murnau in Germany (to name only a few), and the great explosion of cinema across Europe after World War II attest to a strong, independent filmic intelligence. But two issues must be remembered. Films made for *internal* consumption in other countries are as grounded in clichés, in narrative patterns beloved of the particular culture, and banal execution as anything made in the United States. And cinema in Europe or anywhere else in the world never achieved the variety, the sheer energy, or—and this is a key issue in our search for the creative individual in a mass art—the popularity of American cinema.

The Birth of the Auteur

The myth of the individual creator—or **auteur,** which is the French word for "author"—in film grew, indirectly, from political and economic issues between the United States and France after World War II, and it developed directly from the attempts of a group of post-World War II French intellectuals to account for American film and react to what they did not like in the films of their own country. The political and economic issues were of the kind that develop from time to time in all countries where the popularity of American film threatens the economic viability of the country's own cinema. France tried to solve the problem by creating a policy about how many American films could be shown in relation to the number of French films. During the Nazi occupation of France, from 1940 to 1944, no American film was permitted on French screens. In the late forties and early fifties, a flood of previously unseen movies came into the country, and filmgoers were overwhelmed and delighted. French filmmakers hoped to compete against the welcome deluge of American movies and meet their quota of French films by making a "high-class" product. They wound up producing rather stodgy, sometimes stagy films, often based on popular fiction or on big literary works, like Claude Autant-Lara's film of Stendhal's *The Red and the Black*

(1954). That young group of film lovers—who were quickly becoming film critics and who, by the late fifties, under the title of **The New Wave,** became the most influential filmmakers of their generation—railed against their country's movies and held American films up as a model. François Truffaut, Jean-Luc Godard, Jacques Rivette, Eric Rohmer, and Claude Chabrol wrote in disgust about the filmmakers of their country. Jean-Luc Godard said of them, "Your camera movements are ugly because your subjects are bad, your casts act badly because your dialogue is worthless; in a word, you don't know how to create cinema because you no longer even know what it is."

Who did know? According to these Frenchmen, some European filmmakers, such as Jean Renoir and the neorealist Roberto Rossellini, knew. But most important, as far as they were concerned, a handful of American filmmakers knew best. Orson Welles and Alfred Hitchcock; John Ford and Howard Hawks and Otto Preminger; Nicholas Ray, Raoul Walsh, Samuel Fuller—indeed names that many American filmgoers didn't know, then or now, were placed in the pantheon of great directors. For Godard, Truffaut, and their colleagues, these American filmmakers developed and maintained that very quality we've been searching for in this chapter: personal style. These French film critics imagined something so important about American cinema that it enabled them not only to launch their own careers in France and then internationally but to launch film studies as a serious undertaking in the United States. That's because what they figured out gave respectability to the movies. They decided that, despite the anonymity and mass production of the studio system; despite who may have produced, written, photographed, or starred in a film; despite the studio and despite the amount of money a film may or may not have made, continuity could be discovered across a group of films linked by one name: the director's.

The Auteur Theory

The principles of stylistic continuity were suggested by the French critics and then codified in the mid-sixties by the American film critic Andrew Sarris, who imported them to the United States under the name of the auteur theory. The principles of the auteur theory are based on the given—whether true or false—that the director is the controlling force in the structure of a film. For Sarris, that control includes three basic attributes. The first is a technical competence that marks a director's ability to understand and practice the techniques of filmmaking in an expressive way. The second is a coherent personal style, a set of visual and narrative attributes that are recognizable in film after film. Examples would be John Ford's use of Monument Valley as the landscape for his imaginary West; Hitchcock's use of "cross tracking," his variation of shot/reverse shot in which a character, walking and looking at a threatening object, is intercut with that object, drawing closer, ominously; his use of a high-angle shot to show a character in a vulnerable state; David Fincher's dark mise-en-scène, created across the horizontal line of the Panavision screen. The Swedish director Ingmar Bergman's intense close-ups of a character in a profound state of existential despair; the German director Rainer Werner Fassbinder's framing of characters in doorways or behind doors; his colleague Wim Wenders' images of men driving the road from city to city in Germany or America are all ways of perceiving the world, of making images that mark the directors as having special ways of seeing. It is important to understand that these stylistic attributes are formal, sometimes even symbolic expressions of ideas and perceptions. Monument Valley is for Ford a representation of the West and all the myths of the frontier that it represents from film to film. Hitchcock's camera strategies express ways of thinking about his characters and showing them in difficult, often threatening situations. They are expressive of his notions of a precarious and randomly violent universe. Fincher's dark cityscapes in *Seven* (1995), *The Game* (1997), and *Fight Club* (1999) are eloquent expressions of an oppressive world in which nothing is what it seems. Style is not decoration but the visible creation and expression of emotion and thought. This leads to the third and for Sarris, the most important element of the auteur: a consistent view of the world, a coherent set of attitudes and ideas. Sarris calls it "interior meaning" or vision, but it might also be called a worldview, a philosophy, a kind of personal narrative that is either unique to the specific director or a major and consistent variation of larger narrative conventions.

The French director Jean Renoir once said that a filmmaker needs to learn everything about technique, and then forget it. The ability to think cinematically, to know just the right place to put the camera, to create stillness or motion in the frame, to understand exactly where an edit should occur—these are the initial marks of the auteur. Technique that is learned and forgotten becomes style, because style is technique put to imaginative use. Anyone with good cinematic training can create a low-angle shot, in which the camera gazes up at a character looming above it. But only cinematic intelligence can turn this technique into a stylistic trait, and only true cinematic imagination can make it state a view of the world. Orson Welles loved to use the low-angle shot. In his hands, and through his eyes, it became a way of expanding the horizon and distorting the world around a character. He used it to comment ironically on the strength of a character or to predict the fall of a character who might still believe in his own power. It becomes a part of Welles's vision of a labyrinthine world in which the human figure dominates only momentarily. It is matched by Hitchcock's use of the high-angle shot, used to observe a character in a vulnerable moment or a point of moral crisis.

John Ford's figures in the Western landscape transcend compositional stylistics. They articulate a changing vision of the Western myths of settlement and domesticity, of Indians as a force of the land, and of outlaws as impediments to lonely heroes in the inevitable movement of east to west. Ford's visual style fixed individuals in the landscape of a symbolic West; fixed women in the center of the domestic landscape, in the comforting interiors of homesteads, with men riding out to the peripheries, making them secure. The dynamic conservatism of Ford's cinematic inquiry into our memories of the West developed through a variety of films, written by different hands and made for different studios. He was persistent, silent about his work, recessive; a good movie worker who developed his style and his ongoing narrative without fanfare. His concept of the West kept developing and turned to critique. His later films, such as *The Searchers* and *The Man Who Shot Liberty Valance* (1962), began questioning the very notions of frontier heroism he had originally established.

Robert Altman—the director of the original film of *MASH* (1970); *McCabe and Mrs. Miller* (1971); *The Long Goodbye* (1973); *Nashville* (1975); *Popeye* (1980); *Come Back to the 5 & Dime Jimmy Dean, Jimmy Dean* (1982); *The Player* (1992); *Short Cuts* (1993); to name just a few—uses a zoom lens almost obsessively. It is a technique that has become an expected part of his visual style. He uses it as a probe, a way to move to and beyond his characters, and a way to let us, as viewers, understand that watching a movie is, in part, a desire to come close to the image of a face, which is always slipping away from us. Altman's use of the zoom, especially when he combines it with a telephoto lens and wide-screen composition—a combination that flattens the image and makes space claustrophobic—keeps denying our desire. He plays with what we want to see, getting close, sliding away, and finally isolating our look at the characters and the connection of the characters to each other.

The zoom, along with other compositional and editing techniques, becomes part of Altman's style not merely because he uses them all the time (in which case they would just be repetitious) but because they are essential to the way he thinks about the world cinematically. They mediate, represent, and generate to the viewer his particular notions about power, the relationship of people to each other and their surroundings, the way stories get to or miss the truth, the way movies reveal and hide personal and global history.

They all prove a central point about auteurism: once you see a few films by an auteur and learn her or his stylistic traits, view of people in the world, ideas about politics, history, social order, psychology, sexuality, and power, you should then be able to identify those elements as the work of that particular director in any other of his films. The British critic Peter Wollen puts it in structural terms, suggesting that, if we take the body of work by an auteur and strip away the narrative variations that are part of each individual film, we will discover a structure of basic thematic and stylistic traits, a kind of abstract pattern of ways of seeing and understanding the world cinematically. This pattern then becomes a template that we can see generating the form and content of each film the auteur makes. Jean Renoir put it more directly. He said that a director really makes just one film in the course of his career.

At its most fruitful, studying the work of an auteur—like studying the work of a novelist, poet, painter, or composer—becomes a way of discovering thematic and formal patterns, the way similar ideas cohere or oppose each other, how images are constructed in similar ways, how a coherent idea of history and human behavior develops across the artist's work. It is a comfortable kind of discovery, because it breeds familiarity on a personal level. We can get close to a filmmaker by recognizing his or her mark; we can find—as we do in literature, painting, or music—a creative personality. Because of this, the development of the auteur theory made film studies possible as an academic discipline. When we study the novel, we never think about anonymous creativity or a collaboration, unless the novel was coauthored. The author and the work are linked. We study Melville or Flaubert and never refer to the author of a novel as "they." Positing, even inventing, the director as auteur put film in the same league as other humanities disciplines. We could now connect individuals with their work and analyze structures of style and meaning developed by a single imagination. Connecting a singular imagination to a group of films also allowed film scholars to recuperate film from its debased state as an anonymous commercial form to the imaginative expression of a serious artist. Finally, because the French discovered auteurs within Hollywood production, establishing style and vision within the studio system, American film was redeemed from anonymity.

The success of the auteur theory was enormous. Films were rediscovered, reputations were made, methods of analysis were deployed, and a whole new discipline of study developed. Filmmakers themselves were now able to celebrate their medium. The originators of the theory —Godard, Truffaut, Chabrol, and the rest of the filmmakers of the French New Wave—began making films in homage to the Hollywood auteurs they had created. They alluded to American films in their own films —recalling a camera move from a Fritz Lang movie, a composition from a Douglas Sirk melodrama, a character gesture from Vincente Minnelli, a narrative line from Howard Hawks, a snatch of dialogue from Nicholas Ray's *Johnny Guitar* (1954). The New Wave created and honored a universe of cinema and implicitly understood what the poet T. S. Eliot said in his famous essay "Tradition and the Individual Talent." For Eliot, poems coexist and influence each other. So do films. A new filmmaker, like a new poet, responds to, is influenced by, and adds to the existing universe of films; new films absorb the old and then become part of the total film universe.

Many American filmmakers who came to artistic maturity after the auteur theory were influenced by its call to individual expression. Unlike their Hollywood predecessors, who learned their trade by coming up the ranks in the studios, these new directors went to film school and learned filmmaking by learning film history. Like the directors of the French New Wave, they celebrated their knowledge and their medium by referring to other films within their own work and, often, by taking filmmaking as one of the subjects of their films. Unlike their predecessors, who adapted the classical Hollywood style and its invisible access to story, many contemporary filmmakers are less likely to hide style and make us forget we're watching a film. They are more likely to foreground the presence of cinema and its methods and invite us to see the story and understand what allows us to see it. They will often make films of complexity and ideas that run against the grain.

Robert Altman

Let's return to Robert Altman for a moment. Nowhere does Altman articulate his style and his vision better than in *Short Cuts*. Based upon a series of stories by Raymond Carver, it is one of the most powerful statements about gender inequity and the objectifying of women ever made by a filmmaker. And, it is a great narrative experiment. Through a complex intertwining of characters and their stories, all taking place among mostly lower-middle-class Los Angelinos, gender difference, even gender panic, is revealed. Dozens of characters—their stories woven together through chance meetings, through amusing association (a joke about Alex Trebeck and "Jeopardy" run through the film)—and the restless probing of the zoom lens expose their gender hostilities, both open and unconscious. The film seems to discover an almost universal thoughtlessness about feelings and inappropriate actions. A group of men go on a fishing trip and discover a woman's body floating in the water. Rather than call the police, they simply continue fishing. When one of the men returns home and tells his wife, she gets out of bed to take a bath, as if re-creating for herself the dead woman's experience as well as cleansing the wound of her husband's callousness. She goes to the woman's funeral and, when asked to sign the guest book, only makes a gesture of signing, preferring to retain the same anonymity that the dead woman held for the men.

The film is filled with serial cheating (by both sexes), long held anger by one member of a couple toward what the other may have done years ago, and confrontations that lead to deep resentments and finally to violence. One of the men, a pool cleaner, bitterly resentful that his wife engages in phone sex to supplement their income, picks up a girl and kills her. As he does this, an earthquake occurs. The woman's murder is taken by the media as a casualty of an upheaval in nature when in fact it was actually the result of an upheaval between genders.

Short Cuts is somewhat misanthropic, casting a cold and displeased eye on relationships in general, though its sympathies are clearly with the women, who are abused in so many ways. The film is amazingly insightful into the ways gender and sexuality work to keep people cold and apart, as opposed to the melodramatic conventions of keeping them together and happy. It attempts to understand that life in the postfeminist world is no easier than it was when women were supposed to "know their place," and men were content being the dominant gender—as if it were all a given of nature. Altman knows that nothing in culture is a given of nature, especially in the realm of human relationships. His characters struggle against that fact, and his restless, probing camera pushes their struggles to the limits. *Short Cuts* is a summary film. In it are gathered all of Altman's concerns and techniques and views of the world garnered from almost fifty years of filmmaking.

Martin Scorsese

Martin Scorsese—though he is no longer young—is an example of the new kind of filmmaker. A graduate of and part-time instructor at N.Y.U. film school during the mid-sixties, he has since become one of the best-known and most self-conscious filmmakers in the United States. He has worked across a number of genres and for many studios. He has developed a consistent and recognizable style. He has spun off a number of imitators, including Quentin Tarantino and many young filmmakers who make their first and second movies in homage to Scorsese's work (think of *Pulp Fiction, The Usual Suspects,* Bryan Singer, 1995; *Albino Alligator,* Kevin Spacey, 1997). Even more mature filmmakers have done Scorsese imitations, such as the British Mike Newell in *Donnie Brasco* (1997). The popular cable series *The Sopranos* is a riff on *GoodFellas.* More than his equally famous contemporaries—Steven Spielberg, Woody Allen, and Francis Coppola—Scorsese has maintained an unflagging interest in exposing the grammar of film to his viewers. But, at the same time, he understands the nature of working in a popular medium. While he plays and tinkers with the classical style, often exposing its workings, he simultaneously observes the basic rules of narrative and visual construction that allow him to continue to receive financial backing for his films and acceptance from viewers. Like John Ford and Alfred Hitchcock (among two of his major influences, along with Jean-Luc Godard, François Truffaut, and the British filmmaker Michael Powell), he is able to work many aspects of the system at once. He maintains commercial viability and explores and experiments. This was the talent that originally defined the auteur, the director who, while working within the studio system, could also quietly subvert it, using its conventions to develop a personal style.

Scorsese began his career by making films of small but consistent quality, and by varying his output. In the late sixties he made short films and a feature, *Who's That Knocking at My Door* (1969). In the seventies he made *Boxcar Bertha* (1972), *Mean Streets* (1973), *Alice Doesn't Live Here Anymore* (1974), *Taxi Driver* (1976), *New York, New York* (1977), *The Last Waltz* (1978). In the eighties Scorsese made *Raging Bull* (1980), *King of Comedy* (1983), *After Hours* (1985), *The Color of Money* (1986), *The Last Temptation of Christ* (1988); and in the nineties he has made *GoodFellas* (1990), *Cape Fear* (1991), *The Age of Innocence* (1993), *Casino* (1995) *Kundun* (1997), and *Bringing Out the Dead* (1999). Of these films only *Cape Fear* brought in enormous amounts of money, and he made it exactly for that purpose as an offering to Universal Pictures, which had backed the controversial *The Last Temptation of Christ.* Otherwise, he has built both his style and reputation slowly and consciously on films that viewers remember and which influence other filmmakers.

His films are made self-consciously and are, in important ways, about self-consciousness. While, on the level of story, Scorsese's films often concern small-time hoods or individuals on the edge or over the edge of psychosis, they are, on a more complex level, about style and reputation, about how it looks and feels to *be* in the world, looking at people and being looked at, seen, recognized, and hurt by the glance of others. His films are existential and very physical. Bodies as well as personalities are always at stake. Characters kill and get killed, beat up others or get beaten up, thrive and do themselves in by thriving, or are nobodies trying to be somebodies by doing something to their own or someone else's body.

That's what Jake La Motta does in *Raging Bull.* He tries to control his body, which is either damaging other people or getting fat, and he tries to control the world around him by violence and jealous rages—by aggressively imposing his body on others. The film is finally a meditation on the inability to get control, or on always being controlled, just as an actor is controlled by a director and a movie viewer is controlled by a movie. *Raging Bull* focuses on a boxer whose awareness of the outside world and his place in it is dim at best. He is moved by momentary, unthinking whims and responses, and winds up becoming a parody not of himself but of movie representations of a boxer, which is, after all, what Robert De Niro's Jake *is* in *Raging Bull*—an actor, playing a boxer, in a film that grows out of a fairly substantial subgenre of boxing films. In the last shot of *Raging Bull*, Scorsese appears partially reflected in a mirror, telling an aging, fat Jake, who has gone from champion boxer to a nightclub owner to a performer in strip joints, that it's time to go on stage to do his rendition of the "I could have been a contender" scene from *On the Waterfront*. As the film ends, De Niro, as Jake La Motta, urged on by his director, playing a stage manager, does a parody of Marlon Brando playing a boxer from an older film. Jake La Motta is portrayed as a figure made up of self-contradictory parts, a reflection of a reflection. He is "real" and he is a fictional character in a film, there and not there, like film itself. Like Hitchcock, Scorsese impresses his own image on his film (he makes some kind of appearance in almost all of them). He focuses our attention on the artifice of celebrity, the illusory nature of film, and the fact that the film and our response to it are controlled by someone. The illusion totters, though Scorsese never permits it to collapse. The scene so fascinated Paul Thomas Anderson that he imitates it at the end of *Boogie Nights* (1997).

Illusion and celebrity fascinate Scorsese and his characters. Travis Bickle, in *Taxi Driver*, achieves fame without knowing it. Travis is crazy, an uncontrollable psychotic who can see the world only as a brutal, devastating place. His world is created out of a creative use of the most basic aspects of the shot/reverse shot and point-of-view shooting and cutting technique. Travis, like many other Scorsese characters, is menacing and sees menace around him. Paranoia rules. When Travis (or Jake La Motta in *Raging Bull*) looks at the world, the world looks back as a threatening place. One way Scorsese manages this sense of threat is to generate point-of-view shots in slow motion, so that the character's world appears as if it were a hallucination. Scorsese has perfected this technique so that he will change the speed of the motion in the course of a shot. The figures seen by the main character will move slowly and then subtly speed up, until they move at a normal pace. This method, which is a refinement of Hitchcock's technique of intercutting a character in motion with an object or person that character is looking at, also in motion, is disturbing because it plays against the stability of the shot/reverse shot we have come to expect. It generates an unstable space and reflects the perceptions of an unstable character. With it, point of view and the mise-en-scène are joined in an expressive definition of character and the emotional state, the emotional *space*, he inhabits and we are asked to observe.

The result is that Travis's world is one of sharp and dark fragments, created by a mind that is both paranoid and aggressive. Travis believes that he is responsible for cleaning up the very world he imagines, first by attempting to assassinate a presidential candidate and, when that fails, by saving a young hooker—who doesn't particularly want saving. In the process, he murders three people in a nightmarish episode of violence and destruction and is turned into a media hero. A number of films later, Travis is reincarnated in the person of Rupert Pupkin in Scorsese's *King of Comedy,* played by De Niro, an actor who has become part of Scorsese's directorial pattern and mise-en-scène. Pupkin is not a crazy paranoid like Travis. He is an ordinary lunatic who can't be embarrassed. His goal in life is to deliver a monologue on a late-night talk show (hosted by Jerry Lewis), which he manages to do by kidnapping the star and threatening his way on stage. He gets his wish, is put in jail, and is turned by the very media he hijacked into a star.

Blundering violently, lost in the normal world, compelled by madness, high spirits, or some obsessive-compulsive drive, Scorsese's characters, from Rupert Pupkin to Jesus Christ, try to fight the world's imposition on them and impose their own will and spirit back on the world. This question of imposition lies at the core of his characters and also at the core of the classical Hollywood style. That's where Scorsese's cinematic contention lies. Like his characters, he wants to impose his will on the structures of cinema, to undermine the impositions of the classical style by imposing his own style, his own way of seeing the world through cinema. Unlike his characters, he succeeds. He insists that we, as viewers, come to terms not only with the characters but with the way they see and are seen. He asks as well that we question our own ways of seeing movies.

One way is to remind us, even on a subtle level, that his films grow out of other films. In *Cape Fear*—not, by itself, a very subtle film—he constructs sequences that are subtly based upon Alfred Hitchcock's *Strangers on a Train* (1951). You have to be really familiar with Hitchcock to understand what's going on. Both films are concerned with apparently upright characters who become involved with, and are stalked by, figures representing their darker, corrupt natures. In each film, there are sequences in which these characters, these mirror images of dark and light, confront each other. For example, in *Strangers on a Train,* the "hero," a tennis player named Guy, sees his evil other, Bruno, staring at him from the stands as Guy attempts to play a match. All the other spectators except for Bruno turn their heads as the ball flies from side to side. Bruno just stares straight at Guy. In the companion scene in *Cape Fear,* the lawyer, Sam, goes with his family to watch a Fourth of July parade. The crowd watches the procession while in their midst Max Cady, the ex-con out to get Sam, stares straight across the street—the tormentor freezing his victim in his gaze.

Once you see the connections—and there are others—*Cape Fear* becomes an interesting conversation with an earlier filmmaker, as is *Taxi Driver,* which is in many ways a remake of *Psycho* (with allusions to John Ford's *The Searchers*). Sometimes, Scorsese can be downright weird about his obsession with drawing attention to the cinematic roots of his imagery. Early in *The Last Temptation of Christ,* Jesus goes to a tent where Mary Magdalene is performing a sex act. He sits in the audience, and the camera observes him as if he were in a movie

One director sees his work through another's lens. Martin Scorsese overlays Cape Fear *(1991) onto Hitchcock's* Strangers on a Train. *The first image is from* Strangers on a Train, *where the psychotic Bruno stares out at the tennis player, Guy.*

In Cape Fear, *the psychotic Max Cady stares out at Sam among the viewers of a Fourth of July parade.*

theater, looking at a screen. At the end of the film, on the cross, his fantasy of a normal life over, Jesus dies, and Scorsese cuts to a montage of abstract colors and shapes. In the midst of this montage are images of film sprocket holes. Even his meditation on the Christ story is, finally, a meditation on film and the way it represents legend and myth.

He can be very playful, too, almost teasing us about our position as viewers of a carefully made-up tale. This is what he does at the end of *Raging Bull*, and it is the main ploy of *GoodFellas*. This latter film is a more energetic and imaginative version of his earlier *Mean Streets*. It is also an examination of just what we, as audience, think we're doing when we go to see yet another film about New York gangsters. Most especially, *GoodFellas* asks us to consider who tells us stories in films, to think about whom we listen to and tend to believe—an important question in the context of a film that asks us to find gangsters amusing. Henry Hill (played by Ray Liotta), narrator and main character of the film, seems to be our guide and our eyes. His voice talks to us throughout, and we see what he sees. Or do we? One of Scorsese's favorite point-of-view techniques is to use the camera as a surrogate for one of his tough-guy characters as he moves along a bar in a club. He does this in both *Mean Streets* and *GoodFellas*. Early in *GoodFellas*, Henry introduces us, in voice-over narration, to his gangster pals at a bar. The camera tracks along, pausing to look at each face, each character, who smiles and responds to Henry's off-screen presence. Everything here seems to guarantee that we are looking through Henry's eyes, sharing his point of view—until the very end of the tracking shot. The camera moves to the end of the bar, where Henry is heading to examine some stolen furs. A rack of furs appears, and so does Henry. The camera has been moving from right to left, diagonally into the frame. Henry appears on the left, opposite the direction of the camera. So, at the end of the shot, Henry himself emerges, but from the left side of the frame—not from where the camera is positioned. With this slight disruption of expectations, Scorsese brings into question who is actually seeing what, whose point of view we can really depend on.

How is this possible, if we were supposed to be seeing things through Henry's eyes? Well, of course, we are not seeing through Henry's eyes. Henry is a character in the fiction, who is constructed to appear as if he were controlling the fiction. As we've seen, Scorsese is continually questioning the reality of people's control over things. It's one of his recurring themes and a major part of the formal construction of his style. Like Hitchcock before him, Scorsese plays with his characters and his audience and their imagined relationship to the characters. In *Taxi Driver*, for example, Scorsese limits point of view, forcing his viewers to see through the eyes of a madman a dark, violent city. Playing on the conventions of German Expressionism and film noir, drawing upon Hitchcock's ability to define character by how that character looks at the world and how the world looks back, *Taxi Driver* restricts our vision to that of a single, deranged sensibility. The prizefight scenes in *Raging Bull* attempt to create a mise-en-scène of noise, distortion, exaggeration of movement and sound that represents Scorsese's idea of what it must be like to be in a boxing ring. *What it might look like to someone* is a driving force in Scorsese's films. Limiting point of view, fooling us with who is seeing what, even playing with film speed, slowing down motion when he cuts to a character's point of view, are some of the ways Scorsese communicates shifting feelings, uncertainties, and changing responses. For Scorsese, perception is a liquid, undependable, and tricky business. He uses a variety of cinematic properties to communicate this and to make us aware that film can teach us about perception, or keep us fooled.

GoodFellas plays counterpoint between Henry, who seems to be in control of the narrative, and another perspective—Scorsese's, perhaps, or a more abstract "voice" that speaks about film's ability to manipulate perception—with such intricacy that we are left somewhat unsettled. Henry's "story" is punctuated by freeze frames, moments in which the image is frozen while Henry meditates on what's just happened, or what will happen; by virtuoso camera movement, as in the amazing, almost four-minute-long tracking shot that accompanies Henry and Karen as they walk from the street into the Copacabana nightclub, downstairs, through the kitchen, up to their table—all to the tune of The Crystals' "Then He Kissed Me."

At times, Henry's voice is taken over by Karen's, so that the woman's voice seems to run the narrative. Sometimes the editing takes over both and mimics the characters' point of view, as when, late in the film, frantic and high on cocaine, Karen and Henry believe they are being followed by a helicopter. The cutting is quick and nervous: time seems to speed up.

Finally, Scorsese himself takes over completely. It's his film, and one of the things he wishes to do with it is comment upon gangster films in general and our attraction and reaction to them in particular. He wants us to think about stories and their tellers. He makes Henry, the petty thug, the man who betrays his friends, a very attractive character, but he knows this is easy to do. Henry continually seems to take us into his confidence and remains aloof from the violence he and his friends commit. He is good looking, funny, and full of high spirits. But this shouldn't be enough to make us like a small-time criminal, and Scorsese needs to put more distance between us and his character. He does this by continually pointing to the tenuousness of Henry's authority, finally diminishing it entirely. Throughout the film, he plays with Henry's point of view and our sharing of it. Late in the film, after the mob has been busted, Henry goes to meet Jimmy (played by Robert De Niro in a relatively minor role in a Scorsese film). Henry is about to betray Jimmy and everybody else to the police. They meet in a diner and sit in front of the window, the camera placed so that it sees both men in profile against it.

GoodFellas *by Martin Scorsese (1990).*

Suddenly, perspective and space alter. Scorsese executes a simultaneous zoom and track, in opposing directions, so that the background—what's going on outside the diner window—seems to be moving in on the characters as they sit still. This is a technique that Alfred Hitchcock used to represent Scottie's reaction to heights in *Vertigo*. Steven Spielberg uses it to communicate Sheriff Brody's response to his sighting of the shark in *Jaws*, and it has since shown up in many other films. From a self-conscious device used by young filmmakers to pay homage to Hitchcock, it is rapidly becoming a cinematic cliché. In *GoodFellas* it serves as a kind of outside commentary, a caution that the world created in the film is about to slip away, that the character we have been attached to has lost his moorings. Or never had any. It is an artificial gesture of camera and lens used to emphasize that everything we see through the camera's eye is artificial, in the very best sense of "artfully made."

The coup in which the director undermines the point of view of his character and our dependence on it comes in the trial sequence near the end of the film. Here, Henry simply steps out of the scene, literally walks through the courtroom set and addresses the camera, something forbidden by the Hollywood continuity style. By doing so, he acknowledges that it's all an illusion, all going on in somebody's head—Henry's, the director's, ours. As the film comes to an end and we see Henry in the witness protection program, living in some anonymous suburb, complaining in voice-over that he can't find a decent tomato sauce, he once again looks at the camera and smiles, as if to say, "We know what all this is about, don't we?" And just in case we still don't quite know, Scorsese inserts a shot of Tommy, Henry's hilariously violent friend (played by Joe Pesci), pointing his machine gun and firing at the camera. This shot doesn't come from anywhere else in *GoodFellas*. It alludes to another film, made in 1903, Edwin S. Porter's *The Great Train Robbery*. There, a shot of one of the cowboys firing his gun at the camera was put either at the beginning or the end of the film, at the discretion of the exhibitor, to excite the audience.

So, with a wink at the audience and a nod to the history of film, Scorsese lets us know what we like about gangsters and violence. We like to watch. We like to be safe. We like to desire. And we like the delicate balance of control and fear. We also like a wise guy. In *GoodFellas*, Scorsese attaches us to a desirable character who seems to own the world, only to find that he is owned by the film we're watching, as are we ourselves. The director toys with his character and with us, allowing us in on the joke or allowing us to go off in a state of being deceived. It's only a movie, and the choice is ours.

Scorsese's desire to reflect the structures of film back at his audience, to attempt to peel away some of the illusion, is a common trait among modern auteurs. Unlike their predecessors, they want not merely to repeat the old strategies of the classical continuity style but to explore and expand them. American filmmakers like Stanley Kubrick, Robert Altman, Steven Spielberg, Paul Schrader, Spike Lee, and Woody Allen look to their European, Asian, and Latin American forebears and contemporaries, Jean Renoir, Robert Bresson, Luis Buñuel, Jean-Luc Godard, François Truffaut, Michelangelo Antonioni, Joseph Losey, Bernardo

Bertolucci (in his Italian period), Federico Fellini, Rainer Werner Fassbinder, Akira Kurosawa, Yasujiro Ozu, Humberto Solàs, and Andrei Tarkovsky (to name just a few), who explored and experimented. These filmmakers ask audiences not to look *through* the medium of cinema, as if it were a pane of glass, but *at* it. They never sacrifice emotion and narrative, but attempt to ask us to work for emotion by understanding how cinema itself works. Contemporary American auteurs, in various ways, attempt to communicate this approach.

One of them, Stanley Kubrick—whose *Dr. Strangelove* (1964), *2001: A Space Odyssey* (1968), and *A Clockwork Orange* (1971) have become cinematic prophecies of social and political behavior—attempted to avoid completely the public life of a film director. Kubrick lived and worked in London, never traveled, and only dealt with large numbers of people during the actual filming process. He was the one filmmaker who tried to emulate the life of a novelist, painstakingly creating his projects—cool films, filled with strong images and tracking camera shots, weaving complex themes about the cultures of violence and politics and the absolute loss of human agency—which were completed every seven or eight years, in isolation and without any publicity. He made complex films that stay in the memory and keep yielding information on each viewing. These are films that managed the great, barely possible feat of combining the popular and the difficult—high art and popular art at ease with one another yet capable of causing unease in the viewer.

Others do not strain against the system so thoroughly, and all of them know that their experimentation has to be delivered in a palatable package. But the truth is that even a little experimentation makes producers nervous. Briefly, in the seventies, when films like Coppola's two *Godfathers* and Spielberg's *Jaws* and *E.T.* made a lot of money, some directors were given a good deal of control. Some of them went overboard, like Michael Cimino, whose Vietnam film *The Deer Hunter* (1978) was enormously popular. United Artists then gave him a great deal of leeway and money for a somewhat left-of-center Western, *Heaven's Gate* (1980). The film went over budget, over schedule, and flopped. Its failure helped bring down the studio and pretty much put an end to widespread directorial power in Hollywood. These days, even in Europe, where most films must now fit an American blueprint in order to get made, the director is not likely to be a controlling figure, exercising the creative drive that many were able to do up through the seventies.

Women Auteurs

From an article by Nancy Hass, in *The New York Times*, **January 31, 1999:**

When the Hollywood studios announced their 1998 grosses earlier this month, women there raised a quiet cheer. Both Mimi Leder ("Deep Impact") and Betty Thomas ("Dr. Dolittle") had made films that earned more than $150 million domestically. It was the first time ever that two female directors had simultaneously surpassed the magic $100 million mark that certifies a blockbuster.

But another set of numbers, released a few months earlier, made the triumph ring a little hollow. A study by the Directors Guild of America showed that in the year that both Ms. Thomas and Ms. Leder's films were being made, the overall number of women employed on studio projects declined dramatically. Female directors worked fewer than 5 percent of the total days guild members spent on theatrical films in 1997. That represented an almost 50 percent decline from the year before.

Clearly, and sadly, our brief listing of film auteurs has not included the names of women directors. The simple and obvious answer to this is that women are allowed to play only a small role in film production. But in the complex, too-often frustrating world of women and film, we need to discriminate between a number of issues. One is the representation of women themselves: how films "see" women, narrate them and their stories. We've discussed earlier how the basic narrative structure of intercutting shot/reverse shot, especially in the rescue narrative, is built upon men saving women. We have also seen, and will examine even more thoroughly in the next chapter, how the structure of the gaze—the looking of one character at another and the viewer at both—is directed toward women as erotic objects.

The simple point is that, as a part of the larger culture, film reflects the values of that culture and traps women with male-dominated ways of thinking and control. Commercial, narrative film persists in trapping itself within the old and worn-out master narratives of passive femininity and active masculinity, of heterosexuality as the only means of intimacy. Of course, there have been some important exceptions to these narratives. A few films—Donna Deitch's 1985 *Desert Hearts* (a melodrama) and Frank Oz's 1997 *In & Out* (a comedy)—have attempted alternative narratives to those that end in heterosexual union. The Hollywood story machine always responds, however briefly, to alternative cultural currents.

But these are narrative issues. Relevant to our discussions in this chapter is the story of women as filmmakers, behind the camera, making the images, forming the film. Women have been involved in the filmmaking process from the earliest days. They were script writers and, most often, editors. They were "script girls," the important figure who made sure physical continuity was maintained from shot to shot. They were very, very rarely directors.

In the world of avant-garde film, especially in recent years, films and videos made by women have become common, and many of them deal in more complex ways than theatrical movies with gender, race, and alternatives to the norms of society. **Avant-garde** is a difficult term to define and worth a brief digression. In popular usage, almost any form of cinema or the other arts that refuses a linear plot line, simple realism, and the narrative conventions of the mainstream can be called by that term. But, more precisely, avant-garde usually refers to an artist or work committed entirely to small, subjective, even private musings in a medium that is bent and refigured to the artist's aesthetic desire. Avant-garde art is not aimed at a wide audience, does not cost much money to create, and can be perfectly, even maddeningly personal and obscure.

In film, 16 mm photography, repetition, abstraction, single frame shots, outrageous takes on sexuality, or pure aesthetic pleasure can mark the avant-garde. It flourished from the late forties through the sixties, often in small cinema clubs. Some of its practitioners, like Stan VanDerBeek, took academic posts, like poets and novelists often do. Others, like John Whitney, made early experiments in computer-generated imagery that had an influence on the "Stargate" sequence in Stanley Kubrick's *2001: A Space Odyssey* (1968) and has now become the norm in contemporary filmmaking. Avant-garde art is almost always eventually incorporated into the popular, sometimes—as in television commercials—in ways that would make its originators cringe.

These days, video is the chosen medium for much subjective and political filmmaking because of the reduced production costs (with digital production quickly catching up), and it is in video that women filmmakers have come into their own. These are directors such as Pamela Yates, who makes videos on welfare rights issues, and Christine Choy, maker of *Who Killed Vincent Chin?* (1989, originally shot in 16 mm) and one of the founders of the Third World Newsreel, a major distributor of independent political films, which, along with the group Women Make Movies, has given the opportunity to many young filmmakers who might not get their films seen otherwise. But we have to go back a number of years to find the pioneer woman avant-garde director, whose influence was widespread.

Maya Deren

Maya Deren was Russian-born but lived in America since her childhood. Active from the forties through the early fifties—sometimes collaborating with her husband—her films, writings, and activities in promoting avant-garde works helped established the genre among the intellectual underground. Never self-indulgent but always interested in the dreamworld, a subjective, a soft but, at the same time, visually hard-edged and often dark response to the everyday, Deren's short experimental films are lyrical, sometimes lyrically violent, and often surreal. In *At Land* (1944) a woman (Deren herself) climbs out of the ocean, over driftwood, at the top of which is an elegant dinner party in a room. She crawls

Deren on the dinner table. At Land *by Maya Deren (1943).*

along the table, unnoticed by the guests, and at the end of the table sees a chessboard, on which the pieces animate themselves. The images are dreamlike, whimsical, and the result of a mind that associates and connects the unexpected.

Deren's most famous work is *Meshes of the Afternoon* (1943, made in collaboration with Alexander Hammid), an extraordinary work of rich dream images, using techniques, such as **jump cutting** (in which a continuous movement is cut into so that continuity is itself replaced by rapid changes in space; a cinematic version of ellipsis in prose), that were years ahead of their

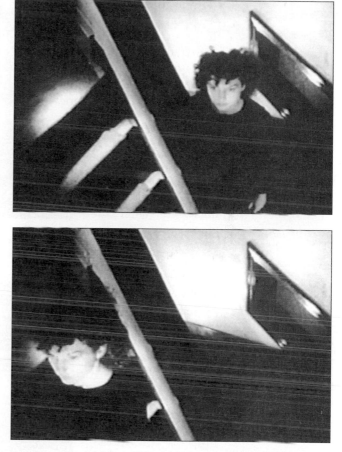

Jump cutting in Maya Deren's Meshes of the Afternoon *(1943).*

most famous appearance in Jean-Luc Godard's *Breathless*. In one sequence, the central figure—Deren—is seen mounting a staircase. But her movement is cut so that she goes up and down in a rapid montage, as if, between the cuts, she had leapt to various places on the stairs.

The film is influenced by the Spanish surrealist filmmaker Luis Buñuel and the French surrealist poet, artist, and filmmaker Jean Cocteau. In its turn, it influenced later directors like the Swedish Ingmar Bergman, Jean-Luc Godard, and another Frenchman, Alain Resnais, as well as the American director Robert Altman, especially as it deals with the difficulties of impressing a feminist sensibility on the world. *Meshes of the Afternoon* touches upon core feminist issues of identity and ownership of the self. The central figure falls asleep in a chair and dreams of two other selves and a figure of death in black, with a mirror for a face (a figure that Ingmar Bergman brought back in his 1957 film *The Seventh Seal*). A key and a knife appear as important images of openings and endings:

they disappear, reappear—one turns into the other. A male figure—a lover or a husband—wakes the woman, and she goes to bed. He caresses her, and in response, the flower lying next to her becomes a knife. The mirror by the bedside shatters, and its shards fly to the sea. When the man returns, the woman is dead—of the knife or broken mirror?

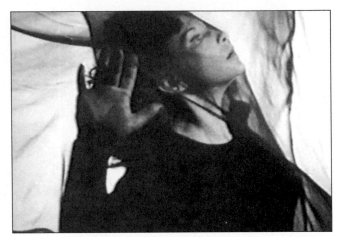

The dream world in Maya Deren's Meshes of the Afternoon *(1943).*

The woman's death is a disturbing moment in a film otherwise dealing with the possibilities of female expression. It may be speaking to the frustration in ever getting the expression made or, on the level of avant-garde aesthetics, to an open-ended question, a lack of comforting closure and explanation that marks off

The figure of death in Meshes of the Afternoon *(1943).*

this kind of filmmaking from the Hollywood style.

Early American Cinema: Alice Guy, Lois Weber, and Dorothy Arzner

Deren is a woman who made films that spoke to the feminine. She was an independent. Her films did not depend upon the studios to finance and distribute them. Since the core of our study is theatrical narrative film, we need to consider how women have fared in that realm. The answer is simple and unhappy: not well. From the beginning through the end of the old studio system in the fifties, there were very few women directors, and the majority of them worked in the silent period, and many of their films are lost. One was a Frenchwoman,

Alice Guy, who, after making films in France, came to America and set up her own production company in 1910. Another woman filmmaker from the early period was Lois Weber, who, in 1916, articulated a strong statement of auteurism. "A real director should be absolute" in her control of a film, she wrote, while she was making progressive films on contemporary social issues. Another was Dorothy Arzner, who, like many women in Hollywood production, started as an editor and a screenwriter. She began directing in 1927 and made seventeen films through 1943. Some of her works—especially *Christopher Strong* (1933) and *Dance, Girl, Dance* (1940)—speak in complex and knowing ways about women and their reduced place in the culture. They address the ways genders are shifting cultural constructs (in *Christopher Strong*, the main character, played by Katharine Hepburn, spends much of her time dressed as a boy) and how women understand their status as things to be looked at by men. In one of the most celebrated feminist moments in film, one of the female performers in *Dance, Girl, Dance* talks to her audience, expressing her outrage at being the object of their gaze. It is a rare moment when a woman is permitted to speak her understanding of what film and gender performance is about from a woman's perspective.

Ida Lupino

Ida Lupino was an actress in many films from the thirties through the fifties (some of her best are Raoul Walsh's *High Sierra* and Michael Curtiz's *The Sea Wolf*, both 1941; and Nicholas Ray's *On Dangerous Ground*, 1952). She wanted control of her work, but instead of fleeing the country and filing a lawsuit against her studio, as the actress Bette Davis had done and lost in the thirties, Lupino, at that moment in the history of the studios in the early fifties when contracts were running out and the monolithic control the studios had wielded for so many years was beginning to dwindle, formed her own production companies so that she could direct her own films.

Lupino was a canny businesswoman as well as a good filmmaker. She also understood the cultural state of the decade in which she worked. In interviews, she always played up her role as mother and family woman, and she spoke about her directing talents as being largely passive and deferential. In the fifties, a woman might conceivably find herself in a traditionally male role, but might also find it necessary to use the more comfortable discourse of the homemaker who—in this case—just happens to be filmmaker as well.

Lupino's films are, at first sight, very much in the manner of fifties noir. Their subjects are, often, lower-middle-class men put in bizarre situations. But there can be an interesting switch. *The Hitch-Hiker* (1953) has no female characters. It concerns two men out on a fishing trip who are kidnapped by a sadistic madman and driven through Mexico until the kidnapper is caught. In place of female characters, the two kidnapped men, Gil Bowan (Frank Lovejoy) and Roy Collins (Edmond O'Brien), are forced into passive, childlike, or—in the terms of cultural conventions—"woman"-like situations. They are completely passive and almost in thrall to their crazy kidnapper, who taunts them for being "soft" and thinking about each other's welfare. At the end, freed of their captor (whom Roy finally beats up, after the madman has been handcuffed by the police), the two family men walk into the darkness. Gil puts his arm around Roy and tells him, "It's all right now, Roy, it's all right."

Men: passive, under the control of a madman. The Hitch-Hiker *by Ida Lupino (1951).*

This is certainly not the only film by a man or a woman in which male characters show some affection and care for each other. However, it is not a male bonding film, because the characters do not work as a "team" or share their joy in the absence of women, despite the fact that no women are present. Both characters are oppressed by their condition: they cannot escape it, and they remain good, middle-class family men. Even though, early in the film, Roy wants to find prostitutes in Mexico, Gil refuses, in fact pretends to be asleep while this is all going on. It is suggested that Roy's would-be diversion is what put them in the path of the mad hitch-hiker. Precisely these kinds of subtleties mark this as a film made by a woman: that the men get into trouble because they want to chase women; because the men are reduced to passive, even weeping childlike characters; because, despite the momentary thoughts of extramarital play, they remain attached to their unseen families through the end. Within the tough, hard lines and rigorous compositions of late noir, Lupino manages to see masculine softness and vulnerability, mock these qualities just a little, and indicate a strength that comes from places other than male braggadocio and a puffed-up sense of the heroic.

There's a similar reversal in *The Bigamist*, a film that shows Lupino's talents at composing and framing sequences which achieve a proximity to her characters in ways that quietly but markedly reveal emotional states. The film is structured in flashbacks as Harry (Edmond O'Brien, again, a kind of icon of the fifties ordinary man) takes two wives. Lupino creates a complexity here that belies the sleaziness of the story. Harry's first wife, Eve, can't conceive a child and turns to running Harry's business. This is a major and ugly fifties stereotype: the childless woman must transfer her maternal yearnings to "man's work" in order to be fulfilled, thereby forgoing her femininity. It is even suggested by Harry that he and his wife don't have sex anymore. But Lupino refuses to take this on face value. The Eve she depicts is a loving wife who wants to adopt a child *and* run a business. Harry, who often has to travel to Los Angeles, is shown as lonely and alienated. He falls in love with, impregnates, and marries a waitress he meets in L.A., Phyllis (played by Lupino).

The melodramatic potential of this conflict—especially when Harry's secret is discovered by the man investigating their adoption request—is underplayed. In this film, Lupino is interested in gazing closely at both male and female faces of loss and loneliness. She condemns none of the characters and gives their neediness equal attention. Even more than *The Hitch-Hiker*, the male character is endowed with what, in conventional film, are considered female traits: shifting emotions, vulnerability, failings, even weakness. Male directors too created "sensitive" men, and we'll examine the phenomenon in detail during Chapter 4. But Ida Lupino, the only female director of the decade—of many decades—understood that gender was not something defined by the movies, only stereotyped by them. Unlike many other filmmakers, she can show sympathy to all her characters and create a film that touches upon such a taboo issue as *The Bigamist:* sympathy across the board, an understanding of what men and women might need and even get were it not for the demands of their culture and gender.

Women Filmmakers Today

With the end of the old studio system and the rise of the feminist movement, there was a hope that filmmaking would be more welcoming to films made by and about women. There seemed to be some opening in the seventies and eighties. Some male directors—perhaps most notably Martin Scorsese in *Alice Doesn't Live Here Anymore* (1974)—attempted to portray women freeing themselves from intolerable domestic situations. But, as in *Alice*, most of these films decided that their women characters had only to find a "better" man, thereby re-creating the traditional narrative closure of heterosexual union.

There was a brief flurry of opportunity for women directors in the eighties and early nineties. Diverse filmmakers undertook a variety of approaches to women's issues, such as Susan Seidelman in *Desperately Seeking Susan* (1985) and *Making Mr. Right* (1987), a film that suggested the perfect man had to be constructed like a robot. Donna Deitch, whose *Desert Hearts* we mentioned earlier, touched on lesbian themes. Barbra Streisand, particularly in films such as *Yentl* (1983) and *The Prince of Tides* (1991), used melodrama to present images of strong women. In *Household Saints* (1993), Nancy Savoca created an extraordinary and surreal film about ethnicity and the feminine. Kathryn Bigelow, most especially in *Strange Days* (1995) (cowritten and coproduced by James Cameron), tried to alter the action genre in ways that redirected male centrality and the focus of the male gaze. *Strange Days* is set in an apocalyptic L.A. at the end of the millennium. The people are up in arms, and the cops are out of control. In the midst of this chaos she creates a technological fantasy in which a recording device worn on a person's head can record and play back experiences as if they were actually occurring. One of these recordings is of a woman being raped, with the recording device placed on her head to capture her terror. The result is a gruesome sequence, and only a woman filmmaker, I think, could have created it in a manner that downplays the inherently exploitative elements and emphasizes how horrible the act is to the woman involved.

The film's "hero" is an African American woman who is in love with a white man, who is definitely not a hero but a kind of human punching bag. In the midst of the uprising, and despite the fact that Bigelow seems to yield to convention by introducing the patriarchal figure of a good police commissioner to set the cops right, this couple emerges, suddenly and openly in love. They kiss—a kiss between a weak white male and a strong African American woman, a kiss that is simply given and offered to the audience, without comment, without sensationalism, in a way that suggests that all the gun play, all the violence and mayhem, are actually a mask that allows the film to present this transgressive act. Like the presence of an African American President of the United States in Mimi Leder's *Deep Impact* (1998), it is a kind of utopian vision of a world that, despite the violence and destruction, can somehow be better. It would be foolish to say that only a woman director could do this; we can only say that women directors did do this.

While some of the original contemporary women filmmakers, like Seidelman and Deitch, seem not to have been able to pursue their careers, others have flourished in different ways. Penny Marshall moved from television sitcom actress to the highly bankable director of engaging films like *Big* (1988), *Awakenings* (1990), *A League of Their Own* (1992), and *The Preacher's Wife* (1996). Penelope Spheeris has carved out a comfortable place making clever comedies based upon television skits and programs, like *Wayne's World* (1992) and *The Beverly Hillbillies* (1993). Amy Heckerling is in the unusual position of making commercially popular films—*Fast Times at Ridgemont High* (1982) and *Clueless* (1995), for example—the latter successfully maintaining a young woman's view of the world without sentimentality.

The Canadian born Mary Harron has made an extraordinary transmutation of a difficult and repulsive source. In 2000, she filmed *American Psycho*, which was based upon a novel that turned the stomachs of most readers with its depiction of a man who mutilated women. Harron overturned the premise and realized the novel not exactly as a feminist film but as one in which the men, and *not* the women of so many conventional films, are preening, fashion-obsessed, narcissists, who have something approaching a sexual experience over their business cards and are enthralled by the most banal of eighties popular music. The central character is so inward looking that he has passed directly through his own personality and come out the other side as a murderous cipher, a madman so undone by the competition of success in business (he refers to "mergers and acquisitions" as "murders and executions") that his violent attacks on both men and women may very well be fantasies. Like so many horror films, *American Psycho* presents women as its main victims; but they are victims not so much of their gender but of a lunatic's notion of gender and his complete absence of

Men: composed, groomed, insane. American Psycho *by Mary Harron (2000).*

self. On its most important level, Harron's film understands that for many men or, more important for our work, for many films, women are not independent figures but the products of an overheated male sexual imagination. She has made a small-budget commercial film that quietly overturns some of the mainstays of the representations of women in film.

Julie Dash, Jane Campion, and Chantal Akerman

In order to find films by women that demonstrate a difference not only in the kind of story being told but in the narrative means used to tell the story, we have to move out of the mainstream. Sometimes out of the country.

Television has been one place where women can work as filmmakers. When Ida Lupino left filmmaking, she went to work on TV in the sixties. One recent director, Julie Dash, an African American, made a film for the now defunct PBS series "American Playhouse" called *Daughters of the Dust*. The film was financed by PBS, the National Endowment for the Arts, and various other government, regional, and corporate grants, and it received a small theatrical distribution.

The film is delicate, filled with beautiful imagery, in which color, the kind of lens put on the camera from shot to shot, the use of slow and fast motion emphasize and form a complex narrative of remembrance and forgetting, past and future, the physical and the spiritual. Set in 1902 in the Sea Islands off the southern coast of the United States, among the people called the Gullah, the film gathers together the members of the Peazant family, born into slavery and now, some of them, reaching middle class, a few about to head north. It is very much a family get-together film, but this is a family from a horrific background of slavery, who have retained not only their sense of self-possession, of coherence, but a wide-ranging religious practice, African, Christian, Muslim.

Daughters of the Dust is concerned with the fuzziness of boundaries between cultures and time, about the joining of traditions and the necessity of progress. We see this in its compositional elements, which depend to a large extent on wide horizontal shots along the beach, often observing people running across the screen. But this linear visual style is undercut by the complex interweaving of the characters' memories, by flashbacks and forwards, by close-ups of objects and faces, creating a series of interlocking stories directly told or suggested. In fact, in her commentary to the film, Dash says that she based its narrative structure on the *Griot*, the traditional African story teller and keeper of tribal tradition. Because of this, there is much magic, much imagery of dream and remembrance. An unborn child appears through the lens of a camera set up to take a family picture. A young man, attempting to sink a powerful African statue in the swamp, walks on water.

Daughters of the Dust is in many ways an ethnographic film with touches of magic realism—a style that combines a conventional realism along with the fantastic. In other words, although a narrative fiction, it also documents a way of life along with its culture and artifacts, but it envelops that documentation with a narrative of marvelous events. It looks lovingly at the women and the men of the Peazant family, at the tensions of their past and their resolution. It is never violent, even when showing the old Indigo slave plantation, where the slaves had to make toxic dyes with their hands. Indeed, the great grandmother, the survivor of the plantation, wears an indigo dress, while most of the other characters wear white. The film proves that a human horror can be effectively communicated without being represented.

Daughters of the Dust is visually beautiful—some might argue too much so, that its prettiness overwhelms the narrative. But I think Dash is consciously attempting to break away from a current convention of African American film-

The former slave and voice of history.

making that concentrates on the bleak, the desolate, and the violent. She is, instead, working in a tradition of some of the great African filmmakers, like Ousmane Sembène, who look to the way cultures and religions call upon the spiritual, remain connected to their past, while staying rooted in the contemporary movements of their own and their culture's history. In this context, the characters are shown in a continuing process of incorporating and not forgetting their past. "There must be connection," says the great-grandmother in

The children on the beach.

Walking on water: the ancient and the modern, the mix of religions and the spiritual. Daughters of the Dust *by Julie Dash (1991).*

Daughters of the Dust. "We came here in chains and we must survive…we must survive." This film is one way to trace the markings of that survival.

Jane Campion, a New Zealander who made a few rather strange, interior, feminist films in her native country, broke into the American market with *The Piano* (1993), a film of some complexity and mixed messages. While observing a woman so strongly attempting to discover selfhood that she removes herself from her world and stops talking, it also engages in some soft-core pornography and can conceivably be read as a film about a narcissistic character who betrays her own daughter with her attempts at sexual experimentation. The film may be addressing the inevitable betrayal that women are led to in a culture that devalues them; or it may be proposing a female strength that must overcome any obstacle in order to survive. The film strongly tries to give the woman back some power over her sexuality, over the gaze, a power lost to women in much narrative film.

One of the most successful attempts to question the female gaze and the entire genre of female melodrama was made by a Belgian director, Chantal Akerman, in a 1975 film, *Jeanne Dielman, 23 Quai du Commerce, 1080 Bruxelles.* The film is available on videotape and well worth a look, because Akerman literally transforms the male gaze at the female character. She makes us look, but removes the pleasure, that is, the male pleasure of gazing at a woman. Akerman's gaze is at a woman, but what we see is not desirable and certainly not erotic. For over three hours, her camera spends much of its time simply watching the central character, a lower-middle-class Belgian housewife, who lives in a tiny apartment with her teenage son and practices prostitution in the afternoons to supplement her widow's pension. The camera looks, unmoving, slightly below eye level, at a distance that prevents intimacy, as this woman goes about her obsessive tasks, cooking, shining her son's shoes, making up the rooms, going to the store, looking after a neighbor's child, talking to her son, entertaining her clients. The camera looks and looks. There is rarely a cut unless there is a change of place, and the change of place is usually to another space in the apartment. Everything is slow, deliberate. The camera looks, relentlessly, but coolly.

The act of looking demystifies everything. The woman and her work, the woman and her sexuality are reduced to the routine of her doing them and our own gazing at them. She and her life become objects, just as so many women characters in film have always been. In the excesses of traditional melodrama, the assumed intimacy of our gaze, and the forward propulsion of the continuity style allow us to identify with the character. We look at her, we look with her. We want her, we want her to succeed, to be punished. Melodrama transfers desire back and forth. But in *Jeanne Dielman* there are no distractions, no excess—except the excess created by the camera's unrelenting gaze. Desire is diverted from the character back to our own looking. We either want to keep looking to see if anything will happen or want not to look. In fact, nothing happens to the woman until late in the film, when her obsessive actions begin to unravel. She forgets part of her routine, does some things over again. Then she sits in a chair for a very long time, the camera gazing at her without a cut. Later, a client arrives. The woman experiences an orgasm with him—perhaps her first—takes a pair of scissors, and stabs him. Her order disrupted, her emotions brought to the surface, she has no recourse but to destroy in an attempt to get the order restored.

Jeanne Dielman is certainly not another postfeminist film about a sexually liberated woman who is really crazy and murderous in the mode of *Fatal Attraction* or *Single White Female* (Barbet Schroeder, 1992) or *Basic Instinct*. Neither is it about a dying mother, after the manner of Carl Franklin's *One True Thing* (1998), where a career woman gives up her independent life to look after her ailing parent and dysfunctional family. Rather it is a commentary on melodrama and its attempts to sexualize and then redeem from sexuality the central female character. *Jeanne Dielman* thinks about what melodrama might look like if we were allowed to look at it without embellishment, given the distance that the classical Hollywood style forbids. *Jeanne Dielman* explores how women are represented in film and how that representation turns them into automatons. It also explores the conditions of our own watching of melodrama and—by draining that watching of all spectacle, of all excess, music, elaborate mise-en-scène, camera movement, and cutting—takes us to the bare level of the gaze and makes us very, very uncomfortable.

Now why should we watch a film that makes us uncomfortable? To understand that there are alternatives; that the language and structure of American film is not the only way films can or even should be made— indeed that film is a kind of language, but with rules that can be bent and alterered. To show up the ways the standard language and vocabulary of film, especially when they speak of women, are not immutable. To have, in a perverse way, some fun. The last time I showed *Jeanne Dielman* to a class, they began yelling at the screen: "Cut. cut, already." There was nobody to hear them; it was only a film, and the shot went on and on. The melodrama had been transferred to the audience.

A woman filmmaker and her film about a lost woman made the class uncomfortable. The radical rupture of the classical style foiled expectations, and the class transferred their annoyance back to the unresponsive screen itself. This transferal was, I think, an interesting lesson in cinematic expectation and the ways we respond when we don't get what we think we should from a film. It was also a good example of why films of such radical experimentation rarely get made, and perhaps explains why women filmmakers take relatively small risks in their work. Perhaps the fear that risks might be taken is one of the reasons so few women are given directorial control.

The Hollywood of today does not "hate" women. But it is always afraid of something different and, like many other parts of our culture, of yielding male authority. Will the public accept a sharply feminist film? Will the business of filmmaking ever be comfortable with women as the directorial "boss" of a production—even as it is becoming increasingly comfortable with women as the producers and, therefore, the controllers of the budget—of a film? These are questions that move far from individual films into the large areas of culture, sociology, and the basics of power and authority.

Auteurism Today

The auteur theory was always a theory, a way of talking and thinking about films, much more than an accurate description of how films are actually made. It was also a way to think about redistributing the hierarchies of power in the filmmaking business. There is no question that in Europe, at least until recently, many directors did exercise an enormous amount of control and usually wrote the films they directed. But this has rarely been true in the United States, at least not since the early twenties when the studio system situated the director as only one among many craftspeople working on a film. Besides, film can never really be reduced to the imagination of a single individual. It is too much a part of the cultural churn, of the thoughts, acts, artifacts, beliefs, and politics of the society in which it is made. It is too controlled by economics and audience response to be left to one person. But the convenience and implied intimacy of auteurism are so seductive. So are the analytical tools it offers, permitting us to understand the structure of film as the clearly coherent stylistic and thematic operation of a singular imagination. Auteurism at least gives power to the film critic. We may often need to sacrifice this clarity and control to the messier realities of film as part of a complex cultural mix. It is perfectly possible to mix various kinds of analysis—auteur, genre, and cultural.

The actual practice of filmmaking—despite the existence of a few directorial stars, like Steven Spielberg, and some who have more control over their work than others, like Martin Scorsese—has pretty much reverted back to the control of the producer and the studio chief, or simply to the current versions of the classical style. The director has become a self-censor. There is little "personal" style, and with the rare exceptions of filmmakers like David Fincher or Todd Haynes (*Safe*, 1995; *Velvet Goldmine*, 1998) or Todd Solondz's wonderfully perverse *Happiness* (1998)—a film more provocative about the suburban experience than *American Beauty*—innovation is tightly controlled. But at the same time, there are opportunities for directors that never existed before. This may be the greatest legacy of auteurism: the recognition on the part of studio executives that directors, after all, can have some imaginative say in the creation of films, even if it is limited. African Americans, though still badly underrepresented, are finding opportunities to make movies, to find a voice within the contemporary versions of the Hollywood style. The success of Spike Lee's passionate social melodramas—such as *Do the Right Thing* (1989), *Jungle Fever* (1991), and *Malcolm X* (1992)—has led the way for strong directors of imagination, like John Singleton (*Boyz N the Hood*, 1991; *Poetic Justice*, 1993; *Higher Learning*, 1995; *Rosewood*, 1997; and *Shaft*, 2000).

Lee's films are deeply and passionately felt, sometimes broadly melodramatic, sometimes, as in *Clockers* (1995), understated and subtle in bringing home a point about how easy it is to stereotype and blame an otherwise deeply sympathetic character. Lee's *Summer of Sam* (1999) is his first film dealing with other ethnic groups. It is part of the serial killer subgenre, but it expands that popular type by showing, in powerful images and big set pieces, that the murderer of

Race in the city. Do the Right Thing *by Spike Lee (1989).*

women is a part of a much larger palette of a cultural violence bred of distrust and hatred, of the terror of difference.

Other minorities are being represented in small-budget films, such as Robert Rodriguez's *El Mariachi* (1992) and *From Dusk 'Til Dawn* (1996), or large-budget studio films, such as *The Joy Luck Club,* directed by the Hong Kong-born Wayne Wang in 1993, who also did a small ethnic film, *Chan Is Missing,* in 1982 and an intricate, understated film about men and families called *Smoke* in 1995. Other Asian directors are at work in Hollywood, most notably John Woo, in the action film genre, and Ang Lee, whose 1997 *The Ice Storm* was a quiet, understated, historically and culturally acute film about early seventies suburban life. His Mandarin-language action film, *Crouching Tiger, Hidden Dragon* (2000), became a major critical and commercial success.

Whether or not any of these filmmakers will break through the restraints of the Hollywood style is open to question. They may occasionally experiment. They are likely to remain content making good, popular films that may or may not reflect their cultural backgrounds. The tendency is for a filmmaker not to remain pigeonholed as a maker of African American or feminist films or Asian films. There is simply too much at stake—too much money, too much fame, too much power.

The commercial and cultural realities of filmmaking largely overpower the desire to be an individual creator with a subjective style and a personal, passionate worldview. The economic realities of production worldwide and the tastes of the majority of filmgoers militate against it. An unusual style takes money but rarely makes it. It costs more to create an elaborate tracking shot than to execute an ordinary series of over-the-shoulder shots. A passionate worldview usually comes from a passionate ego, and there is little room for a big ego in directors, whose job is usually to carry out the orders of the ego with the money, the producer. And audiences are too often uncomfortable with flights of cinematic imagination, a problem made clear in the spate of recent "independent" films, most of which are independent of neither studio money and distribution nor the conventions of the Hollywood style.

And that, finally, is what this book is about, the development of a comfortable style that negotiates with its audience a series of predictable, and flexible, responses. Flexibility, however, only yields so far. The work of negotiation has its limits. Too much experimentation, too much irony, and a film is in danger of losing its audience. A filmmaker must always be concerned with her audience. We admire the idea of the artist, even though we're too often uncomfortable when an "artist" exercises an unusual imagination in film.

I don't want to end this chapter on a pessimistic note. For almost ten years, from the late sixties to the late seventies, a vital, sometimes experimental film culture thrived in the United States and abroad. Many of the filmmakers we have discussed here began their work during that period, and new ideas thrived. Many, many people throughout the culture were thinking and talking and writing seriously about film. The serious study of film was developed and established during this period. Given the great cyclical nature of culture and creativity, and the occasional signs of creativity in a variety of films during the past decade, such a period is bound to come around again—though perhaps in different forms.

Film, Form, and Culture: The CD-ROM

The CD-ROM provides a variety of visual demonstrations of the production processes described in this chapter, including the way cinematographers work in the *Camera* section; the work of the editor in *Continuity Editing;* of the composer in *Sound and Music;* and the director's work in *Mise-en-scène.*

NOTES AND REFERENCES

Individuals and Creativity   An excellent, though challenging, source for information on the individual subject and its shifting positions is Kaja Silverman's *The Subject of Semiotics* (New York: Oxford University Press, 1983).

The Ideal Viewer   A brave reader may want to tackle Jean-Louis Baudry's essay "Ideological Effects of the Basic Cinematographic Apparatus" in *Film Theory and Criticism.*

Film and the Individual Talent   The best and clearest theorizing about the existence of the author is Michel Foucault's "What Is an Author?" trans. D. F. Bouchard, *Screen* 20, no. 1 (1979).

Cinematographer   One of the finest works on cinematographers is a film called *Visions of Light,* available on VHS and (preferably) laserdisc. It contains good commentary and excellent visual examples.

Editor   One of the best books on film editing is by the director Karel Reisz, *The Technique of Film Editing* (New York: Hastings House, 1968).

Composer   Because few people combine the talents of a film critic and music expert, there has not been a great deal of work on film music. One recent book is Kathryn Kalinak's *Settling the Score: Music and the Classical Hollywood Film* (Madison: University of Wisconsin Press, 1992). For the use of popular music in film, see Jonathan Romney and Adrian Wootton, eds., *Celluloid Jukebox: Popular Music and the Movies since the 50s* (London: British Film Institute, 1995); and I. Penman, "Juke Box and Johnny-Boy," *Sight and Sound* 3, no. 1 (April 1993), pp. 10-11. Stories of Stravinsky in Hollywood can be found in Otto Friedrich, *City of Nets: A Portrait of Hollywood in the 1940's* (New York: Harper & Row, 1986), pp. 38-39; and John Baxter, *The Hollywood Exiles* (New York: Taplinger, 1976), pp. 220-21.

Screenwriter   Here is a story that demonstrates how difficult it sometimes is to arbitrate a screenwriting credit. In 1995, a film named *Bulletproof* appeared. The screenwriting credit was given to one Gordon Melbourne, a Canadian. In fact, the film was written by Mark Malone, an American. The bogus name was put on the film in order to register it for a Canadian tax shelter. (See *New York Times*, May 21, 1995, pp. H11-12.) For a good survey of Hollywood screenwriters, see Richard Corliss, *Talking Pictures: Screenwriters in the American Cinema* (New York: Penguin Books, 1975). For some stories about writers in Hollywood, see Tom Dardis, *Some Time in the Sun* (New York & Middlesex, England: Penguin, 1981).

Actors   There have been two recent books on acting: James Naremore's *Acting in the Cinema* (Berkeley and Los Angeles: University of California Press, 1988); and Christine Gledhill's edition of essays, *Stardom: Industry of Desire* (London and New York: Routledge, 1991). See also Richard Dyer's *Stars* (London, British Film Institute, 1979). For Kubrick's work with actors, see Vincent LoBrutto, *Stanley Kubrick: A Biography* (New York: Donald I. Fine, 1997); and John Baxter, *Stanley Kubrick: A Biography* (Carroll & Graf, 1997). The cultural historian Garry Wills has written an important book on John Wayne: *John Wayne's America: The Politics of Celebrity* (New York: Simon & Schuster, 1997).

Producer   The biography of Welles is by Frank Brady, *Citizen Welles: A Biography of Orson Welles* (New York: Scribner, 1989). Welles's *It's All True* has recently been found and edited together. It was released in 1993, more than fifty years after it was shot, seven years after its director's death. Welles's original material for *The Magnificent Ambersons* has still not come to light.

The Auteur: The Birth of the Auteur   The quotation from Godard is from *Godard on Godard*, ed. Jean Narboni and Tom Milne, trans. Tom Milne (New York: Viking, 1972), pp. 146-47.

The Auteur Theory   Sarris's essay "Notes on the Auteur Theory in 1962" is in *Film Theory and Criticism*, pp. 585-88. Peter Woolen's work on auteurism is in his book *Signs and Meanings in the Cinema* (Bloomington and London: Indiana University Press, 1972). Sarris's *The American Cinema: Directors and Directions*, 1929-1968 (Chicago: University of Chicago Press, 1985), is the classic survey. T. S.

Eliot's "Tradition and the Individual Talent" is widely reprinted and can be found in the collection *The Sacred Wood* (New York: Barnes and Noble, 1960).

Martin Scorsese   If you look for Scorsese's reflection in the mirror in *Raging Bull,* you may not see it because the edges for the frame are cropped in the videotape version. Try the laserdisc.

Women Who Make Movies   For Dorothy Arzner, see Judith Mayne, *Directed by Dorothy Arzner* (Bloomington: Indiana University Press, 1994). The quote from Lois Weber comes from Anthony Slide, *The Silent Feminists: America's First Women Directors* (Scarecrow, 1996). For Weber also see Diane MacIntyre, *The On-Line Journal of Silent Film,* http://www.mdle.com/ClassicFilms/index.htm. See also Claire Johnstone, "Women's Cinema as Counter-Cinema" in *Movies and Methods,* I. Two excellent books on avant-garde cinema and Maya Deren are P. Adams Sitney, *Visionary Film: The American Avant-Garde 1943-1978* (New York, Oxford University Press, 2nd ed., 1979); and Gene Youngblood, *Expanded Cinema* (New York, E. P. Dutton, 1970). Professor Patty Zimmerman of Ithaca College helped me identify some contemporary avant-garde women filmmakers.

4

FILM AS CULTURAL PRACTICE

We have been examining film from the minute particulars of the shot and the cut to the economics of production, to the people responsible for the various parts of movie making. We have seen that film is a part of industrial production (the making of films follows principles of mass production and, in purely economic terms, is now one of the largest commercial endeavors in Los Angeles). We have begun examining how film creates and satisfies its consumers' desires. But unlike other industrial goods, and conforming more closely to what we usually think of as art, movies have emotional and moral designs on us. They ask us to respond with our feelings and to think of the world in moral certainties, to assume there are clearly defined good people and bad, ethical acts and unethical ones, clearly discernible. They even suggest ethical solutions to the problems of how we should act in the world. Yet when compared to a novel or a painting or a symphony, the emotional demands made by a film seem shallow and unambiguous. Unlike the traditional high arts, film—with the exception of the so-called European art film (films by such as Godard, Bertolucci, Antonioni, Fellini, and Bergman made during the sixties and early seventies)—does not demand great intellectual powers to understand it. Film is too often condemned, like popular music and fiction, as being exploitative, commercial, and stupid.

While many movie studios do have units that produce "independent" films for an adult audience, who want—the producers believe—to see such things as romanticized adaptations of a Henry James or Jane Austen novel, many producers believe that the targeted audience of filmgoers lies between the ages of fifteen and twenty-five, and that they need sexual titillation and vicarious experience delivered in the most banal and violent ways. Such films feed the notion that the people, young and old, who admire and enjoy popular culture are being pandered to and willingly enjoy the bad effects of the pandering. That willingness somehow reflects a debasement of the culture. Fear that cultural standards are being lowered by popular culture and mass media causes distrust, which is followed by condemnation. But condemnation seems to have no effect. We still love movies; we still watch television and listen to rock and roll and rap. Distrust then turns to cynicism.

CULTURE AS TEXT

There is an element of truth in everything negative that is said about popular culture, although blanket condemnations are not useful in helping us understand its richness. It will be useful to attempt a broader definition that takes into consideration the negative things about pop culture, but also sees it in all its seriousness and playfulness. In this larger view, we need to start with a definition of culture and then an examination of popular culture (or, more accurately, cultures) to discover ways to fight cynicism with the understanding of unexpected complexity.

Culture can be understood as the text of our lives, the ultimately coherent pattern of beliefs, acts, responses, and artifacts that we produce and comprehend every day. Coherence, system, and order are the highlights of what constitutes a text. We usually think of a book as a text, but anything with known boundaries that produces meaning—even self-contradictory meaning—can be a text. The idea of culture as text means, first, that culture is not nature; it is made by people in history for conscious or even unconscious reasons, the product of all they think and do. Even the unconscious or semiconscious acts of our daily lives can, when observed and analyzed, be understood as sets of coherent acts and be seen to interact with each other. These acts, beliefs, and practices, along with the artifacts they produce—the music we listen to, the clothes we wear, the television we love, the films we watch—have meaning. They can be read and understood. By "read," I mean that we can understand the musical and lyrical complexities of popular music, just as we can analyze a score by Beethoven or a Philip Roth novel. Reading as a critical act is applicable to all meaning-making entities or texts. People drive cars and select certain makes of cars, go to school, open bank accounts, make paintings, watch television, accept racial and sexual differences (or don't), hate Democrats or Republicans (or don't), believe in free will and a free economy (or don't), behave well or badly, love classical music or rock, and somehow make perfect sense of most of this behavior. With a little study and an open mind, we can understand the sense we make of it and the needs that are fulfilled by the choices we make and the things that entertain us. We can understand why and how our entertainments affirm or deny our beliefs. We can see that none of this is natural; it is all born of class, gender, race, education, acculturation, and the ideologies that drive them.

Subcultures

Now, our culture—or that part of our culture that makes divisions between high and low, serious and popular art—defines culture much more narrowly than we just have. It defines as culture those serious works made by independent imaginations that are complex, difficult to understand, and acceptable only to the few who have, want, or like "culture." In other words, culture segments and segregates itself. The culture's culture is what we normally think of as the difficult, personal art we have to engage deeply in order to understand: paintings in museums, symphonies played in concert halls, poems and novels analyzed in the classroom, foreign films that used to be shown in "art houses." If other kinds of imaginative products are allowed in, they become part of a hierarchy and are referred to as "low" or "popular" culture and relegated to the margins. Popular culture is scorned by admirers of "high" culture, and the high is scorned by the popular. This mutual antagonism is sometimes expressed through allusions to stereotypes. Classical music, art, and poetry lovers are the effete, the intellectual elite, with all the implications of class and sexual otherness this implies. People who enjoy the popular arts are sometimes represented as working-class slobs, or women without a life, or people of color who threaten dominant values. The negative view of the popular is further nourished by the fact that mass culture is commercial culture ("commercialized" would be the popular, pejorative term). Movies, television, rock music, romantic novels, and newspapers are commodities, objects of commercial desire. The companies that manufacture them seek a profit. Popular culture commodities are the product not of the individual imagination but of the calculations of the large organizations that construct them to appeal to the largest part of their audience. The results are then positioned for the most appropriate segment of that audience; marketed according to age, gender, race, class; and promoted and sold accordingly. The commodities and their audience become part of the cost/price, profit/loss, asset/liability, manufacture/distribution structure that makes up industrial practice.

There are even wider, more profound, and potentially dangerous splits between subcultures who enjoy the products of popular culture itself. Religious and political differences mark divergent interests in radio programs, kinds of music, and films. People who listen to National Public Radio are identified as different from those who listen to right-wing talk shows—both by themselves and by others. People who watch action movies are seen differently—even by the moviemakers themselves—from those who watch adaptations of Jane Austen novels. In such divisions, the resentment and anger felt by one group toward another are marked and sometimes unsettling.

Media and Cultures

The roots of all this are complex and indicate how any narrow definitions of culture are insufficient to describe the strong and changing elements of the larger culture we belong to. What follows is a very abbreviated sketch of some complex events and movements that created subcultures within larger cultural groups, but it will give an idea of how culture keeps generating itself, how vital groups within it create its art, and how that art changes and transforms the culture.

In European culture, the "serious" production of music and painting and literature goes back to the Middle Ages, when it belonged to the royal courts. The "lower classes," illiterate peasants mostly, had cultures indigenous to their country and place, based on crafts and oral traditions, a phenomenon that is true of most non-European cultures as well. The formation of a property-owning and goods-trading middle class began in the Italian Renaissance, and it is this new group that brought high culture out of the palaces and into the villas, the homes of wealthy traders and property owners. Owning or sponsoring fine art was part of the movement of the burgeoning middle class toward owning cultural property. Well-to-do Italian merchants became patrons of the arts, commissioning painters, for example, who, in gratitude, would paint an image of their benefactor at the feet of Christ. Ownership was a sign of wealth. Owning or patronizing art was a sign of wealthy good taste. It still is.

During the eighteenth century, the property-owning middle class grew across Europe, small shopkeepers flourished, and an industrial working class began to expand. Each of these classes developed its own cultural forms. The novel, for example, was developed in the early eighteenth century and was originally directed at middle-class women, who read, for example, the romantic adventures of the heroine of Samuel Richardson's *Pamela; Or, Virtue Rewarded* (1740) and *Clarissa* (1747–1748) with a devotion and identification (and, sometimes, a sense of irony) that many people still devote to soap opera. Melodrama, a popular working- and lower-middle-class form, was born of the novel and the theater, especially the late eighteenth-century theater of post-revolutionary France. It started as pantomime with music—"melodrama" means drama with music—in response to laws that forbade traditional theatrical performances in which actors spoke their lines. Early melodrama in Europe and in the United States was broad, moral, and political, with exaggerated gestures and simplified structures of good and evil—too broad and "common" for upper-class tastes. It was broadly participatory as well, inviting emotional and even verbal response. Melodrama was a form of satisfaction and gratification, a communal expression of a class desire for stability, place, and confirmation of simple moral values. In various forms, it has thrived in many cultures in the West and the East, and its cinematic version will be examined in the next chapter.

Music Hall variety entertainments were, by the mid-nineteenth century, another working-class site of comedy, popular music, parody, and gender lampoon (cross-dressing in British variety shows remains popular, accepted without embarrassed innuendo). Music Hall was and is performed in a space that encourages lively audience response. The American version of Music Hall, vaudeville, along with melodrama, were to prove enormous influences on the development of film.

In order for popular culture to become mass culture, storage and distribution methods had to be developed. Print culture was well advanced by the eighteenth century, and novels and newspapers enjoyed a fairly wide circulation. In the case of the novel, some transmission occurred through people reading aloud to groups. In order for the music, images, and narratives that were enjoyed by mainly working- and lower-middle-class audiences to become mass culture, other means had to be developed, which they were by the late nineteenth and early twentieth centuries. The new technologies of photography, telephony, the phonograph, and the movies served everyone well, and especially those who did not have the time or the means to contemplate the complexities of high culture. These new technologies quickly became dominant. When this happened, the culture of print—with its demands of education, leisure time, and access to the quiet and solitude that reading fiction or poetry demands—ebbed.

We have examined one new form of storage and distribution in some detail: the photographic emulsion on plastic strips, which, when exposed to light and developed into a series of high-resolution images, can be cut together in various ways, put in cans, and sent around the country and the world to be projected on movie screens. Electronic transmission was another important nineteenth-century development. The telephone, phonograph, and radio delivered voice and music, news and entertainment, into the most intimate of spaces, the home. When film began its gain in popularity, people had to go out of the house to see it, with all the planning and expense that entails. By the twenties, radio was omnipresent in the domestic sphere and became the dominant form of entertainment. When sound came to film in the late twenties, a vigorous interchange between the two media began. Radio carried film advertising as well as programming based on current films. Radio stars played in films; film stars appeared on radio.

One version of print media expanded along with movies and radio by becoming integral to them. Newspapers advertised and reviewed radio and film. Movie magazines and newspaper gossip columns extended the work of studio publicity by keeping the stars and their personal lives in the public eye. It would be no exaggeration to say that, by the end of the twenties, an elaborate, integrated network of popular culture had evolved in which listener and viewer had access to an intertextual web of radio, movies, magazines, and newspapers. By intertextual, I mean that all of these elements referred to one another, reproduced or represented each other. Radio broadcasts were used as narrative elements in film; films were turned into radio drama; newspapers reviewed both and printed film publicity and scandal; film music and popular music were connected so that a movie theme was available on record and on the radio. By the 1940s, a film might include a theme song composed especially so that it could be released as a single.

The only thing missing was a means of delivering moving images to the home, and that problem was solved after World War II. With the coming of television (which began development in the thirties), the web of mass-mediated popular culture was ubiquitous, available to anyone who could afford it. By the mid-1950s, almost everyone could. The intertextuality of this cultural web grew as well. Radio ceased being a medium for drama and assumed a major role, first, as a delivery system for popular music and, recently, as a site for the expression of various political views. Film and television took immediately to one another, even though television cut deeply into film attendance and moviemakers pretended nothing but scorn for the new form. Television became the delivery mechanism for old films and for films made specifically for television.

Movie studios bought television outlets and assisted them with product. With the advent of the videocassette and cable television in the late 1970s, movies and television became, on a very important level, functions of one another. Filmmakers depend upon videocassette and DVD sales and rentals to round out the profits of a film. Moviegoers balance viewing at home with going to the movie theater.

Meanwhile, the domain of "high" culture shrank. It remains proscribed by class and education and finds a home in museums, concert halls, and bookstores with some airplay on radio and television. But it was always marginalized and is growing more so. The "popular," in particular the American version of the popular, is the dominant form around the world. Within it thrive many varieties and subforms, many national inflections. In almost all cultures, film is ubiquitous, and the most ubiquitous of all, the dominant of the dominant, is American film.

THEORIES OF CULTURE

In order to understand the place of popular culture in general and film in particular within the larger complex of cultural practice, it will be useful for us to look at some theories of cultural studies that discuss mass media and film. **Cultural studies** looks at various kinds of texts within the context of cultural practice, that is, the work, production, and material stuff of daily life, marked as it is by economics and class, by politics, gender, and race, by need and desire. It examines the form and structure of cultural texts as they create meaning or have meaning created by the people who produce them and the people who are entertained by them. Cultural studies thinks about meaning as an ongoing process built out of complex relationships between people in their daily lives and the works of imagination they look to for emotional and intellectual sustenance and release.

The Frankfurt School

An early wave of cultural criticism that took mass media as its subject found it deeply troubling, and for very good reason. The Frankfurt Institute for Social Research was founded in Germany in 1924. Its function was to integrate the study of sociology, psychology, culture, and politics. Among its members and associates—known as the **Frankfurt school**—were some of the most important left-wing thinkers of the twentieth century: Max Horkheimer, Theodor Adorno, Herbert Marcuse, Erich Fromm, Siegfried Kracauer, and Walter Benjamin. Because they were left wing and, many of them, Jewish, the Institute was closed down by the Nazis in 1933. Many of its members came to America, where they taught and pursued their work.

A core part of that work was the study of film and mass media. Siegfried Kracauer wrote two major studies of film, *Theory of Film: The Redemption of Physical Reality* (1960) and *From Caligari to Hitler: A Psychological History of the German*

Film (1947). The latter was an attempt to describe a cultural mood, one that would lead to the cultural and political catastrophe of fascism, by looking at the films the culture had produced. Theodor Adorno wrote books and articles on philosophy and music and coauthored with Max Horkheimer *The Dialectic of Enlightenment* (1944). A chapter of this book, "The Culture Industry," along with Walter Benjamin's magisterial essay "The Work of Art in the Age of Mechanical Reproduction," laid the foundation for future studies of media, culture, and politics. It proved to be a difficult foundation to build on. Given the society they observed, the conclusions about mass culture reached by Adorno, Benjamin, Kracauer, and others of the Frankfurt school were either very negative or ambiguous.

Germany in the 1920s was a society going through a massive political upheaval that would lead to the most brutally destructive regime in modern history. The Frankfurt school viewed the rise of popular culture in this society as part of the growing authoritarianism in Germany's political culture. Instead of a web of interrelated texts in which the listener or viewer is part of a complex structure of commercially produced and distributed music, news, images, and sound, the Frankfurt school saw a vertical structure where government and industry worked in close collusion with each other, producing mass media that was distributed downward to the people, dominating the masses with films, music, and radio. The audience for popular culture was an undifferentiated and passive mass, robbed of subjectivity and individuality by an authoritarian government, which swayed the people to its needs by manipulating the popular media.

To the Frankfurt school, the audience for the popular was in fact created, given form, made compliant, turned into a willing tool of the ruling political party. Again, this view was based in a strong reality. Hitler's Nazi government was the first to use mass media—radio and film especially (they were busily developing television)—as a controlled means of communication, fashioning information, entertainment, and outright propaganda in such a palatable way that its audience could not, did not want to, resist.

The Frankfurt school looked upon the government and its associates in industry, journalism, broadcasting, and film as strong and controlling, the audience as weak, willing, and easily fooled. Horkheimer and Adorno wrote: "Life in the late capitalist era is a constant initiation rite. Everyone must show that he wholly identifies himself with the power which is belaboring him. . . . The miracle of integration, the permanent act of grace by the authority who receives the defenseless person—once he has swallowed his rebelliousness—signifies fascism."

The Frankfurt school understood that mass media did not have to clobber its audience into submission, that people have free will that can be easily, willingly subdued. They understood the comfort that comes with joining a group, swallowing rebelliousness, integrating oneself into the mass, and receiving authority's grace. They saw and noted how easily popular culture accepted anti-Semitism, agreed to abstract calls for sacrifice to the fatherland, to the promises of redemption from a despairing and oppressed life. Totalitarian power—along with the offerings of banal entertainment in the form of musicals, melodramas, and comedies made by the ruling powers—was hard for most Germans to resist.

Under Hitler, cultural difference, individual expression, artistic experimentation were not simply discouraged but destroyed. Serious art, modern and critical art, was declared decadent and was banished. Books were burned. Artists fled the country. Popular art was molded into the narrow spectrum of hatred of Jews and communists, adulation of Hitler, and celebration of a lower-middle-class life of home, family, and fatherland, driven by exhortations to keep sacrificing in order to perpetuate Nazi ideals. Fascism became a model for the Frankfurt school's analysis of the culture industry as a conspiracy of politics and business to form, out of the most profound and uninformed aspects of a culture's collective fears and desires, superficial entertainments that confirmed and reinforced the basest instincts of that culture. The culture seemed to yield unquestioningly.

The Critique of American Popular Culture

Unsurprisingly, Frankfurt school scholars tended to look down upon popular culture from an elitist perspective. Anything that was part of such an abominable political culture could not have any value. They took this elitist position with them when they came to the United States in the late thirties. Theodor Adorno particularly disliked the popular and wrote often of the debasement of jazz and popular music. The worst part of Frankfurt school elitism was popularized in the United States during the 1950s and became integrated with the general concern over what some people perceived as a decay of the culture and a rise in adolescent misbehavior. The fifties were a period of serious cultural instability, during which post–World War II anxieties were heightened by the Cold War with the Soviet Union. A paranoia about being subverted and infiltrated took over the country during the first half of the decade, and popular culture became a main target of its fears.

The anti–popular culture discourse of the 1950s was carried on by many sides. Attacks by right-wing politicians and journalists were not very sophisticated, though they stirred up many anxieties. They did not present the Frankfurt school's complex portrait of a culture industry that was an interrelated process of the government and the producers of entertainment crafting their products to manipulate the willing masses. Indeed, some Cold War writers and politicians put the argument of the Frankfurt school on its head. Where the Frankfurt school analyzed a top-down control of media and the population, fifties critics of the media argued that the media—especially film and television—were elitist and left wing. Rather than controlling the belief system of the people, the media subverted it, destroying their values.

Less virulent ideologues, indeed many fifties intellectuals on the left, argued that popular culture was simply too debased and shallow. If people were entertained by mass media, they were already diminished in intellectual and emotional response by contact with films, pop music, and television, or soon would be. Some critics of popular culture saw it—and some still do—as a promoter of violence and sexuality. Comic books, movies aimed at teenagers, and, near the end of the decade, rock and roll music were deemed the worst offenders. Congressional hearings investigated their influence. And, of course, the explosive growth of television in the fifties was looked on with dismay. While its manufacturers, producers, and promoters saw it as a miracle that would placate bored housewives and keep families together, its detractors saw it as a further degradation of cultural standards. Television was yet another sign that the culture was being reduced to a featureless, homogenized mass.

High Culture, Masscult, and Midcult

The social and cultural complexities of mass media were not as important to fifties critics as the pronouncements of decay and corruption. In the fifties and early sixties, elitist categories maintained a strict segregation of the arts and their audience based on matters as vague as taste. The film reviewer and cultural critic Dwight MacDonald categorized fifties culture into three parts. Creating a less ethnically and racially biased metaphor than the old "low brow, middle brow, and high brow" classification, he spoke about **high culture**—the complex, resonant art for the elite—but concentrated his attention on what he called **Masscult** and **Midcult**—the first being popular culture produced for mass consumption, the second something in between, not high, not low, but peculiarly middle class. By splitting popular culture into two groups, MacDonald could address a decade that was entertained by a new range of entertainment from Elvis Presley records and movies to plays and films written by Tennessee Williams and live television drama.

These new categories began to introduce an element of complexity into the American discussion of popular culture. They were still derogatory and judgmental: Masscult, MacDonald says, "is bad in a new way: it doesn't even have the theoretical possibility of being good." Midcult only reproduces the bad in a better light: "It pretends to respect the standards of High Culture while in fact it waters them down and vulgarizes them." Midcult gives the impression of seriousness, while reproducing the same banalities of Masscult (films made from eighteenth- and nineteenth-century novels might be considered recent examples of Midcult). However derogatory, these classifications at least began to recognize or point to the fact that popular culture was not monolithic, that issues of class and taste could be used to achieve a finer definition. But, without the Frankfurt school's complex ideological analysis and with the conservative bias so many of them held, the mass media critics of the fifties and early sixties mainly railed and raised alarms. These were the views from above. Meanwhile, the culture of the popular expanded.

By the late fifties, rock and roll, which began as African American rhythm and blues that was then integrated with country and western formats, became an important component of a revived, activist youth culture that began to have purchasing power to match young people's desire for a unique entertainment. In cinema, the influence of foreign films began nudging movies in the direction of high culture. At the same time, because of population shifts to the suburbs, movie attendance began to fall off and television viewing went up. In response, American cinema changed and began targeting specific age groups with specific kinds of movies, trying to pinpoint an ever-changing audience with both Masscult and Midcult films. Popular culture—both its products and its audience—grew more complex and needed new theories to deal with it.

Benjamin and the Age of Mechanical Reproduction

New theories began to converge from many directions. The growth of film studies in the 1960s and the development of feminist theories in the early 1970s laid the ground for a growing interest in serious analysis of popular culture. Some of the new theories grew out of an essay by an associate of the Frankfurt school, originally written in 1936. It helped form the basis of a nonjudgmental, appropriately political, speculative, and complex meditation on popular art and its relation to the larger matrix of cultural practice. Walter Benjamin's "The Work of Art in the Age of Mechanical Reproduction" takes as its starting point the new elements of reproduction, storage, and distribution that made film and other forms of popular cultural practice possible. For Benjamin, the difference between the old art of the elite classes and the new popular art of the masses is that popular or mass art is readily available outside the usual sites of museums and libraries. The image (film is Benjamin's main object of study, though his ideas can usefully be applied to recorded music, photography, television, and now to digital media) is not a unique, one-of-a-kind event, kept in one place and viewed with awe and reverence. The image is now infinitely reproducible and available. It has lost that which makes it special, even worthy of worship, what Benjamin calls its aura.

Aura can be thought of as the uniqueness of a work of traditional high art. An original painting has aura. It is one of its kind, visible in its originality only where it is hung, looked at with the privileged relationship of viewer and the work itself. The autographed first edition of a novel might have an aura, as would the live performance of a play or symphony. Aura is the nonreproducible, the authentic, the original production from the hand of an artist or ensemble. Popular, mass-produced art is without aura. The compact disc by a rock group that you own is the same as thousands—hundreds of thousands—that were cut from the same master. The print of a film viewed in a mall multiplex in Cleveland is the same as a print viewed in a multiplex in West Palm Beach or (except for the redubbing of the sound track) in Frankfurt, Germany. There is nothing unique about it. In fact, there is nothing about it. Nothing is there but digital, electronic, or optical data; no human presence but the beholding eyes and ears of the viewer, who the producers hope will respond in the same way as every other viewer anywhere—by paying for access.

Benjamin, unlike most of his Frankfurt school associates, did not look at this development with alarm. He looked at it as historical fact—something going on despite what social and cultural critics might think about it. He thought about the growth of popular culture as something to be understood not as an oppressive reality but as a potentially liberating one. Loss of aura and ease of access meant two things. Everyone could come into contact with works of the imagination, and everyone would be free to make of the auraless work what she could. Curiously, the loss of aura could lead to a greater intimacy with the work. The ritual and awe that surround the work of original genius might be replaced by the intimate interpretation of each viewer. "The progressive reaction," Benjamin writes, "is characterized by the direct, intimate fusion of visual and emotional enjoyment with the orientation of the expert." Every person becomes a critic, able to make sense and make judgments. Every person's perception becomes enlarged. "By close-ups of the things around us, by focusing on hidden details of familiar objects, by exploring common place milieus under the ingenious guidance of the camera, the film, on the one hand, extends our comprehension of the necessities which rule our lives; on the other hand, it manages to assure us of an immense and unexpected field of action."

Film and other mass media offer a place of entry and participation in the imaginative representations of the world. Certainly, Benjamin was not out of touch with the realities of mass media and politics, especially in his own country. He knew that the larger an audience, the more difficult it would be for mass art to present progressive ideas. He knew as well what the Nazis were doing with mass media and to the culture as a whole. He experienced it directly. Forced out of his country in 1940, this Jewish, mystic, Marxist intellectual, who wrote about angels as well as the mass media, would take his life on the Spanish border. He understood that fascism attempted to reintroduce a false aura into the mass-produced art, turning it into spectacle and putting it into the service of political ritual and, inevitably, of war. Communism, he believed, might work the other way, by liberating the viewer and the work of art into a politics of communal action. While such a view is out of fashion at the moment, it reflects an understanding that an art of the masses can mean a participation of the masses in the political work of the culture.

The Aura of State Intervention   There have been important examples of governments working with artists to promote a popular art that involved many people on many levels, including the political. The artistic activity that immediately followed the Russian Revolution—and formed the model for Benjamin's idea of a communal, politicized art—is one successful example. The work of Eisenstein, Dziga Vertov, and other filmmakers, writers, and visual artists in the twenties exhibited an energy and a desire to reach their audience and actively engage the audience's intellect and emotions unparalleled in the century. Stalin put a stop to all that. Elsewhere, throughout the century, there have been many attempts at state intervention in the arts. Germany revived its film industry in the 1970s through state subsidies to television. Films were made for television and also exhibited in theaters. Popular response was mixed, but most of the films made under the subsidies were excellent. By and large, public funding has helped to foster a serious and engaged, personal and political cinema—as we saw in the example of *Daughters of the Dust*. But public funding has been less successful in forging a large-scale interaction of audience, work, and culture at large that Benjamin hoped might occur in the age of mechanical reproduction.

Mechanical Reproduction Online   Only recently has such an interaction occurred, and not in the cinema. The government, university, corporate-supported Internet is proving to be the one arena in which individuals form large communities of interaction and communication, where mechanical (in this case, digital) reproduction offers groups of people who have access to the appropriate equipment the ability to penetrate beyond the restrictions of personal and national borders, dissolving both into a large communal space. Nothing is so entirely without aura as the digital; there is nothing that allows such direct participation of one and many imaginations. And there is nothing that so immediately demonstrates the desire of the corporate world to own everything.

Nothing is as elitist as the digital. Although access is rapidly spreading, it still remains restricted to a middle class who can afford the equipment. Cyberspace is different from the movies, which, for Benjamin, offered access to everyone. For Benjamin, the age of mechanical reproduction offered the utopian possibility of integrating everyone into the work of the culture. To use a current cliché, it would be empowering. Benjamin's analysis also introduced a new way of thinking about the popular, a way of seeing culture as multifaceted, as having dimension and difference. Rearticulated, brought up to date, many of Benjamin's ideas—along with those of a contemporary of Benjamin's, the left-wing Italian intellectual Antonio Gramsci—have formed the foundation of new approaches to culture and media. These approaches do not condemn the popular as vulgar and unredeemable, but attempt to understand its attraction, and its interactions. Benjamin insisted that popular culture was a culture of involvement in which viewers actively engaged the work, where everyone was an interpreter, molding the popular to our needs. The critical approaches that emerged from these ideas go under the heading of cultural studies.

The Birmingham School of Cultural Studies

Cultural studies is less a movement than a loose affiliation of intellectual agreements about how to think of culture and its productions. Influenced by the British cultural theorist Raymond Williams, and given its name by the British Birmingham Centre for Contemporary Cultural Studies, this wide-ranging discipline has some important foundational principles: the study of culture is interdisciplinary and broad. All events are seen in the context of cultural practice, and that practice is determined not only by the elite culture industry but by the activities and interventions of many subcultures, which are determined by class, race, and gender. Cultural practice involves both the production of works and their reception by an audience. Culture and all its various components can be understood as coherent, legible, interactive "texts."

These texts can be briefly isolated for the purpose of study and then placed back in their cultural context. I can analyze Alfred Hitchcock's *Psycho* or James Cameron's *The Terminator* (1984) as unique texts, as I might a novel. I can examine their formal structure, their images and narrative form. But I must also integrate them within the culture of the late fifties and the economics of the end of the studio system (in the case of *Psycho*) or the apocalyptic consciousness of the 1980s and the melding of the superhero into the science fiction genre (in the instance of *The Terminator*). I can read parts of these films as cultural texts: the way the automobile in *Psycho* reflects an ambiguous response to mobility and security, and how the old dark house recapitulates familiar images from gothic literature and Hollywood horror movies. I can look at the way robotics in *The Terminator* is a sign of the culture's long-term attraction to and repulsion from the image of the automated human. *Psycho* and *The Terminator* can be analyzed as another entry into the popular imagination of Freud's story of Oedipus: *Psycho* talks about a child destroyed by his mother; *The Terminator* addresses the unending and impossible search for patriarchal figures who destroy and are destroyed. *The Terminator* can be figured as a response to the end of the Cold War and the unknown terrors that occur when we discover that the enemy is really us and not them. Both films can be seen as ways in which the culture continues to come to terms with the modern world, with despair, emptiness, and terrors of the unknown, how it deals with issues of the feminine and masculine, with its attraction to and repulsion by sexuality, with its fascination with and fear of otherness and difference.

Text and context—in their usual senses of the work of art and its cultural and historical surroundings—are reconfigured in cultural studies. The individual work, the work of culture, our acts of looking, understanding, and participating can all be read as interacting texts. The very interaction of viewer and film is a kind of text that can be interpreted. Form and meaning make sense only when we examine their intersections in all their complexity. The key is legibility, the ability to read culture and its work, to understand, dissect, and then reassemble what we have read into a coherent analysis. No one element can be taken for granted. The whole is made of its parts.

Reception and Negotiation

Reading Benjamin, we introduced another principle of cultural studies that opposes many of the ideas of the Frankfurt school and almost all of the ideas of mass media studies of the fifties and early sixties. Instead of positing a "culture industry"—a conglomeration of governmental, political, and business forces that determines the commodities of popular culture and conforms the culture from the top down—cultural studies sees a complex interaction of production and response and reception. The consumers of popular media are not a dumb, cowed, undifferentiated mass, repressed and oppressed by the banal homogeneity of what they see and hear. People consume in many different ways, and with varying degrees of comprehension and ability to make interpretations. Individuals, as well as small and large groups, determined by their economic and social classes, make up subcultures who negotiate (a key word for the Birmingham school of cultural studies) meanings with popular texts, much like readers of high cultural products do. Negotiation implies a relationship between the work of popular culture and the consumer, with the latter taking what she wants from a song, a television show, or a movie, and possibly not taking it at all seriously. People have different backgrounds and different needs, which they put to use in negotiating with the text meanings that are most useful or pleasurable. People are capable of comprehension and of articulation, of struggling against the desire of the producers of the popular to inundate them with sounds and images. Everyone interprets; everyone responds. What the Frankfurt school sees as a monolith, cultural studies sees as a complex group of class-, race-, and gender-marked individuals, with desires and with intelligence. We don't merely accept what the culture industry hands down: we deal with it and use it.

Along with the process of negotiating with the text comes the work of unpacking. Earlier I spoke about the economy of the image. Films made in the classical style—as well as television, advertising, and other popular forms—pack a great deal of information into a small space. Much narrative detail is stored in a glance, a gesture, a nod, a camera movement, a cut. We understand films because we know the conventions, we know how to read and interpret. Cultural studies holds that we can move through the conventions and unpack more subtle meanings, that we decode according to what we want or need to understand about a film or a song or a television program: think, for example, how much information and emotional response about gender and the power of women is gathered from the television show *Buffy the Vampire Slayer*. We open the text, pick, choose, and interpret. What we interpret might not necessarily be what the producers intended. Women fans of *Star Trek* and *X-Files*, for example, write highly erotic, homosexual stories—"slash fiction"—about the heroes of their favorite programs and publish them on the Web. Freddy Krueger, the evil dream figure of the *Nightmare on Elm Street* films, becomes a figure of fearful admiration for adolescents. Weekend soldiers in Serbia dress up like Rambo. Many popular culture phenomena do have their intended effect: Madonna is taken by teenagers as an icon of sexual liberation. Rap music and its lyrics provide the rhythms and narratives of African American street life. *The Terminator* moves, by means of subtle negotiation between filmmaker and audience and movie star, from destructive monster to substitute father. Forrest Gump becomes a role model for simpleminded courage. The class-crossed lovers of *Titanic* (James Cameron, 1997) become objects of adoration and a confirmation of teenage despair. But even here, viewers respond in different ways and understand with a touch of irony the intentions such events have on them.

Judgment and Values

Not all the negotiations, unpacking of codes, and rereadings of cultural texts are for the good (Serbian nationalists playing Rambo only means that real people get killed; Forrest Gump is a role model only for dumbness); rarely are they ennobling in ways that we expect works of high art to be. But the idea of "ennoblement" may be as much a cultural cliché as is the notion that popular culture is debasement. That some individuals or groups use culture badly is not unique or new. The Nazis made Jewish prisoners who were musicians play Mozart in the concentration camps. The point is that cultural studies attempts to be nonjudgmental while, we can only hope, maintaining a moral center. It seeks to describe and analyze and broaden. Judgment comes after comprehension.

But judgment must come. The interplay of perception and analysis, guided by methodology, that makes up critical thought must lead any critic to abstract what she finds about the culture into broad, general patterns and then analyze those patterns for subtle meaning. The description and evaluation of these patterns will be subjective, based upon the values and moral beliefs held by the critic. Some aspects of popular culture will be found wanting, even intellectually or morally degrading, but this judgment will not then become an all embracing condemnation. Perhaps the key element of cultural studies is its ability to analyze broadly and make judgments discriminatingly.

Intertextuality and Postmodernism

This discrimination is difficult, largely because of the simple attractions of the works of popular culture and the desire of one part of the culture to put them down and the other to embrace them and make them their own. The works themselves make discrimination difficult because they tend to feed upon themselves, interact, and absorb one another to a remarkable extent. Films refer to other films; musical styles are filled with quotations from one another—sampling, for example, is a popular formal element of rap; news gets confused with sensationalism; sexuality and violence constitute the major elements of almost all mass media, substituting themselves for more rational explorations of the world. The culture seems to be enthralled with images and sounds rapidly edited together. Fragmentation rules. In rock videos, the unifying elements of the classical style in film are sacrificed to the sensation of rapidity. The classical style made fragments look like wholes, and while that style still predominates in narrative films, in other forms—music videos, television commercials, news reports—fragments are presented as fragments while at the same time moving in a flow that is almost undifferentiated. Commerce, imagination, culture, and news intermingle and move us along in a process that makes analysis difficult.

This is the style of the postmodern, where hierarchies, definitions, and separations are broken down, and the quickly seen is substituted for the deeply understood. Cultural studies discovered the postmodern and, as if by necessity, adopted it. No one can look at popular culture for long and not recognize—with delight or with horror—the often indiscriminate flow of images and ideas. In film and television, images of extraordinary violence become as commonplace as the sentimentality of the characters who are the targets of the violence; images of the poor and the starving appear on television news, call upon our emotions and as rapidly disappear again. When images disappear, so does sympathy. A clothing manufacturer uses images of the dead and dying, or of prisoners on death row, to sell his goods. Everything seems to be occurring on the same plane of comprehension, or willing incomprehension. Popular culture appears to be in a steady state of assertion and denial, of claiming the importance of what is shown and then denying that it really means anything.

This has made media historians and critics of all of us. **Intertextuality**—the interpenetration of various texts, one within the other—keeps reminding us how wise we are to the popular culture we've grown up with. The rapid association of images in film, television, and advertisements forces us to analyze and make sense of the image inundation. Staccato shrieks of violins in a television commercial will make us all think about *Psycho*. A commercial for a local car dealer will play the opening of *Also Spake Zarathustra*, and we will recall *2001: A Space Odyssey*. Any episode of *The Simpsons* will contain references to a dozen movies. Everyone is wise to the sounds and images of the culture, though, perhaps, no one is the wiser.

If you detect overtones of the Frankfurt school as well as fifties critiques of the popular in this argument, it is because of the tension between the open embrace offered by cultural studies and a need to maintain some balance between what may be important and what may not be. Cultural studies insists on accepting all aspects of the popular with an understanding that individuals take from it what they feel is important to them. More traditional criticism asks for value judgment, discrimination, and a preservation of hierarchies. Some practitioners of cultural studies may applaud the undifferentiated flow of the postmodern, while other critical schools look in horror at its surrender of judgment and discrimination. As always, an intelligent compromise works best. The concept of negotiation, the recognition that the audience for the popular is not stupid, helps us understand that there may indeed be discrimination at work. A postmodern critic might argue that it is precisely because viewers and listeners are so sophisticated that sounds and images can be used in a rapid-fire, punning, intertextual structure. Perhaps it is because we have seen and heard it all before that no one accepts the old meanings, and the new ones have yet to be invented. At the same time, any critic must be aware of boundaries even as they are being broken down. Making judgments depends upon recognizing boundaries. We may not always want to keep them in place, but we must note their location, their history, and where they might be moved.

CULTURAL CRITICISM APPLIED TO *VERTIGO* AND *DIE HARD*

How do we combine a theory of cultural studies with an understanding of the formal structure of film and come up with a reading of cinematic texts that situates them within larger cultural practices and within the culture as a whole?

Such a task would involve looking closely at a film and how it is put together—including its form, its narrative structure, the function of the actors and stardom. We would need to address the thematic structure of a film—what it is saying. We would want to place the film in the context of other films of its kind and examine its intertextual structure. We would then need to take all of this and look at the film through the eyes of the period in which it was made, as well as the period in which it is being analyzed. In other words, we would try to see the film as its contemporaries did and then see it again as it looks to us now. We would have to place all of this information in line with larger social issues: technology, politics, questions of gender, race, and class, of ideology and how the film in question fits or contradicts those general ideas and images we hold about ourselves and our place in the world. We would want to draw some value judgments about the film. This should not be done mechanically, because the best criticism is written in a comfortable, integrated style, in which ideas are set forth and analyzed, grounded by the film being studied. There will be digressions along the way, but they constitute part of the complex weave of a film and its cultural surround.

I would like to attempt such a criticism of two films that could not seem more different and distant from one another. They are *Vertigo*, a film made by Alfred Hitchcock in 1958, and *Die Hard*, the Bruce Willis film directed by John McTiernan, thirty years later, in 1988. *Vertigo* is a film of great complexity and high seriousness, made by one of the few filmmakers in America whose name was as recognizable as that of a movie star. Hitchcock's popular television program, *Alfred Hitchcock Presents*, started airing in 1955 and had made his name a household word. Combined with his appearances in his own films, Hitchcock's weekly introductions to the television show made him among the most recognized filmmakers in the world.

Vertigo appeared during Hitchcock's most fertile filmmaking period, right after the popular films *Rear Window* (1954), *To Catch a Thief* (1955), *The Man Who Knew Too Much* (1956), the less popular, darker film *The Wrong Man* (1957), and just before *North by Northwest* (1959) and *Psycho* (1960). *Vertigo* bears every sign of a careful, deliberatively crafted film, structured with a master's understanding of his own time and the methods of his art. Hitchcock attended to every last detail of his films and his career. A self-conscious artist, Hitchcock tried to gauge public taste and his own imaginative needs, to make the commercial and the subjective work together.

Die Hard appears to have come out of nowhere, like most Hollywood films. But we know by now that "nowhere" really means the anonymity of studio production. *Die Hard*'s director, John McTiernan, came to film from television commercials, a major breeding ground—along with MTV videos and the University of Southern California film school—of new directors. He had made two feature films before *Die Hard* (*Nomads*, 1986, and *Predator*, 1987). After *Die Hard*, he made two more successful films—*The Hunt for Red October* (1990) and *Die Hard*'s third sequel in 1995. In a business in which "you are no better than your last movie," McTiernan's career tottered with the expensive flop *Last Action Hero*

(1993); the success of *Die Hard with a Vengeance* gave him a boost, though he has never shown quite the inventiveness that he did with the first *Die Hard* in this or any of his other films. Hitchcock is an example of a filmmaker who worked and thrived within the Hollywood system, using it to his advantage, stamping his personal mark on the films he made. McTiernan is a figure of the new Hollywood. While not a contract director, as he might have been in the old studio days, he is still typical of a decent commercial director. A better-than-average craftsperson, working as part of a large group of collaborators who are experts in the action/special-effects movie, he is sometimes able to bring together a film that is ultimately greater than its parts. With *Die Hard* he succeeded once in making a film that was successful on all counts.

The Cultural-Technological Mix: Film and Television

Analyzing films in their cultural contexts leads us into interesting, sometimes unexpected byways: we need to think about the technologies of film and television, about actors and acting styles, about the size of the viewing screen itself, because they all speak to the cultural context of the works in question. Both *Die Hard* and *Vertigo* owe a great deal to television. Both Hitchcock's and Bruce Willis's fame had blossomed because of their respective television programs, *Alfred Hitchcock Presents* in the fifties and *Moonlighting* in the eighties. *Vertigo*'s debt to television, while playing on the audience's recognition of Hitchcock, is more indirect, more technical, and driven by economics. It has to do, interestingly enough, with screen size, which becomes part of the film's aesthetic.

Film is made to immerse us in the process of its narrative. Part of that immersion is the consequence of the sheer size of the image. Larger than life, the image engulfs the viewer, overwhelms his space. Television, on the contrary, is overwhelmed by the space around it. Small, with (until the advent of high definition TV) poor resolution, its image is not comparable to the large, sharp image projected on the movie screen. So, during the fifties, when audiences left theaters by the hundreds of thousands to stay at home and watch TV, Hollywood responded by making movie screens larger and wider. Hollywood pretended not to get what television was all about—namely, visual narratives delivered for free in the comfort of home—and thought their films could conquer the desire for TV by further overwhelming the viewer with the image. Of course, to hedge their bets, they also bought television stations and produced films and series for TV.

Various wide-screen processes were developed, invented, and reinvented in the early fifties (actually, Hollywood had been experimenting with wide-screen formats from the early part of the century). Cinerama used three cameras and three projectors to show an enormously wide image. Cinemascope (and, later, Panavision) squeezed the image onto the film—called an **anamorphic process**—and then unsqueezed it with a special projector lens. The result was that the standard ratio of the movie image, which had remained the same since the early thirties, permanently changed. It had been in an **aspect ratio** of 1:1.33

or 3 × 4 (three units wide to four units in height). Cinemascope and other anamorphic processes turned it into 1:2.35 (more than twice as wide as it is high). Other processes involved matting the image in the camera or projector—putting a black mask across the top and bottom—to change the image size to 1:1.66 or 1:1.85, creating a wide screen.

A few people came back to the theaters to see the novelty of wide screen, but its legacy has not been a happy one. Cinerama went the way of 3-D, another visual gimmick of the fifties, which demanded glasses be worn to see the 3-D image. Hitchcock actually made a 3-D film in 1954, *Dial M for Murder*, but he never used Cinemascope or Panavision. Both Cinerama and 3-D were too ungainly and not well suited to narratives. Panavision and other wide-screen processes have remained and, in fact, permanently changed the size of the film image. But because the screens of mall theaters are sized to fit the auditorium and not the film, directors can never be sure what will be seen on the edges of the frame. Therefore everything tends to get composed toward the middle. Television and videocassette have never become comfortable with masking the image top and bottom, presumably because viewers would complain that something is missing, and so they crop the image off at the sides, guaranteeing that something is definitely missing (about one-third of the Panavision or Cinemascope frame). Compositional precision was the victim of Hollywood's attempt to conquer television by drowning the viewer in image size. Viewers were subjected to experiments in the size of the image that resulted, ultimately, in a loss of the image. Only now, with the advent of DVD, can we see a film at home in its proper ratio.

Paramount Pictures, Hitchcock's studio during most of the fifties, developed its own wide-screen process called "VistaVision" and used it to compete with Twentieth-Century Fox's Cinemascope. All of Fox's films from 1954 to the end of the decade were filmed in 'scope. All of Paramount's films during the same period were filmed in VistaVision, *Vertigo* included.

Hitchcock turned necessity to advantage. *Vertigo* is, in part, a film about a man wandering and searching. In the first part of the film, Scottie, the central character played by Jimmy Stewart, tails a friend's wife. He falls in love with her, and when she dies, he searches for a replacement for her. Much of the first half of the film is taken up by shots of Scottie in his car, driving through San Francisco, following the woman, Madeleine, to a museum, a flower shop, Golden Gate Park. While these languid sequences of driving, looking, spying constitute a major narrative expression of Scottie's deeply obsessive personality, they are also a kind of travelogue of San Francisco, presented in VistaVision. Hitchcock was a studio director and paid his debt by filming in the studio's proprietary format. At the same time, he made the wide screen part of the film's mise-en-scène and narrative structure, using its horizontal frame to show Scottie's wanderings and also his boundaries. The screen opens point of view and limits it as well.

*Scottie drives around San Francisco in VistaVision (top). Shot/reverse shot—
which is also a point-of-view shot (bottom). Alfred Hitchcock,* Vertigo *(1958).*

Bruce Willis, TV, and Movies

By the 1980s, the screen-size wars were over. Films were, and continue to be,
made in a variety of wide-screen formats. *Die Hard* is in Panavision (the ratio of
1:2.35). It makes excellent use of its broad horizontal scope especially by framing its characters in the corners of large architectural spaces so they seem overwhelmed and diminished by their surroundings. (*Die Hard* looks particularly
dreadful on videotape where the sides are cut off: as with *Vertigo*, a letter-boxed
DVD is the best place to see it). *Die Hard*'s connection to television is not via the
circuitous route of screen size, but directly through its star, Bruce Willis. He
came to the film with an enormous reputation as a character on the popular
television series *Moonlighting*, in which he played a snickering, wise-cracking

detective—a somewhat overgrown adolescent with some conventional characteristics of self-assurance and an ability not to take himself too seriously. *Die Hard* was only his second film (the first was *Blind Date* in 1987), and it launched the second phase of his career, which followed an unusual track through the culture of American entertainment.

There is, generally, a lack of exchange of actors from one medium to the other. Some movie stars, like Willis, start on television, move to film, and never go back. Most stay in one medium or the other. The reasons have partly to do with old antagonisms between the two forms, despite the fact that those antagonisms are now gone on the economic front as the ownership of the companies that make or distribute television programs and movies converges. One reason has to do with salary: movies pay more. But mostly it has to do with status. Movies, even though they are seen by fewer and fewer people in theaters, retain a higher status than television. Willis has often returned to television in small roles or limited runs. He seems more in the British tradition, where crossing over between the two media carries no stigma.

The Actor's Persona: Bruce Willis and James Stewart

As we discussed in the previous chapter, movie stars are a combination of personality constructed by their films and their publicity. Big stars become part of the culture, recognized, identified with, gossiped about in the tabloids, their "private" lives becoming public business. Both Bruce Willis and James Stewart shared these qualities of stardom, but in very different ways.

Bruce Willis is a television link in *Die Hard*, where he expanded characterizations already familiar to millions of people. Within his own brief career, Bruce Willis has tried various roles, serious and comic, but keeps returning to the tongue-in-cheek adventure figure he does so well. His range is limited, his expressions restricted mostly to sneer and smirk with a small amount of vulnerability or deadpan seriousness as in *The Sixth Sense* (M. Night Shyamalan, 1999). He is a very physical presence: he uses his body as an expression of effort and turmoil, violence and revenge. Through physical stamina and wiliness, he transmits a sense of smartness, an engaging quality at a time when many people—men in particular—are uncertain how to express themselves in the world and are liable to choose dumb rather than smart.

James Stewart, the star of *Vertigo*, was also familiar to millions, but as a movie actor who had been in films since the 1930s. Stewart's acting range was also limited, but his was a limitation that allowed him, in the course of a very long career, to become something of a cultural barometer. Stewart's on-screen persona embodied, until the fifties, variations of a passive, sweet, vaguely embarrassed and self-effacing character. His public persona was as quiet and reserved as the roles he played. That very passivity and self-effacement seemed to make him into a kind of rubber stamp, onto which could be impressed not only the characterizations demanded by a particular role but the responses of the audience as well. The illusion of simplicity and gentleness made him something of a mirror for everyone's best intentions. Until the fifties, he specialized in comedy roles, often assuming a foot-shuffling, head down, aw-shucks characterization, whose simplicity was irresistible. His characters were nonthreatening; a viewer could feel both kindly and superior to him.

The role of George Bailey in Frank Capra's *It's a Wonderful Life* (1946) simultaneously summed up and altered this persona that Stewart, his various directors, and the audience had so carefully nurtured. Stewart and Capra added a measure of anxiety and despair to the character of George Bailey. The film's narrative is driven by George's attempt to get out of Bedford Falls and his continual frustrations in realizing this dream. The frustrations and anxieties reflect the lack of clarity about how an individual of ordinary means would make it in the new, unfamiliar world that had formed at the end of World War II, a world where old institutions and accepted ways of life were changing. *It's a Wonderful Life* is a rare Hollywood film that refuses to give its hero his life's dream and forces him instead to accept another role—almost literally forced upon him by the film. Indeed, the frustration George feels at the way his story refuses to come out the way he wants it to leads him to attempt suicide. Only through angelic intervention does he understand that, without him, the town he wants so desperately to leave would be a dark, violent, corrupt place. With this understanding, he takes the more "responsible" path and becomes a family man, a banker, and a protector of his town's interests.

It's a Wonderful Life is one of the great postwar narratives of uncertainty about the present and the future, a statement of the culture's discomfort and yearning for fantasies of simpler times. It still strikes a chord and remains, along with a World War II film, *Casablanca*, one of the favorites of old, black and white movies. It launched Stewart's career in a different acting direction. His roles became more serious, and that aspect of despair and moral confusion that he manifests in *It's a Wonderful Life* is played out through a succession of roles, most notably in the films he made for Hitchcock and in a series of Westerns he made for Anthony Mann, such as *Bend of the River* (1952) and *The Naked Spur* (1953).

Hitchcock began playing on the changes in Stewart's acting persona in *Rope* (1948), *Rear Window* (1954), and *The Man Who Knew Too Much* (1956). In *Rear Window*, a serio-comic film about the unpleasant consequences of being a voyeur, Hitchcock began to elicit from Stewart a worried, somewhat obsessive performance. Playing a photographer confined to a wheelchair because of an accident, the character spies on his neighbors and forces his girlfriend to investigate a murder he believes occurred in an apartment across the way. Beneath its jokey surface, the film raises serious points about the gaze, about the morality of looking and seeing what you are not supposed to see. It is a virtuoso riff on the technique of shot/reverse shot. In *Vertigo*, Hitchcock plays up further the obsessive characteristics he gave Stewart in *Rear Window*, and the two of them create one of the best portrayals of near-psychosis in contemporary film.

Vertigo and the Culture of the Fifties

To understand *Vertigo* and *Die Hard*, we have to understand what happened in the late forties and the fifties to bring about the despair in Hitchcock's film and, ultimately, the various questions about heroism we will find raised in *Die Hard*. The end of World War II did not bring a feeling of victory and power to American culture. Instead it created a churning discomfort, an uncertainty about the future and a lack of clarity about the past. The revelations of Germany's attempted extermination of the Jews and the explosion of two atomic bombs over Japan that ended the war shook the culture and confirmed how easily our myths of civility and order could fall. The revolution in China and the expansion of the U.S.S.R. into Eastern Europe in the late forties further upset a society that thought the second great war of the century might settle things down overseas.

At home, major changes involving economics, race, gender, and class began in the early forties, continued throughout the war years, and generated anxiety for years to come. Labor expressed its unrest through a number of strikes during the war. There was a migration of the African American population to the North, creating economic opportunities for some who had not experienced them before, while disturbing the majority white population. Meanwhile, African American soldiers fought bravely in a segregated army overseas. Other minorities expressed their presence at home. Attacks against Hispanics resulted in the "zoot suit riots" that spread from southern California to Detroit, Philadelphia, and New York. The outbreaks of violence not only signified the willingness of minorities to express themselves but set the stage for the creation of the myth of the juvenile delinquent after the war.

By the early fifties, the culture was wracked with events it could barely understand. Huge internal and external changes continued to occur, such as suburbanization and the flight from the central cities, the formation and institutionalization of the multinational corporation, the slow, painful progress of civil rights, the continued redefinition of gender roles. However, the United States sublimated these and many other pressing issues into a struggle against a mostly mythical external enemy, the "communist threat." Almost every issue was absorbed into the Cold War discourse of anticommunism.

Beginning in the late forties and continuing through the fifties, the House Committee on Un-American Activities, the various committees run by Joseph McCarthy, newspapers, magazines, and much of the language of political and popular culture condemned as communist almost anyone who had once held or continued to hold liberal or left-wing views. People informed on friends and colleagues. Government workers, teachers, screen and television writers, directors, and actors lost jobs. Intellectuals were discredited. The blacklist thrived. American culture and politics underwent a purge. Women were, in analogous way, also purged from the culture. Their roles changed dramatically during the years of World War II. With most young men fighting abroad, women came flooding into the workforce, did quite well, and enjoyed financial power, many of them for the first time. While few women rose to executive positions, they kept factories and shops operating and discovered a welcome liberation from old domestic routines. The liberation was such that, when the war was over, a massive ideological retooling had to be put into place. Men were returning from battle and wanted their jobs back. Women had to be reinserted into their former passive routines. Movies, magazines, and newspapers once again extolled the importance of motherhood and family, the submissive role of women, the nuclear family in which mother was anchored to home while father was free to move like a satellite out of the home, into the office and back.

Discussions about gender got caught up in the absurd momentum of the anticommunist discourse. The political and the personal, the power of the state, the workplace, the family, the sexual all became confused and self-contradictory. The larger fears of subversion and conformity, of being taken over and changed by enemies from without were filtered down into the more immediate concerns of the role of men and women in the culture and the way gender determined the structure of power. Fifties culture was as much obsessed with sexuality and gender roles as our own. It tried to assuage obsession through control. The decade's most conservative desire was to maintain a perfect imbalance of male domination and female subservience, male mobility at work and female stability in the domestic space. But at the same time people feared that this desire for control in matters of gender and throughout the entire patriarchal structure would bring about an unwelcome conformity.

People seemed to find security in sameness while fearing that too much conformity would be dangerous. For example, while the growth of corporate culture was recognized as the source of secure jobs for men and a secure consumer economy for the country, it was also seen as something that interfered with the image of the free, unfettered male, who should be making his own way in the world. Voices were raised and books were written about men being unmanned by their new subservience to the corporation and the family.

Some popular literature was quite direct about this anguish over conformity, the apparent diminishing of male potency, the growth of corporate culture, and communism. Articles in the popular *Look* magazine, gathered in a 1958 book called *The Decline of the American Male*, claimed that women control male behavior, from the early formation of men's psyches, to the kinds of jobs they take, to their competitiveness. Because women now demanded equal or greater satisfaction than the male, they were beginning to control his sexuality. The subjugation to women and the pressures brought by the culture had produced a broken shell of a man, without individuality, without power, overworked, stressed-out, unable "to love and to make moral decisions as an individual." Men were weakened and regimented, made impotent and recessive. "In the free and democratic United States of America, he had been subtly robbed of a heritage that the Communist countries deny by force." As males went, so went the country. Communism by female control.

The Kinsey Reports   Sexuality, control, anticommunism: the triad of fifties cultural obsessions. The gender problem was further aggravated by the publication of two scientific reports that became, next to anticommunism, among the most influential and disquieting cultural events of the fifties. The Kinsey Reports on male and female sexuality (published in the late forties and mid-fifties, respectively) were works of scientific analyses, presenting themselves as objective, methodical surveys. They frightened almost everyone by claiming that there was no normative sexual behavior, no controllable, conventional way of defining what people do in the bedroom. In a world where moral, cultural, and political safe harbor was becoming increasingly harder to locate, the Kinsey Reports seemed to remove yet another anchor. Somehow, what the Reports seemed to be saying about sex became part of the general concern about subversion—cultural, political, and gender. Nothing seemed secure.

The Vulnerable Male in Film

Many films of the decade examined questions of gender (as they did with racial issues) with some delicacy and complexity. They were able to put aside the anticommunist hysteria. Many of them created interesting narrative combinations out of the culture's fears of conformity, out of juvenile delinquency (which the culture invented as one more way to scare itself about what was happening to masculinity, meanwhile creating another reason to excoriate mass media), out of notions about gender that somewhat altered the old stereotypes of the rugged male hero. Some of these films, such as *A Place in the Sun* (George Stevens, 1951) and *The Man in the Gray Flannel Suit* (Nunnally Johnson, 1956), presented male characters who in their passivity, sensitivity, and vulnerability took on characteristics and attributes usually associated with female characters.

A number of postwar film actors—Montgomery Clift, James Dean, Marlon Brando, and Paul Newman, in films like *A Place in the Sun, Rebel Without a Cause* (Nicholas Ray, 1955), *The Wild One* (Laslo Benedek, 1954), and *The Left-Handed Gun* (Arthur Penn, 1958)—expressed a search for new ways of expression under the guise of a withdrawn sensitivity. Their acting styles were a major break with prewar movie conventions; their roles spoke to the repressed anger and sexuality of the culture at large. In *The Wild One*, Marlon Brando plays a biker with a very sensitive soul, who, in one scene, alone with his motorcycle in the night, weeps. Early in the film, a girl asks him, "What are you rebelling against?" "Whaddya got?" he asks. This film, along with *Rebel Without a Cause*, spoke to many people's feelings about the constraints and confusions of

On the face of it, The Wild One *(Laslo Benedek, 1954) is a fifties juvenile delinquent–motorcycle gang movie. But it is also a fifties vulnerable male movie (like its near cousin, Nicholas Ray's* Rebel Without A Cause, *(1955). In this close-up, Brando emotes his sensitivity and despair over being misunderstood and mistreated.*

the fifties. *The Wild One* was considered subversive enough to be banned in England for many years, but its interest is really not in the rebelliousness of the male character but in his ambiguous expression of anger and passivity. Despite the gang brawling, the film's representation of masculinity plays against conventions of heroism and strength; it is, finally, the feminizing of the male that makes this and other films of its kind attractive and curious.

Vertigo is not a film about youthful rebellion. Nor is it on any explicit level about fears of conformity or communist subversion. Quite the contrary, it is about a middle-aged man who implodes under the weight of sexual repression and despair, bringing about the death of other people in his wake. It is more closely related to the fifties films of constricted and destroyed businessmen, films like *The Man in the Gray Flannel Suit* and Nicholas Ray's *Bigger Than Life* (1956), than to Ray's *Rebel Without a Cause* or to *The Wild One*. But it is of a piece with the decade's concerns with change and betrayal, with power and passivity, domination and servitude, and sexual panic. It quietly addresses all of these concerns and the culture's general sense of incompleteness, its feeling of unfinished, perhaps unfinishable personal business, its pervasive anxiety. It touches, in an oblique way, on the Cold War obsessions of containment. The political culture of the fifties was obsessed with containment of the "communist threat." *Vertigo* personalizes the political by creating a deeply repressed man, contained by his fears and driven by his obsessions.

Die Hard would seem to be *Vertigo*'s opposite. It is a film about getting things done, and its hero is uncontained. The film has evil villains who are taken care of by a strong and resourceful man. *Die Hard*, unlike *Vertigo*, is about male strength and heroism, about action that is not questioned. Yet resourceful and heroic as he is, Bruce Willis's John McClane bears a relationship to the sensitive men who began appearing during the fifties. He carries pain with him. Not the vague cultural anxieties that afflicted characters thirty years earlier, John's is a much more contemporary pain—though its roots lie deep in fifties gender ideology as well as conservative 1980s notions about individual initiative. John's wife has left him, and *Die Hard*'s narrative is set into motion by his traveling from New York to Los Angeles to attempt a reconciliation. John's responses to his wife's newfound independence bear traces of the same sexual anxieties that marked his predecessors. There is even a touch of the fifties fear of corporate strength mixed in. But John McClane is a man of the late eighties. His insecurity is marked by the cultural discourse of women's independence, not male dependence, by the fact that his wife left him to take a corporate job, even to reclaim her last name. Such an event in a fifties movie would be the cause of derision, not anxiety. More accurately perhaps, it would be anxiety turned into derision. We noted the reaction in Lupino's *The Bigamist*.

Die Hard's John and *Vertigo*'s Scottie do have a common lineage. Both characters are policemen. John comes from a long line of movie cops, those tough New York Irishmen with soft hearts. These are figures unique to film, yet reassuring in their mythic qualities. Scottie's lineage is more local—he is a San Francisco cop—and more engaged with fifties film images and narratives of damaged men. He cannot live up to the expectations of his job. While John McClane is sick at heart over his separation from his wife, Scottie is sick in soul and mind, a sickness that manifests itself as vertigo, a paralytic response to heights. This results in the death of a colleague at the very beginning of the film, when a rooftop chase leaves Scottie dangling, paralyzed, unable to save one of his men. Scottie leaves the force and is made vulnerable to a monstrous plot by a businessman who plays upon his sincerity, insecurity, and self-doubt, and destroys his life and that of a woman with whom he thinks he's fallen in love. Scottie is left at film's end alive but reduced, staring into the void. John McClane, through a series of explosively adventurous acts, saves his wife, develops a profound emotional attachment to an African American policeman, and emerges from a series of apocalyptic events alive, triumphant, but a somewhat conflicted supercop.

Scottie's despair and John's conflicted state are partly the result of gender confusions we spoke of earlier and are specific to the times of their stories. Scottie Ferguson is the timid fifties male, reduced in stature, capability, and agency in the world. There is little he can do. He is, in his small fictional container, a metaphor of the fifties middle-class, middle-aged man, undone by forces over which he has lost control. John McClane is a collective fantasy of exactly the opposite response. By the late eighties, fear of loss of control had turned into the reality of lost control. The succession of blows to the culture's self-esteem and to the power of the individual over anything in the world had taken their toll. While there were some major victories in the sixties and seventies—gains in minority and women's rights, effective mass protests against the Vietnam War—there were greater, more profound defeats. A lingering unhappiness was the result of the Kennedy and King assassinations, the frustrations caused by Vietnam experienced by those who supported and opposed it, the corruption of the Nixon administration, culminating in Watergate, the stagnation of real income, and a more subtle, yet farther reaching realization that America had little power in an increasingly complex and fragmented world, that an individual's power over everything had diminished. Fifties anxiety became the helplessness of the eighties, figured in its quest for suitable heroes, reflected in the election of Ronald Reagan, the movie star hero–president.

The role of the hero, intimately tied to issues of masculinity in any cultural period, is always under question. It was being questioned in the fifties, and it was again in the late eighties. The notion of the strong, moral, righteous, and courageous man of action, who would cleanse the entire culture of corrupt and violent forces—by means of greater violence—has never held up very well when tested in reality. After World War II, the premise of heroism was examined in film across the board. The great Western director John Ford was exploring the corruption of the Western hero as far back as *Fort Apache* in 1948. In *The Searchers* (1956), Ford was pressing his and America's favorite heroic figure, John Wayne, to give a performance in film that explored the proximity of heroism to psychopathic obsession.

This examination and debunking continued, particularly in the Western, through the early seventies and resumed in the late eighties in other genres. *Die Hard* thinks a lot about the old movie hero, and John Wayne in particular. I pointed out that the Bruce Willis character is related to the movie stereotype of the Irish cop. But there is more. His character is named John McClane. In 1952, John Wayne played the title character in an anticommunist cop film called *Big Jim McLain*. John Wayne as Jim McLain becomes Bruce Willis as John McClane. But this is not a simple substitution or even a complicated reference to the great film hero. It is an attempt to embrace and deny heroism, all at the same time. At one point in *Die Hard*, the terrorist Hans, frustrated by John's clever and heroic efforts to outsmart him, calls to him in desperation, "Who are you, just another American who's seen too many movies . . . ? Do you think you are Rambo or John Wayne?"

Sylvester Stallone's *Rambo* was, just three years before *Die Hard*, one of the last action-adventure films to take its central character with deadly seriousness. Rambo became a right-wing icon. It was not until *The Terminator*, in 1984, that the action film hero began to take on some of the reflective qualities that the Western hero had in the fifties. Arnold Schwarzenegger, ex–muscle man turned actor, moved his career forward by not taking his characters too seriously. There was always something safe and nonthreatening in Schwarzenegger's posturing, and it became even safer after *The Terminator*, when he began actively poking fun at his earlier characters and went on to play comic roles. His presence is invoked by John in *Die Hard*, who says, at one point, "There's enough explosives in here to blow up Arnold Schwarzenegger."

John McClane is a hero and would be directly in the John Wayne–Rambo tradition if he would take himself more seriously. He fights manfully; he gets bloody (or "blooded" as some die-hard believers in trial by violence would say); and he demonstrates uncanny recuperative powers, so uncanny that they became a model for action-adventure films that follow. He becomes John Wayne and Rambo and a parody of both. *Die Hard* begins a new phase of movie violence that is now called cartoon violence. The damage being done to human bodies in film is so enormous that "real" people would never survive it. These films—which include the *Die Hard* and *Lethal Weapon* series and Bruce Willis's film *Hudson Hawk* (Michael Lehmann, 1991), as well the Stallone vehicles *Demolition Man* and *Cliffhanger* (1993, directed respectively by Marco Brambilla and Renny Harlin) or *Judge Dredd* (Danny Cannon, 1995)—are some of the contemporary popular movies that begin to reveal the fact that the image and the narratives made from them are not of the world but of film, and that film violence is a visual trick. They can, of course, go only so far. Audiences do not seem to want a full-scale revelation of artifice and self-reflection. *Hudson Hawk* and the Arnold Schwarzenegger film *Last Action Hero* (1993, directed by *Die Hard*'s John McTiernan) failed partly because they did not take themselves seriously enough and revealed a sense of play that went beyond some viewers' desire for a necessary illusion. We want heroes to be self-mocking, but we don't want them mocking us.

Heroically antiheroic might best describe John McClane. He is the confused late twentieth-century man turned into a courageous, resourceful, and indestructible defender of his wife and her fellow workers. He is always a little befuddled, but always ready for action.

In order to understand more clearly where these two films and their heroes diverge and converge, we need to consider for a moment their narrative approaches, which determine the way they speak to their contemporary experience. *Vertigo*, with its dark, ironic structure, is a modernist narrative. Modernity—the movement of technological advancement, increased urbanization, rapid fragmentation of dependable, cohesive structures such as the family, religion, dominant race or ethnicity, and government, along with the falling away of individual agency—climaxed in the seventies and eighties. The responses to modernity are represented in various ways, including the stories the culture tells itself. Movies and television bring our fears to our attention, sometimes confirming them, sometimes attempting to assuage them with narratives about mastering our destiny, overcoming great odds, and recuperating our emotional losses. In the fifties, science fiction films spoke to our terrors of vulnerability to alien forces (allegories of the "communist threat" back then)—stories that are being retold again today, in less immediate political terms. Melodrama tended to confirm the loss of individual power by insisting that the family, the married couple with children rather than the individual, was the best bulwark against modernity—all the while confirming the fragility of the family. *Vertigo* is an unusual affirmation of the disintegration of both the family and the self in modernity. It has romantic elements and touches of fantasy. But it is concerned mainly with the coming apart of the modern male.

Scottie is lost, unable to act or to love. His female friend, Midge, has been unable to get him to respond to her sexually. Her simplicity and directness frighten him. So does her sense of humor. She is a designer, currently working on a brassiere ("You know those things. You're a big boy now," she tells him). The brassiere she's designing has "revolutionary uplift," based on the principle of the cantilever bridge, and it parodies the fifties fetishism of the female breast, the formulating of women's bodies into preconceived male fantasies.

Scottie's own fantasies are so powerfully conceived that women are unattainable for him, and he suffers from either impotence or sexual incompetence. Immediately following the banter about the brassiere, Scottie and Midge talk about a moment, years ago, when they were engaged for three weeks. Scottie insists that Midge called it off. She doesn't respond. But Hitchcock does. He cuts twice to a close-up of her, very tight, and high enough to knock the balance of the frame off center. She simply frowns a bit and looks slightly off into the distance. It's a very typical Hitchcockian gesture, exploiting the standard grammar of the reaction shot to expand the viewer's comprehension of the situation. In this case, the reaction shot of Midge indicates to us that Scottie not only is in trouble sexually but is unaware of it. He is unaware of who he is and what he is capable or incapable of doing.

Scottie is an emotional void, into which a rich businessman pours an incredible plot about his wife, who thinks she is inhabited by the spirit of a nineteenth-century woman who committed suicide. (A major best-seller in the early fifties was *The Search for Bridey Murphy*, about a woman who, under hypnosis, revealed a past life. In 1956, Paramount, the studio that produced *Vertigo*, made a VistaVision film of the book. Hitchcock may be consciously parodying the Bridey Murphy story in *Vertigo*.) The businessman asks Scottie to follow a woman he identifies as his wife, who is actually someone pretending to be her, and report on her actions. She becomes the obsessive core of Scottie's life, which is so lacking a strong center that it barely survives. Scottie is the man of the postwar age, without power, without a sense of self and able only to re-create his desires in other people, who are not who he thinks they are.

Everything is false, a huge ruse created by the businessman—and by Hitchcock, who gives nothing away until much later in the film—to cover up the murder of his wife. But the ruse itself, as is typical in a Hitchcock narrative, is less important than its effects on the characters and the viewer. We are privy to the decay of Scottie Ferguson from someone who is already weak and afflicted to an obsessive-compulsive, to a sadomasochist, to a shell of a man gazing down at the abyss, having finally caused the death of the woman he has tried to re-create into another's image. If this sounds melodramatic, it is. *Vertigo* is in the tradition of fifties melodramas about repressed desires exploding and then imploding back onto the central character—who is usually a woman. *Vertigo* makes its figure of melodramatic suffering a man. It is unusual too because its narrative plays ironically with Scottie's perception and the viewers'. We must disentangle ourselves from Scottie. In the first part of the film, we tend to identify with him; in the second, we are asked to pull away and judge. There is no comfortable closure. Neither the character nor his world is redeemed at the end of the film. Scottie is left utterly, unrecuperably alone and in despair. In short, *Vertigo* has aspects of tragedy about it.

Modernity, and its narrative expression, modernism, speak to the loss of a center through an ironic voice with a whisper of tragedy. Postmodernity sees the center—the binding stories and beliefs of culture—as already lost and decides to get on with it through many voices, many images, spoken and shown with irony and cynicism. *Die Hard* builds its structures by borrowing from wherever it can and using or alluding to whatever fits—or doesn't. It is a ping-pong game of pop-cultural memory and contemporary cynicism. It plays havoc with any serious moral structures other than the sentimental affirmation of individual heroism. Like the postmodern in general, *Die Hard* is a roller coaster of images, a feast of the intertextual, the junk food of the indecisive and confused.

As a postmodern work, *Die Hard* tries, and largely succeeds, in being everything to almost everyone: an action-adventure movie, a political thriller, a buddy cop film, a discussion of race, an ironic commentary on movie heroism, and (though it may not be quite serious about doing this) a study of gender conflict in the late 1980s. *Vertigo* is a movie conscious of its seriousness, a slow, thoughtful, and formally acute meditation on gender and male anxiety. *Die Hard* is a big, loud, explosive ball of fire that is built out of one of the oldest narrative structures in cinema, the alternation of scenes of pursuers and pursued, an alternation of action and reaction. It is a captivity narrative, entranced with violent action and a hero who doesn't take himself too seriously and can't be killed, who is compared to John Wayne and Rambo but thinks of himself as Roy Rogers.

Postmodern Villains

Scottie is an almost tragic figure; John McClane is confused as a hero. The villains they fight are confused even more. Scottie's enemy is none other than himself: his own weakness and insecurity. Gavin Elster, the businessman who makes up the huge lie that kills a woman and destroys Scottie's spirit, is, in a way, a reflection of himself. In *Die Hard*, the villains are clearly present and mean in the way villains of action films always are. But remember, in this film nothing is as it seems. John has flown into Los Angeles from New York to see his estranged wife, Holly, who works for a rich Japanese company, the Takagi Corporation. He visits her in the middle of the company's Christmas party, which is attacked by a group of terrorists, who kill the boss and take the rest hostage.

The 1980s were a decade of swiftly changing attitudes toward foreigners as well as women. The latter had found their voice, and men were uncomfortable with what that voice was saying. The former were creating other kinds of confusion. The Japanese were particularly frustrating to Americans. We had been victorious over them in World War II. Now their economy was booming and their products, from VCRs to automobiles, were used by almost everyone. They seemed to be buying up everything in this country from movie studios to golf courses to major tracts of real estate in large cities. They were held up as a model of productivity, yet demonized as a strange, alien culture. Though it was never quite spoken, they remained in memory as our dark-skinned enemies. There were other enemies as well, and *Die Hard* seems to acknowledge them all. If the Japanese seemed to be threatening us with economic takeover, then Europe and the Middle East were threatening us with terrorists: people with less than comprehensible political goals that they attempted to achieve by the most appalling violence. In all cases, we responded with fear and loathing to the cultures that scared and threatened us, that we did not understand, or that provided convenient diversion from the complex economic and social processes occurring at home.

Die Hard plays with these complexities and confusions and turns them inside out. Holly's Japanese company is apparently quite benevolent, and her boss, Mr. Takagi, is a kindly and paternal man. He talks gently and has the rare quality of dignified self-mockery. "Pearl Harbor didn't work out," he tells John, "so we got you with tape decks." In fact, the villain in the company is not the foreign boss but another paper tiger of the eighties, the yuppie Ellis. The yuppie was the eighties version of an old cultural stereotype once called "nouveau riche," and yuppies became figures of resentment and ridicule to the working- and lower-middle-class people who were not part of the eighties boom. They were the subject of a number of "yuppies in hell" movies—such as *Fatal Attraction* (Adrian

Lyne, 1987) and *Pacific Heights* (John Schlesinger, 1990)—in which yuppie characters had to go through humiliating, often violent, events in order to redeem themselves.

Die Hard's yuppie is a coke-snorting, sniveling fool, who shows off his Rolex, comes on to John's wife, and betrays both her and John to the terrorists. In return, the terrorists shoot him dead—much to everyone's delight. Mr. Takagi is also brutally murdered by the terrorists, much to everyone's horror. This kindly, civil man stood in contrast to everyone else but John and Holly, and his murder clearly marks the ruthlessness of the terrorists—who turn out not to be terrorists.

Midway through the film, Hans, their leader, is discovered to be not the politically driven terrorist he pretends but just a thug whose gang is out to steal from Takagi's safe. Suddenly the film is stripped of the problematically political and becomes simply a struggle between good and bad. Even when depoliticized, Hans's gang is a strange model of cross-cultural diversity: there is a violent Russian, a number of Asians, and an African American who is both a computer wizard and a heartless murderer. This is an international cross section of the bad, and it mirrors the film's unusual treatment of race.

Ethnicity in *Die Hard*

The major reference to ethnicity in *Vertigo* is in Gavin Elster's fantastic story about his wife, who, he says, is possessed by the spirit of a nineteenth-century Hispanic woman, stereotypically marked as sensual and exotic. Scottie becomes fascinated with "the mad Carlotta" as he becomes more obsessed with her supposed reincarnation, Madeleine. Although there were a number of films throughout the fifties that did deal with racial issues, usually in very positive, liberal ways (films like Joseph Mankiewicz's *No Way Out*, 1950, and Martin Ritt's *Edge of the City*, 1957, to name only two), there existed another kind of segregation. In most cases, if race was not a central subject of the film, it was not considered at all. Therefore, in most films, people of color either did not exist or were treated as servants or, as in *Vertigo*, another reflection of the character's vulnerable imagination. By the eighties, race was a consciously pursued issue in popular culture, almost always present though treated with various degrees of sincerity and enlightenment. In good postmodern fashion, *Die Hard* plays its race card in an indecisive and noncommittal way, giving and taking, leaving us in a quandary. John is picked up at the airport by Mr. Takagi's driver, a young black man named Argyle, who, throughout the film, sits in his limousine, listening to music, seemingly oblivious to the mayhem going on in the skyscraper above him. He threatens to be another in the long, ugly history of stereotypes of the dopey black man—until he becomes a hero by driving his limo into the van of the escaping gang.

Early in the film, as John is cornered by the gang in the unfinished floors of the skyscraper, another African American makes an appearance. This is Al, the cop. He is introduced as a bumbling, good-hearted soul, buying junk food for his pregnant wife, driving his car into a ditch when he learns what's going on in the building. However, he quickly emerges as the only representative of authority who has any sense. When the police arrive in force, their leader proves to be a dope. Two FBI men, Johnson and Johnson (one of whom is black), arrive and are pompous fools. A representative of the media turns out to be a self-serving, dangerous man, whom John's wife, Holly, punches in the mouth. But Al quietly endures, out on the street, in phone contact with John, remaining calm amidst the growing chaos, supporting John in his isolation, providing our point of view from the outside. The cross cutting between the two of them creates their bond and assures us that John will be saved, no matter how perilous his situation seems. Al becomes more than a black cop, and this transcendence is important, because it leaves the race issue unresolved. He becomes—after Takagi is killed—a paternal figure, John's surrogate father. He also becomes John's surrogate wife and mother, falling into the stereotype of the protective black mammy.

The Buddy Film

Vertigo is one of the most potent investigations of heterosexual panic undertaken in the fifties film. (Hitchcock visits the problem again in *Psycho*, where he solves it in an especially perverse way, indicating that the male personality can be entirely absorbed by the maternal female.) By the seventies, Hollywood found other ways to deal with the crushing difficulties of men living up to the image of themselves produced by the culture. One was the buddy film, in which two men—most often cops—are paired in a loving union of support and good humor in which everything is possible but sex. Buddy movies always insist that the two male figures are heterosexual. They have wives or girlfriends. But the women are peripheral; true nonsexual love and unfettered pleasure are derived from the relationship between the men. It is a narrative construct that avoids the painful introspections of the fifties films of male despair, skirts issues of race by having one buddy white and the other black—providing a weak pretense of racial equality—and avoids more complex investigations of male-female or same-sex relationships.

Die Hard is a great riff on the buddy film. Al and John are given a multifaceted relationship. They are father and son, mother and child; they embrace almost like lovers. Near the end of the film, most of the villains having been killed off, John emerges from the skyscraper; he and Al recognize each other through a rapturous exchange of point-of-view shots. Al, once afraid to shoot his gun, redeems his manhood by shooting the last of the bad guys. John walks away from Holly and embraces Al passionately. Holly is marginalized on the edge of the frame as the two friends express their love.

The sequence echoes one early in the film when John has his first reconciliation with Holly in Takagi's office. Holly enters the male space where John is talking to Takagi and Ellis. There is an exchange of glances between John and Holly; they walk over to each other and embrace. In the sequence at the end of the film, the same pattern occurs, but the genders are reversed. John and Holly meet again, but now the exchange of glances and the final embrace are between two men. The bond between the buddies is sealed.

The romance of the buddies. These stills represent the parallel sequences of recognition and embrace in John McTiernan's Die Hard *(1987). In the first sequence, John greets his estranged wife, Holly. Then, after his adventures in the skyscraper, he greets Al, the cop and John's new buddy (his new love? note how Holly is marginalized on the edge of the frame). The gestures and the affection are mirrored.*

Were the film to end here, interesting questions would be raised and the line between buddies and lovers might be confused. But remember, this is a film that will not allow any statement or idea to stand without presenting its opposite. And, as postmodern as it may be, it must also, finally, conform to the master narrative of domestic, heterosexual love. Al soon yields his embrace. He tells Holly to take good care of John, and the husband and wife are sent out of the picture arm in arm. John is saved, his marriage is saved, Al is redeemed, and the love between two men is strong and protected from a tantalizing suggestion that it might be something more. Al changes from potential lover to protective mother. The domestic, nuclear family is saved. After all, the premise that begins the film is John's coming to Los Angeles to see his estranged wife and save his marriage. After so many trials, he may now assume his place as the heroic head of the family. He has proved himself. But, in the process, he has made a strong male bond with Al, the kind of bond, movies keep telling us, men need to be comfortable and free; to be protected, finally, from those domestic bonds that always seem to be so difficult for men to maintain.

The End of Redemption

Scottie is not saved or protected by anyone. He wants to be the hero who saves the heroine in distress, except that the heroine is not in distress; he is. First he pursues the lie that Elster manufactures for him, then he attempts to re-create the lie by searching for a woman who never existed. In the second part of the film, Scottie discovers Judy—who was the woman who "played" Madeleine in Gavin Elster's hoax. Scottie forces her to remake herself as Madeleine. He denies her personality and tries to suck her into his. They return to the Spanish mission, and she falls from the roof of the bell tower. There is no triumph over evil here, or even the triumph of good, because, unlike *Die Hard*, *Vertigo* does not externalize its moral structure into stereotyped characters . Everything, finally, is a manifestation of Scottie's lack of moral center, a lack shared by the decade of the fifties itself. Where love and friendship are offered to John McClane, Scottie is left with only his own narcissism and madness. *Vertigo*, like its name, is about an unbreakable, downward spiral.

There is much falling in both *Die Hard* and *Vertigo*. Hans falls from the skyscraper. John falls down an elevator shaft and swings out a window supported only by a fire hose. But these falls solidify his heroic stature, even as he downplays it. He returns from the struggle bloodied but unharmed, saves the captives, and appears reunited with his wife. The film quietly admits it's all too fantastic, as fantastic as Scottie's obsessive attachment to Madeleine/Judy. But *Die Hard* asks us to join in the joke. *Vertigo* asks us to observe Scottie with pity, seriousness, and even tragic awe as he destroys his life. The relationship between viewer and *Vertigo* is as serious as Hollywood ever demands such a relationship to be. We are asked to read this film carefully, to understand its subtleties, to stay with it as it reveals to us the secrets that aren't revealed to its central character. There are no secrets in *Die Hard*, only spectacle. Its internal confusions about gender, race, nationality, politics, and authority are meant to be taken only as passing jokes, as momentary bits of relevance, or irrelevance.

We could conclude from this that the Frankfurt school and the fifties media critics were correct, that there is an unalterable breach between high and low culture and that, at its best, *Vertigo* falls into Dwight MacDonald's category of Midcult and, at its worst, *Die Hard* is irredeemably Masscult. *Vertigo* attempts to be tragedy, though, at bottom, it is a strong romantic melodrama, well constructed, dark and complex. *Die Hard* makes no such reach and comfortably accepts its Masscult status as a simple entertainment, acceptable as straightforward action film or as a sarcastic, cynical, even ironic, play on serious issues.

Its refusal to take seriously any of the issues it raises only emphasizes its lack of commitment to serious intellectual inquiry.

But our reading suggests another path. By noting the different directions the films take—and recognizing that despite their different intentions, they are very serious about using film form expressively—we discover a common base. Then, analyzing their proximity to their cultural contexts and the ways, consciously or not, they address those contexts, we see that it is possible to understand both films as serious, imaginative statements that come out of commercial intent. We could argue that *Vertigo* is a less cynical film than *Die Hard* because it is structurally and thematically more complex and makes more demands upon the attention and the intellectual and emotional response of the viewer. But ultimately, this is a difference in address, in the way the filmmakers and their films decide to talk to us. The address requires a difference in response, the ways in which we choose to react to the film.

This brings us back to the cultural studies position. The imagination operates in many different ways and for many different reasons, none of them completely pure or completely corrupt. The imagination of a viewer responds in different ways to different films. I find the racial and gender ambiguities of *Die Hard* extremely interesting and revealing, and the overall structure of the film irresistible in its confidence and engaging in its mixture of humor, action, and absurdity. *Vertigo* impresses me with the fine care and detail of its structure and moves me with the depth of its insight into male vulnerability. Both films are impressive in the ways they deal, subtly but pointedly, with the culture from which they emerge.

On another level, both films, fascinating as they are in their differences and similarities, clarify the ways all films tell their stories, sometimes the same or strangely similar stories in various guises, various forms. Even two such different films as the ones we have analyzed here converge at sometimes unexpected points. One reason for this is that stories are a limited resource. Another is that what we seem to want our stories to tell us is limited as well; we demand convergence and repetition. We find security by having the same stories told over and over again. Even more important, all stories can be connected, and when we look beyond the old split between high and low culture, we find that we can learn, respond to, and understand films that seem, on their surface, to be as different as Bruce Willis and Jimmy Stewart.

Film, Form, and Culture: The CD-ROM

The "Screen Frame" section in *Mise-en-scène* demonstrates the differences in screen sizes that have occurred during the past fifty years. This segment also includes a complete visual analysis of the sequence in Elster's office in *Vertigo* and—in the section on sound—a clip of the close-up of Midge when she responds to Scottie's discussion of marriage.

An example of intertextuality is offered in *Continuity editing*.

NOTES AND REFERENCES

Definitions of Cultures: The Roots of Cultural Differences Two standard works on the history of melodrama are Peter Brooks, *The Melodramatic Imagination: Balzac, Henry James, Melodrama, and the Mode of Excess* (New Haven, CN: Yale University Press, 1976); and David Grimsted, *Melodrama Unveiled: American Theater and Culture*, 1800–1850 (Chicago: University of Chicago Press, 1968).

Theories of Culture There is another branch of media research known as mass communications research. This is mainly statistical and, while it may make analytic judgments about its numbers, rarely addresses the cultural and political ramifications of what the numbers reveal. A book that combines mass media and cultural studies is James W. Carey, *Communication as Culture: Essays on Media and Society* (New York: Routledge, 1992).

Theories of Culture: The Frankfurt School The quotation is from Max Horkheimer and Theodor W. Adorno in *Dialectic of Enlightenment*, trans. John Cumming (New York: Herder & Herder, 1972), pp. 153–54. (Original publication, 1944.)

Theories of Culture: Masscult and Midcult The quotation is from Dwight MacDonald, "Masscult and Midcult," in *Against the American Grain* (New York: Random House, 1962), pp. 4, 37. One writer in the early fifties attempted a somewhat neutral analysis of popular culture. Although much of his work is marked by Cold War rhetoric, Robert Warshow wrote some groundbreaking analyses of the Western and gangster film genres. See his book, *The Immediate Experience* (Garden City, NY: Doubleday, 1962). Another critic, Gilbert Seldes, also wrote against the grain in his book *The Seven Lively Arts*, originally published in 1924, the early, formative period of mass culture (New York: A. S. Barnes, 1957).

Theories of Culture: Benjamin and Aura The Benjamin quotation is from "The Work of Art in the Age of Mechanical Reproduction," in *Illuminations*, trans. Harry Zohn (New York: Schocken Books, 1968), pp. 234, 236.

Theories of Culture: Mechanical Reproduction Online For a serious discussion of fans and their work, see Henry Jenkins, *Textual Poachers: Television Fans and Participatory Culture* (New York: Routledge, 1992).

Cultural Studies The literature on cultural studies is quite large. Here are a few titles: Stuart Hall, ed., *Culture, Media, Language: Working Papers in Cultural Studies*, 1972–79 (London: Hutchinson, 1980); Stuart Hall, *Critical Dialogues in Cultural Studies*, ed. David Morley and Kuan-Hsing Chen (London and New York: Routledge, 1996); Richard Hoggart, *On Culture and Communication* (New York: Oxford University Press, 1972); Lawrence Grossberg, Cary Nelson, Paula A. Treichler, eds., *Cultural Studies* (New York: Routledge, 1992); and John Fiske, *Television Culture* (London and New York: Routledge, 1989).

Cultural Studies: Intertextuality and the Postmodern Raymond Williams first articulated the concept of "flow" when he noticed how various television events moved together without being differentiated. See his *Television: Technology and Cultural Form* (Middletown, CN: Wesleyan University Press, 1992). A sharp, concise summary of postmodernism can be found in Todd Gitlin's essay, "Postmodernism: Roots and Politics," in *Cultural Politics in Contemporary America*, ed., Ian Angus & Sut Jhally (New York: Routledge, 1989). See also Stuart Hall, ed, *Representation: Cultural Representations and Signiflying Practices* (London: Sage Publication, 2000).

Cultural Criticism Applied to Cinematic Texts: *Vertigo* and *Die Hard*   For a study of Hitchcock's popularity, see Robert E. Kapsis, *Hitchcock: The Making of a Reputation* (Chicago: University of Chicago Press, 1992).

Cultural Criticism Applied To *Vertigo* And *Die Hard*: Screen Size   The best work on screen size is John Belton, *Widescreen Cinema* (Cambridge, MA: Harvard University Press, 1992). David Parker of the Library of Congress pointed out to me the connections between Scottie's driving around and VistaVision.

Cultural Criticism Applied to Cinematic Texts: *Vertigo* and the Culture of the Fifties   For a good history of the fifties, see James Gilbert, *Another Chance: Postwar America, 1945–1968* (New York: Knopf, 1981). On the zoot-suit riots, see Stuart Cosgrove, "The Zoot-Suit and Style Warfare," in Angela McRobbie, ed., *Zoot Suits and Second-Hand Dresses* (Boston: Unwin-Hyman, 1988), pp. 3–22.

Cultural Criticism Applied to Cinematic Texts: An Age of Anxiety   There is a large literature on the work of the House Committee on Un-American Activities in Hollywood. Two excellent sources are Larry Ceplair and Steven Englund, *The Inquisition in Hollywood: Politics and the Film Community, 1930–1960* (Berkeley and Los Angeles: University of California Press, 1983); and Victor S. Navasky, *Naming Names* (New York: Penguin Books, 1981).

Cultural Criticism Applied to Cinematic Texts: Gender and the Cold War   One of the most popular books voicing the fear of conformity in the fifties was William Whyte's *The Organization Man* (New York: Simon and Schuster, 1956).

Cultural Criticism Applied to Cinematic Texts: The Decline of the Male   The quotations about declining masculinity are from J. Robert Moskin, "Why Do Women Dominate Him?" and George B. Leonard, Jr., "Why Is He Afraid to Be Different?" in *The Decline of the American Male*, by the editors of *Look* (New York: Random House, 1958). One of the best new studies of the changing ideas of masculinity in the fifties by a scholar whose work led me to the *Look* articles is Steven Cohan, *Masked Men: Masculinity and the Movies in the Fifties* (Bloomington, Indiana: University Press, 1997).

Cultural Criticism Applied to Cinematic Texts: The Hero's Role   Susan Jefford's *Hard Bodies: Hollywood Masculinity in the Reagan Era* (New Brunswick, NJ: Rutgers University Press, 1994) offers an interesting political take on contemporary action/adventure films.

5

THE STORIES TOLD
BY FILM

MASTER NARRATIVES AND DOMINANT FICTIONS

Internal Tensions

In the last chapter, we spoke about the tensions that emerge in *It's a Wonderful Life*, a film that pulls its hero and its audience in many directions as it tries to reconcile post–World War II anxieties with a story that wants to be upbeat and morally responsible in a conventional way. In the process, the film tries to make up its mind whether it is a comedy, a fantasy, or a melodrama. It is full of high emotion but also has plenty of jokes and silly characters; angels guide the main character; and it ends, as comedies do, with a reconciliation, a reaffirmation of harmony and happiness. Everyone forgives; everyone appears ready for long-term happiness. But the film's central character, George Bailey, is not a comic figure. He is wracked with doubts; he fights against the calls of his community, wishes to break from his father, to leave the constraints of the small town of Bedford Falls. During much of the film, he is represented as a man on the verge of a nervous breakdown. He attempts suicide and is saved only because he has a guardian angel, who brings George to his senses by presenting him with a vision of the town as it would have been without him, dark, corrupt, violent—almost like the inside of George's mind.

The film, like George, is a bit schizophrenic, split between various fantasies and nightmares of its own making. Coming at the end of World War II, it tried to create a story that would bring the culture together, remind it of its responsibilities, reinstate the nuclear family headed by the working man, nurtured by the stay-at-home mother. It wanted to be a good populist warning about the need to shift large capital out of the hands of single owners into the community.

But it too fully absorbed the uncertainties of the moment, and all it can do in the end is breathlessly proclaim a happy ending. Its vision of George's conversion, and the town's sudden unity; its images of the smiling family and presumption that everyone will live happily ever after are as great a fantasy as Clarence the angel's vision of the town without George.

Closure

Despite the tensions within the film that threaten to break it down, it manages to reach closure, that conventional narrative event in every kind of fiction that stitches together the loose ends, the broken lives, the ruined love affairs, the villains still at large, the people physically and emotionally lost, what has come unwound as a narrative moves along. More than simply ending a story, the act of closure brings back into harmony and balance lives and events that have been disrupted. That harmony and balance is always contrived to fit with what filmmakers believe to be dominant cultural values: victory over evil, as defined by the film, comfort to the previously afflicted, redemption of the lost and abused, reassertion of the family as the most valued cultural unit.

Despite the tensions, *It's a Wonderful Life* manages to position itself within the framework of what might be called the Hollywood master narrative of harmonious closure and, by so doing, positions us within it as amused, intrigued, and delighted spectators. Like *Casablanca* (Michael Curtiz, 1942) before it, *It's a Wonderful Life* has become even more popular than when it was first released, not only because it tells a universal story, a grand narrative applicable to all people throughout time (keep in mind that "universal" is a culturally generated idea) but because it generates a large and inviting fantasy out of a style that carefully and invisibly propels us through a narrative of desire, sadness, fear, reconciliation, to a final proclamation of self-worth and fulfilled communal need. A master narrative contains the elements that please us with their ease of access, with the way they raise our expectations and satisfy them, generate fears and then quiet them, and conclude by assuring us that all is right with the world.

Narrative is a general term indicating the construction, development, and telling of a story. We use it in many contexts. The concept of master narratives is of large culturally, historically, and economically determined constructions, many of them formed long before film. Master narratives drive the dominant fictions—the reigning stories of the culture—that address those most comforting abstractions of love, family, sin and redemption, life and death, and our deepest fears of disruption of order, of violence and despair. *It's a Wonderful Life*'s story of a man who overcomes his fantasies of independence to settle down and be the center of his family and community derives from a dominant fiction of how men should act, and it is driven by a master narrative of disruption and harmonious closure. Master narratives drive the dominant fictions that are articulated in the particular stories told to us by film. Even the classical Hollywood form that we spoke about in detail in Chapter 2 is, in effect, a master narrative. It is not only the form that so many films use to tell their stories but a story itself. It offers an invitation to pleasure without work, invites us to see without really having to understand what we see, and gives us an illusion of continuity and process without asking us to understand the way the links work. The classical Hollywood form enfolds us within a comforting space between the gazes of the characters and constitutes—no matter what other story is being told—a tale of desire for excitement, danger, transgression that is satisfied by film's end. It is the form that embraces the others, the particular stories that eventually make up individual films. These are the large dominant fictions not only of love and hate, fear and desire, but of male heroism, female dependence, the liberal virtues of racial equality, the conservative virtues of demonizing and destroying selected enemies, the imperatives of family, self-respect, and all of the other good and bad stereotypes of human behavior that films talk to us about.

Narrative Constraints

Master narratives and dominant fictions do not exist "out there," though many exist outside of film and have been constructed out of the long lineage of our culture and others. They have a history, and most important, they can be varied, told and retold, reworked at different times and for different needs. Film can trace the lineage of its narratives back to Renaissance comedy and nineteenth-century melodrama, stories of love lost and reclaimed, virtuous women attacked by corrupt men, families and other beloved institutions imperiled by greedy and immoral individuals, the sanctity of home and the order of the nuclear family, the innocence of children, the patience of women, the resolvable confusion of men.

The structure of the master narratives and the fictions that result is based on constraints. Cultural contexts, social norms, and dominant beliefs dictate their form and evolution. In a capitalist society, cultural constraints encourage narratives that promote close families and dependent women because this is a manageable structure that urges the woman to stay at home and care for children—future homemakers, workers or managers—while the male is freed to be in the workplace. Socialist countries may generate narratives of communal activity rather than families and celebrate the laborer's and the farmer's work. Socialist narratives are constrained by state ideological necessity—celebration of the revolution or of workers, for example. In a commercial system, constraints are created by the need for a film to make a profit. Story and structure that push too hard against what has already been proved to work are discouraged. There are still other ideological constraints that we will need to examine.

Censorship   In the history of Hollywood film, events occurred in the early thirties that further restricted the contours of the master narratives. Responding to pressures raised by the Catholic Church over what it perceived as licentiousness in film—especially the films of the sexy actress Mae West and the violence of the gangster film—and faced with falling revenues caused by the Great Depression, the film business decided to censor itself before the government stepped in. The studios adopted a "Production Code" written and administered by a Catholic layman, a Jesuit priest, and a Catholic publisher. The Code essentially forbade films from showing anything sexual—even married couples had to be shown sleeping in separate beds—or allowing any crime to go unpunished. Films could not show the details of a crime or any explicit violence. There was to be no profanity or any other activity suggestive of the ordinary or the extraordinary behavior of flesh and blood individuals, nothing that wasn't conventionalized by the formalized code of cinematic representation and the restricted behavior it portrayed. No one in a film narrative could be allowed to get away with anything that transgressed the culture's most conservative notions of legality and morality. Films had to restrict themselves to the stereotypes of heroism, virtue, and reward that they themselves had imported from the Victorian stage and reworked into their native language.

If the Code had been followed religiously, movies of the thirties, forties, and fifties would have been banal to the point of being unwatchable. But screenwriters and directors created their own codes through images and editing that suggested things rather than stated them. Rain and cigarettes, for example, were often coded to signify sexuality. A look or gesture was loaded with meanings that might not otherwise have to be spelled out in dialogue. Often, screenwriters put in outrageous sequences in early versions of their scripts—a visit to a brothel, perhaps—guaranteed to throw the censors off so that they would not notice more subtle elements elsewhere.

A good argument can be made that the Production Code forced film to be more indirect, more implicit and subtle than it is now in the post-Code period. Today, even with the Code long gone—and with violence, profanity, and sexuality rampant across cinema—the stories films are telling remain largely the same. In the great majority of films, evil is still punished, the complexities of individual, communal, political, economic, and cultural behavior are largely ignored. Redemption stands as the promise offered by every film and demanded by every audience: the promise that lost men will find their way, that a confused and threatened people will find clarity in the action of a male hero, that women desiring more than the culture allows will finally understand that the love of a man and the raising of a family will bring their lives to fruition, that domestic harmonies will be restored, that the right way will be found.

All of this constraint and repetition must be understood within the cultural contexts of film. The ability to repeat the master narratives means that they respond to important individual, social, and cultural needs. We respond to films because we want to; we want to because films show and tell us the things we want them to. Subtleties and variations are continually added to the dominant fictions driven by the master narratives. They have to be rearticulated at different times, for different audiences. The narratives always have to be given the concrete details of a story. They are abstractions that become concrete in individual films. But the concrete stories are themselves structured against the regular patterns, the recurring themes and characters of *genre,* literally the *types* of film narratives that relate the stories we want to see. There are many layers and terms here—master narratives, dominant fictions, genres—and they are useful to help us understand how film gathers its materials and moves from the large fictions of its culture to the concrete, recognizable conventions of form and content that are repeated and varied from film to film to our continued delight.

GENRE

We invoke **genre** whenever we classify a film narrative. Video stores do it when they arrange their titles by categories such as "Action," "Comedy," "Drama." Like any generic classification, they help prepare viewers for what they will see, though the video store categories are often broad and imprecise. To better understand genre, we need to create categories that are not only inclusive but also more definitive. When we do this, we find there is a moderately stable group of major genres—comedy, melodrama, action-thriller, crime, film noir, war, musical, Western, science fiction, horror—that flesh out and individualize the master narratives and tell us the stories we like, with the variations and invention that keep them interesting.

Subgenres

From within these large groupings, **subgenres** emerge. The action-thriller genre, for example, spawns such subgenres as spy films, and chase and caper films. Under and around crime film are its satellites, the gangster movie, the detective film, and film noir, which began as a subgenre and quickly emerged into a full-fledged genre of its own. Road movies like *Bonnie and Clyde* (Arthur Penn, 1967), *Thelma and Louise* (Ridley Scott, 1991), and *Natural Born Killers* emerge from the crime genre. Comedy and melodrama often cross. *Forrest Gump* is a melodrama with comedy; *Sleepless in Seattle* (Nora Ephron, 1993) is a comedy with melodrama. *Mars Attacks!* (Tim Burton, 1996), *Men in Black* (Barry Sonnenfeld, 1997), and *X-Men* (Bryan Singer, 2000) mix the genre of comic book and trading cards with the action/science fiction genre. Genres are often inflected and changed by gender. The Western, a genre in steep decline since the early seventies, has seen recent attempts to revive it. One attempt, *The Ballad of Little Jo* (Maggie Greenwald, 1993), makes a strong case that a generic narrative can be retold by imagining what would happen were a women in the role usually reserved for a male.

Genres can be quite supple, stretching and moving with the cultural demands of the moment. They help the viewer negotiate with the film, promising to provide certain narrative structures and character types that the viewer finds satisfying. But they have definite limits. For example, we saw in the last chapter that the action-adventure film can stretch to contain a great deal of self-mockery and exaggerated, cartoon violence. But when the mockery becomes too severe, as it did in *Hudson Hawk* and *Last Action Hero,* audiences rebel. If a film is too self-conscious, the narrative bonds are in danger of being broken. If the audience feels it is not being taken seriously enough, it may not show up.

Genre and Gesture

Genres began to form as soon as films developed a narrative sense, as they moved quickly from merely showing things, such as a train leaving the station or two people kissing, to telling stories. When stories began to be told, they quickly fell into recognizable types: romances, melodramas, chases, Westerns, comedies. As we said, much of this was familiar to audiences of the Victorian stage, vaudeville, and popular fiction. Types and stereotypes of villain and hero, bad woman and faithful wife, stories of captivity, heroic action, individuals wronged unjustly and then saved, chases and rescues both comic and serious were constructed, developed, and conventionalized into film from the stage within a matter of years. Acting styles, borrowed from the stage and further exaggerated into the pantomime of silent films, established the conventions of demeanor and gesture that, modified over time, are still used and still specific to particular genres. A man or woman may no longer raise the back of a hand to the forehead to indicate melodramatic distress, but a man will bury his head in both hands and a woman will put both hands up to her mouth to show us she's shocked and frightened. Men still jut out their jaws to represent determination in an action film, and both sexes will look to the floor to show contrition, part their lips and roll their heads upward as a sign of passion in a romantic melodrama.

Generic Origins

Melodrama is an especially interesting case in point. The genre had its origins in the eighteenth century, when the English novel gave a voice to middle-class romantic fantasies aimed at a female audience. In the drama of pre- and postrevolutionary France and America, melodrama at first personalized great political aspirations of a middle-class yearning to be free of aristocratic baggage. After the revolutions in both countries, melodrama expressed middle-class moral principles of virtue rewarded and vice punished. In nineteenth-century French and English novels—Dickens and Balzac, for example—melodrama still combined the personal and the political, addressing issues of gender and class, discovery of lost identity, strenuous pursuit of freedom from oppression, and self-sacrifice for the cause of others. These master narrative principles would become embedded in melodrama's transformation to the cinema.

The transformation was made through the Victorian stage, where the passions of melodrama were played out with exaggerated abandon and the clichéd gestures that are now referred to whenever the genre is parodied. These gestures were, in fact, codified, illustrated, and written down so that actors would know how and when to use them. Exaggeration was required in the pantomime of silent film. Intertitles, which interrupted the action with printed words, might represent the intended dialogue or summarize narrative events, but emotional continuity needed to be maintained by physical movements and facial expressions. In many countries during the silent period a live speaker might be present at a screening to narrate the events on the screen. Music also provided continuity and emotional support for the images. Melodrama means drama with music. Silent films were rarely shown silent. By the 1910s, orchestral scores were distributed with major film productions and were played by orchestras in urban movie theaters. In smaller theaters, a pianist might play from a score or improvise music to the film. Music provoked the emotions and made connections between what the characters on the screen and the viewers in the audience were supposed to be feeling. It still does this on the sound track and remains a major element of film in general and melodrama in particular.

The great dynamics of emotion generated by melodrama were supported by the economic dynamics of an audience willing to pay to see virtue rewarded and vice punished, to be assured that heroic men would save women from disaster and that the moral balance of the world would be restored. These dynamics were set into motion by writers and producers who worked in concert with what they intuited or analyzed as audience desire. Audience desire and creative supposition were more often in sync than not.

In literature, genres were born out of the complex interactions of form, structure, individual imagination, and social need. Forms of story telling developed and were repeated, rules were constructed, obeyed, and repeated, in acts of collusion. An artist's imaginative needs, the audience's desire (originally, a limited, upper-class audience), and larger cultural events conspired to establish specific forms and formulas that generated specific meanings and maintained them in the social conscience. Tragedy, originally stories of kings and rulers, evoked the social profundity of the cyclical movements of power and pride, authority, self-deceit, and fall from power. The pastoral became the form for discriminating between the simplicities and complexities of a culture by contrasting an innocent, rustic world against the corruptions of the city. The epic told the large, complex story of the origination and formation of the culture and its politics from the perspective of a great hero. In film, genres are also born out of social need and continue as long as the need is there. But while they have literary and theatrical origins, film genres rarely emerge out of the work of individual artists. In fact, many have argued that, in film, individual imagination is the enemy of generic purity. The genre transcends the artist and is therefore the perfect example of the mass production of narratives that constitutes studio filmmaking. A genre film is the result of many imaginations, including the collective imagination of the audience and the dominant fictions that nourish it. And, as in all imaginative issues relating to film production, it is economically determined.

Generic Patterns

Establishing a genre means establishing a pattern—a blueprint—and, as in the making of a car, once the pattern is established, it is easier and cheaper to turn out many versions of the same pattern than reinvent a new one for each unit. During the thirties, when Warner Brothers decided to make a gangster film—a genre that the studio came to specialize in and, with Mervyn LeRoy's *Little Caesar* in 1930 and William Wellman's *Public Enemy* in 1931, practically invented— a number of events would occur almost automatically. A basic story line would be at the ready: a young man from the slums would wander into a life of crime. Since this was the period of prohibition against alcohol, the life of crime would usually be illegal trafficking in booze. The young man would collect around him a close male friend and a girlfriend. They would all be seduced by fame and fortune, build a gang, gain riches through violence, reach for more than they could grab. The young man would become entranced by his fame and wealth, fall out with the friend, the girlfriend, or his mob, be betrayed, and finally get gunned down by the cops. This narrative appealed to the Depression audience's desire to break out of the difficult, poor life many of them suffered during the decade and helped them fantasize a life of power, riches, and comfort that ran parallel to the "legal" system. At the same time, it appealed to a dominant fiction that spoke about the moral prohibition against easy money and provided a cautionary restriction on the too easy satisfaction of desire. If wealth came too easily and illegally to someone, he needed to be punished. The gangster film offered the fantasy of wish fulfillment and the reality of cultural restraints all at the same time. The audience was tempted and was redeemed from temptation, though apparently not redeemed enough to keep censors from getting nervous.

Along with the gangster narrative, the apparatus for the gangster film could be easily constructed. The studio would have everything at hand: the city street already built on the back lot, a cutout of a car placed against a rear-screen projection of a city street in motion, guns of all kinds, fedora hats, sharp suits for the men, low-cut gowns for the women. The actors were under contract: Edward G. Robinson, Humphrey Bogart, James Cagney. Writers and directors, also under contract, could be assigned to the latest gangster production. In short, all the elements were there and ready to make a genre film. As long as the audience and the censors remained receptive, the economies for this kind of production were sound and returns on investment guaranteed. Unfortunately, the censors soon cracked down on the studios and so they modified the genre, sometimes turning the actors who played gangsters into FBI agents, repeating the patterns but with the "good guys" in the foreground.

Genre and Narrative Economy

By the thirties, as the studios geared up production, many of them releasing a film a week (six major studios and a number of smaller ones averaged over 300 narratives a year for almost twenty years), originality in story line was not a practical or affordable quality. Genres—fed by adaptations from existing novels, stories, plays, or other films—allowed this vast production of narratives to go on with ease. The question of originality was rarely raised. Audiences became habituated to seeing variations on a theme with apparent ease. The studios continued the variations on a theme with obvious ease. Each part of the process—production and reception, filmmaker and audience—remained in contact through genres. The studios negotiated generic form and content with an audience that signified its acceptance of the contract by buying tickets.

In the days of the studios, executives would hold previews in the Los Angeles suburbs. The film's director and producer, perhaps even the studio head himself, would travel to a theater and, from the back of the house, watch the audience watching the film. Afterward, they would collect note cards from the audience. Depending on the audience's reaction during the film and on their written comments after the screening, the executives might order retakes, demand an alternative ending be filmed, ask to have more funny lines added, or have the entire film recut to increase or slow down its rhythm. Based on audience response, the film would be reshaped, the variations on a theme reworked.

Previewing still goes on. Some moviemakers hold focus groups, in which a representative group of people are invited to discuss their attitudes about a particular film or about film in general. But currently the main negotiating power of the audience is mediated through the money they pay in film admissions and videocassette rentals. The main "preview" is a film that makes a great deal of money. If a film is successful, it becomes a model for films to follow. The audience resides mostly inside the gross receipts a film earns. On the basis of those receipts, writers, agents, producers, and directors attempt to guess what variations on the successful genre or story might make them more money still. They guess wrong more often than right. But every right guess usually pays for the wrong ones. Think of how that single variation of the old thirties action-adventure film, *Raiders of the Lost Ark*, led to a string of imitations. When *Batman* (Tim Burton, 1989), a variety of the heroic thriller and the fantasy film, came along, filmmakers seized the opportunity to combine comic book action, heroism, fantasy, and elements of the science fiction film in a variety of ways. There were the sequels of the films themselves (two for *Raiders: Indiana Jones and the Temple of Doom*, 1984; *Indiana Jones and the Last Crusade*, 1989; both directed by Spielberg; and three for *Batman*: Burton's *Batman Returns*, 1992; and Joel Schumacher's *Batman Forever*, 1995; and *Batman and Robin*, 1997), and there were spinoffs from both films like Robert Zemeckis's *Romancing the Stone* (1984), Sam Raimi's *Darkman* (1990), *The Crow* (Alex Proyas, 1994), *The Shadow* (Russell Mulcahy, 1994), and *Stargate* (Roland Emmerich, 1994), to name a few.

But we cannot simply blame the studios for churning out generic clones. In fact, no one is to blame. The key to genre is the circulation of stories, and as long as audiences enjoy the product and pay for it, the circulation continues. As long as the stories keep shifting and changing shape, the studios keep making them applicable and acceptable to a large enough audience, and audiences keep reading them and making them applicable to themselves, a large enough generic community will be achieved. The films will be successful and the genre will thrive.

DOCUMENTARY

At first thought, documentary—sometimes called nonfiction—film seems to stand outside of the usual categories of film genres: Westerns, science fiction, action-adventure, comedy, romantic comedy, melodrama, thriller, gangster film, and so on. It stands outside because it is not fiction, not "made-up," and therefore not driven by the large narratives and dominant fictions of make-believe. The master narrative of documentary is its truthfulness, a faithful gaze at the world and the lives of the characters it observes. Observation is the guiding force of documentary, and the illusion of neutrality of the documentary filmmaker makes up its central generic elements.

In fact, the history of documentary, which is as long as the history of fiction film, proves otherwise, and the documentary turns out to be not only a genre but, like narrative film, host to a number of subgenres. Earlier we spoke about the old notion that fiction film derived from the work of the Lumière brothers, who often set up their cameras and simply recorded the events in front of it, while Georges Méliès crafted fictions inside his studio. In fact, Méliès also filmed historical events and the Lumières set up little fictions to film. Between them, they set the complexities of documentary filmmaking that all the way through *The Blair Witch Project*—a fiction film made to look like a documentary—have made it a difficult genre to define with any certainty.

Newsreels

Documentaries break down into a number of subgenres. Originally, documentaries were made to observe and record events that would go on even without the camera's presence. Newsreels were one manifestation of this kind of documentation. They were a part of almost every filmgoer's experience from the thirties throughout the fifties. In cities, there were theaters devoted to showing only newsreels. One major hybrid of newsreel documentary was *The March of Time*, a weekly newsreel produced in the thirties through the early fifties by Louis de Rochemont and *Time Magazine* (*The March of Time* is parodied in the "News on the March" sequence in *Citizen Kane*). *The March of Time* rarely depended on newsreel footage alone and, like many turn-of-the-century silent newsreels, would boldly create sequences in order to achieve maximum dramatic effect.

Today, television has taken over the work of the newsreels that were common in theaters, and while the re-creations of events are less radical than the theatrical versions, TV news skews and shapes the events it observes in other ways. Television news loves to show blood and tears, and it is the major outlet for political messages. While much of the footage is of events that have actually taken place, it is edited for maximum emotional effect, like a movie. And because everyone from politicians to special interest groups is now quite savvy about the power of television, events—especially political ones—are more often than not staged by their participants to be filmed rather than filmed as they are. If *The March of Time* pointed the way to the mixture of fact and fiction to produce what appeared to be fact, television news turns fact into fiction and attempts to control viewer attention to maximize viewership itself.

Early Masters of the Documentary

Newsreels, news footage, and television "infotainment" programming—shows like *Dateline* or *20/20*, which take banal events and shape them into heartrending melodrama—are in fact a special and one might say especially corrupt aspect of documentary filmmaking. Much more prominent and lasting are films made by a variety of independent filmmakers whose purpose is to show an aspect of human activity, promote social programs, or record societal problems. Some of these filmmakers worked entirely on their own. Others—especially in the thirties and forties, in Russia, the United States and Great Britain—worked for government agencies and created some of the most important and exploratory films that we have.

Dziga Vertov and Esther Shub   We have examined, through the work of Sergei Eisenstein, the powerful, structurally complex political films that were made after the Russian Revolution. Other filmmakers of the period made films that were documents of events before, during, and after the revolution. Dziga Vertov, best known for his surreal celebration of filmmaking, *Man with a Movie Camera* (1929), also made a long series of films about daily life in the postrevolutionary U.S.S.R. The *Kino Pravda* films were instructive, observant, and playful. They would, for example, demonstrate the making of a loaf of bread by running the process in reverse, from the loaf to the bakery, the flour mill, the field of wheat. Vertov's "kino eye" made the camera a kind of reality probe to show people how the world worked.

Esther Shub, on the other hand, rarely filmed out in the world and instead made her films out of found footage. Called compilation films, nothing is shot

Dziga Vertov found and manipulated his documentary images. Man with a Movie Camera *(1929).*

specifically for the new work, which is created in the editing room. Like so much of postrevolutionary Russian film, Shub's compilations are about editing, about choosing available images and so ordering them that they are given new meaning. Unlike Eisenstein's muscular, dynamic montages, Shub's *The Fall of the Romanov Dynasty* (1927) is amazingly linear, a history lesson moving across revolutionary time.

Found footage of the revolution, Fall of the Romanov Dynasty, *by Esther Shub, 1927.*

Robert Flaherty   The American Robert Flaherty still holds a place as a founding figure of the documentary. In fact the Flaherty Seminar for Independent Video and Cinema is held regularly as a forum for discussion and exhibition of documentary and experimental work. Flaherty was a perfectionist and a creative force, pulling together his material, the people whose lives he was documenting, and literally arranging their environment to create the perfect scene and effect that, though often staged, would bring home the points he was making about his subjects even better than unmanipulated observation. His most famous film, the silent *Nanook of the North* (1922), despite its mildly patronizing attitude and stereotyping of the "simple savage," creates a kindly, engaged, and often lyrical observation of daily Inuit life in the twenties. Flaherty loves to look into the faces and actions of his characters with both an anthropologist's curiosity and a desire to find the homely and comprehensible attributes of what, to an outsider, is an exotic culture: Nanook listens to (and tries to eat) a phonograph record, the family gives medicine to a child, the group builds an igloo, or they simply engage in play. In some of the film's most famous sequences, we observe Nanook fishing (he kills the fish with his teeth,) and his capture of a walrus and a seal.

The latter event is a fake. Flaherty had a dead seal placed beneath the ice. But this production history does not take away from the power of the sequence and representation of authenticity of the film as a whole. Flaherty's talent at placing his camera at exactly the right place to compose the person in the landscape, and the time he allows for events to take their course, mark the film as kind of touchstone for documentary filmmaking to come. Unfortunately, Flaherty's own career did not fare well. Film was a perfect vehicle for the culture's desire for the exotic: foreign people in strange lands who fit stereotypes of the primitive and childlike. *Nanook* fit that desire well enough that the studios attempted to cash in on it. Flaherty went to work for Paramount on a variety of projects, often with a codirector whom the studios either trusted or—in the case of the

German filmmaker F. W. Murnau, who collaborated with Flaherty on *Tabu* (1931) until the latter abandoned the project—apparently thought would add to the exoticism and make it more sentimentally attractive.

These films barely adhere to anything but the vaguest requirements of documentary, and it wasn't until Flaherty turned to government and corporate sponsorship that his talents shined again. He made *Man of Aran* (1934) for the British, and it is one of his best and least compromised works. The rawness of the life of a fisherman in an inhospitable environment is presented with little flinching; the brutal landscape and hopeless labors of its inhabitants are represented with little sentimentality. Flaherty ended his career with *The Land* (1942), made for the U.S. Information Service, and *Louisiana Story* (1948), sponsored by Standard Oil. Somewhat compromised because of its sponsor, which wanted a film to show what a good environmental neighbor it was, the film is a lyrical glorification of both place and alleged corporate goodwill.

Government Sponsorship

Pare Lorentz   Documentaries are never big moneymakers, and filmmakers often have to turn to government and corporate support in order to make their films. This does not, of course, mean that the films are automatically more ideologically charged than films financed by the studios, or that they have to toe a particular line. *Louisiana Story* survives as a well-made documentary apart from its corporate sponsorship. There have been periods in the history of film when many governmental bodies understood the importance of film in representing the culture, creating images for it, and, yes, propagating some important ideas that the sponsoring bodies wished to have known.

The U.S. government under Franklin Roosevelt in the thirties became, briefly and through various agencies, the funders and producers of some of the best documentaries we have. Pare Lorentz, for example, made two films about the work of the government in land reclamation—*The Plow That Broke the Plains* (1936) and *The River* (1937)—in which a precise photographer's eye composes the shots (indeed Lorentz used prominent still photographers to film his work) and an editor's rhythm, heavily influenced by the montage practice of Sergei Eisenstein, drives the films forward with a grace and purpose. Indeed, it is the visual rhythm of *The Plow That Broke the Plains* that turns a powerful statement about the reclamation of the thirties' dustbowl into a splendid piece of filmmaking with political urgency. Its precise montages of land and people, of the deadness of the first threatening the lives of its inhabitants, make it a strong prelude to the saving of the land by government intervention.

Leni Riefenstahl   Lorentz was one of many American documentary filmmakers in the thirties who used government sponsorship to provoke their political and aesthetic imaginations into visually stimulating cinema. There were also many European documentarists, perhaps most famously Joris Ivens, who worked through a variety of subjects, including *The Spanish Earth* (1937), a film about the struggle of the Spaniards against the right-wing insurgency of Francisco Franco, with a commentary by Ernest Hemingway.

One filmmaker, however, did not use her government sponsorship well. Or perhaps she did—too well. Leni Riefenstahl remains to this day one of the few prominent women filmmakers across the

Leni Riefenstahl's staged Nazi documentary, Triumph of the Will *(1935).*

history of world cinema and one of the most controversial. She was the filmmaker of the German Nazi Party. Her two best-known films, *Triumph of the Will* (1935) and *Olympia* (1938), were financed for and made in the service of Adolf Hitler and his Minister of Culture, Joseph Goebbels (the man who was reported to have said, "When I hear the word 'culture,' I pull out my gun"). *Triumph of the Will* is a film about a gigantic Nazi rally that was staged precisely so that Riefenstahl could film it. The purpose of the film is to provide visual and ideological stimulation to the viewer of people in large, geometric masses, marching, saluting, looking at and listening to Hitler, the object of their adoration. Stimulation is not the same as stimulating, however. The incessant parading and the huge massing of people, along with Hitler's harangues, may have had a hypnotic effect on a willing and ideologically committed fascist audience. Today the film is long, noisome, and tiring. A part of the hypnotic effect lies in Riefenstahl's cutting, which proved so tight that filmmakers were unable to extract footage from *Triumph* to compile an *anti-*fascist film. Curiously, the film maintains some kind of perverse influence. For reasons best known to himself, George Lucas imitated not the cutting but the compositions of *Triumph of the Will* to celebrate the victory of the heroes at the end of the first *Star Wars*. Perhaps there is something in the composition of geometrically massed people that attracts an innocent (or not so innocent) cinematic eye.

The film, obviously, has remained in the global cultural consciousness and has sparked many arguments about aesthetics versus politics. This argument reaches as far back as the nondocumentary film *Birth of a Nation*, D. W. Griffith's groundbreaking work that celebrates and led to the renewed popularity of the Ku Klux Klan. With Riefenstahl's *Olympia*, which at casual glance really does give the impression of an artful recording of sports events, the aesthetics versus politics argument grows stronger. It appears to be a "neutral" documentary of the 1936 Olympic Games in Berlin, in which Riefenstahl even had the authority to include the (for the Germans) humiliating win of Jesse Owens, the African

Riefenstahl's composition imitated by George Lucas in Star Wars *(1977). Why celebrate the triumph of good by imitating a film about evil?*

American Olympic athelete. The climactic high-diving sequence of *Olympia* is among the most delirious and expertly cut visions of the body in motion. But here is where the problem lies, and it ties in with much of what we are talking about in regard to film throughout this book. The cultural, political context of the film, its maker, and its intended audience bring it under suspicion. If *Triumph of the Will* is a peon to the totalitarian massing of fascist forces, *Olympia* is a celebration of the Nazi cult of the body: the perfect Aryan body, which   with the brief, begrudging exception of Jesse Owens—is what Riefenstahl concentrates on the most. Hers is a politicized erotic gaze of the body under stress and sacrifice, two major elements of Nazi ideology. The very structure and image content of her films make them part of the ideology of destruction, no matter what those images seem to show.

John Grierson and the British Documentary Movement   Leni Riefenstahl is (at the time of this writing) still alive, still proclaiming her innocence, her interest in art not politics. She has even become the subject of someone else's documentary, Ray Müller's *The Wonderful, Horrible Life of Leni Riefenstahl* (1993). She remains, perhaps with D. W. Griffith, among the most interesting, unredeemable figures in film history.

Happily, while she was making Nazi films in Germany, John Grierson, a Scotsman with large humanist-socialist leanings, began overseeing a complex filmmaking process in England through funding first by the Empire Marketing Board and then—more in keeping with his notion of film as a means to disseminate information—through the General Post Office. Though Grierson directed only two films himself, he produced or oversaw many, many others. The films were as varied as they were brilliantly made. Harry Watt and Basil Wright's *Night Mail* (1936), with its narrative written by the poet W. H. Auden and music by Benjamin Britten, showed how the British mail system worked. The same director's *Song of Ceylon* (1935) demonstrated the growing and production of tea.

All of the films represented information through a synthesis of word, sound, and imagery photographed in bold, large compositions, edited with an Eisensteinian imagination, a rhythm that drives the viewer through and with the film's information.

If this weren't enough, Grierson went to Canada in the late thirties and founded the Film Board of Canada, which was in its time a major and influential government filmmaking agency. Grierson also wrote. He invented the very word "documentary" in a review of Robert Flaherty's *Moana* (1925) and propagandized the social power of the documentary film with grace and persistence:

> The "art" of documentary is, as always with art, only the by-product of an interpretation well and deeply done. Behind the documentary film from the first was a purpose, and it was the educational purpose . . . to "bring alive" to the citizen the world in which his citizenship lay, to "bridge the gap" between the citizen and his community.

World War II

During World War II, the U.S. government, through the Office of War Information, continued the production of documentary films, all of which were "propaganda" films in the sense that they propagated the rightness of the American cause and pushed, sometimes to extreme racist proportions, the horribleness of the Germans and Japanese. Many of these films were produced or directed by major Hollywood figures: Frank Capra, for example, oversaw production of a large number of films grouped into two categories, *Why We Fight* and *Know Your Enemy*. These films combined narration, war footage, reenactment, and animation (supplied by Walt Disney) in films that compelled the viewer to an assent to the rightness of the war.

Other directors of great stature also made wartime documentaries. John Huston, for example—the director of films like *The Maltese Falcon* (1941), *Treasure of the Sierra Madre*, *Key Largo* (both 1948), and *The African Queen* (1951)—made two dark, troubling nonfiction films about the war and its aftermath. *The Battle of San Pietro* (1945) is something like an engaged (though partially reenacted) newsreel with a probing, troubled intelligence behind it, so troubled that the army itself was uncomfortable with its unrelenting images of destruction and cut it for public release. Similar trouble confronted Huston's *Let There Be Light* (1946), a documentary of emotionally disturbed soldiers in an American rehabilitation facility. In this case, it was fear of revealing the identities of these emotionally disturbed prisoners of war that kept the film out of circulation until a few years ago.

Cinéma Vérité   Later in this chapter, we will be discussing a kind of film that emerged in post-World War II Italy called "neorealism." Neorealism was fiction film, but its use of actual locations and nonprofessional actors gave it the air of documenting life in the streets and tenements of a war-ravaged country. As we will see, the influence of Italian neorealism was enormous, and it extended to the documentary as well.

Much of early documentary was carefully planned and structured. Flaherty's films, as we pointed out, contained staged sequences, and the best of the thirties and forties documentaries were composed and edited more artfully than fiction films. There was a tendency in many studio-made documentaries to use voice-over narration, providing a shell of words to envelop the images. The term "voice of god" was coined to describe the stentorian tones of the narrator of the *March of Time* series. But the influence of neorealism led to a change in these documentary structures. Beginning with the work of Jean Rouch in France in the fifties—and moving to the United States in the films of Richard Leacock, D. A. Pennebaker, Fredcrick Wiseman, and David and Albert Maysles—a surge in new documentary, often referred to as cinéma vérité, occurred in the sixties. **Cinéma vérité** is marked by the absence of voice-over narration and strives to achieve a perfect illusion of ongoing life, casually observed by the camera. Vèritè is meant to appear seamless: in other words, it attempts to imitate some aspects of the Hollywood continuity style. But this continuity is meant to communicate the on-goingness of life, of people doing their work, conducting their personal affairs.

For example, David and Albert Maysles' *Salesman* (1969) follows a Bible salesman on his door-to-door rounds, watches and listens to him give his pitch to prospective customers, talk to his colleagues, and ruminate about his profession. The film attempts to represent a neutrality, which, given the very nature of its subject and his work, it cannot quite manage. While not melodramatic, and never reaching for the large insights of that other great work about salesmen, Arthur Miller's play *Death of a Salesman*, the film cannot avoid pulling our emotions toward the comprehension of a rather small, sad life devoted to the selling of religion. It also cannot avoid a very careful editorial structuring of events. The film's sequences may actually be recorded as they occurred, but they are arranged to create a particular and affecting narrative flow.

It was another Maysles brothers film, *Gimme Shelter* (1970), that brought the vérité movement to its climax. One of a number of rock music documentaries following in the wake of Michael Wadleigh's *Woodstock* (one of whose editors was Martin Scorsese), *Gimme Shelter* had one major difference: it showed a murder. The film documents the infamous Rolling Stones' Altamont concert, for which the band hired Hell's Angels as guards. The Angels fought with the crowd, and one of them stabbed to death a man brandishing a gun. In the film, the Stones are very aware that trouble is afoot; they ask the audience to "chill out." But in a sequence staged for the observing camera, the Maysles sit the members of the rock group in front of an editing machine and show them the footage of the fight. Mick Jagger asks, "Can you roll back on that, David?" And in slow motion the stabbing is clearly seen.

From one point of view, *Gimme Shelter* is a perfect documentary in that it shows us events happening that even the crew shooting them at the time were unaware of. At the same time, it is so edited that the discovery of the murder becomes the film's climax, and the filmmakers' presence is clearly announced. The Maysles argued that it couldn't have been done otherwise, given the notoriety of the event. However, it does demonstrate how carefully a good documentary is structured and crafted, given form not by the passing of the daily world in front of a neutral lens but by the creative intelligence of the filmmaker. *Gimme Shelter* and the cinéma vérité movement spurred documentary filmmakers to further experimentation, including the often strange, hypnotic, and surreal documentaries of the German filmmaker Werner Herzog, one of whose films, *The Great Ecstasy of the Woodcarver Steiner* (1974) consists of long, slow-motion shots of a skier, his mouth opened in a strange oval of awe at his own flight. In his documentaries and his fiction films, Herzog's images of people, animals, and landscapes, often taken at unusual distances or with a disconcerting combination of lenses, greatly influenced the nature films so prominent on Public Television.

Other filmmakers, in particular Errol Morris in *The Thin Blue Line* (1988) and *Mr. Death: The Rise and Fall of Fred A. Leuchter, Jr.* (1999), pushed harder and harder against the generic principles of documentary. In *The Thin Blue Line* he uses the policemen and the accused in a murder case to reenact the incidents and, in the resulting film, prove the accused's innocence. *Mr. Death* is an example of how the talking-head style of television documentaries can be put to insightful and even subversive ends. The film consists mainly of interviews with its subject, a former inventor of and consultant for execution devices, who becomes, through his own obsessive behavior, a Holocaust denier—that is, someone who claims that the Nazis did not kill six million Jews. The latter part of the film intercuts the interviews with images of Leuchter endlessly chipping away at the walls of a Polish concentration camp, gathering samples to prove that gas was never used. Another interview, with someone who actually knows what he's talking about, completely demolishes Leuchter's theory, and the rest of the film allows Leuchter to reveal himself as a kind of innocent, amoral idiot, who seems simply to have followed ideas without actually having any. The film joins with the great documentaries of Marcel Ophuls—*The Sorrow and the Pity* (1970) and *Hotel Terminus* (1987)—which allow past and present participants in human atrocity to expose themselves before the gentle, ironic, and completely knowing eye of the documentarists.

Morris and others have themselves proved that neutrality and the illusion of objective observation are not generic givens. Some documentarists, like Michael Moore in *Roger and Me* (1989) and his subsequent television work, make themselves the center of observation, the agents provoking actions that *wouldn't* have occurred without the camera's presence. MTV has revived cinéma vérité in a teenage soap opera format in its "Real World" series, and those endless series of network voyeur programs we've already mentioned prove that, just as with fiction film, we love to look at what other people are doing.

Television Documentary

Grierson's drive toward the well-made educational and civilizing documentary has, today, devolved into the talking-head mode of Public Television nature, science, and history documentaries. In the thirties, there was a notion that governments could help produce progressive and artistically adventurous films that could influence for the good a good many people. And, certainly in Great Britain and the United States, this proved true. But American ideology hardened after World War II, and the notion took hold that art and politics should never mix and the government should not have a large hand in the making of art. We see these battles being fought to this day. Public Television, par-

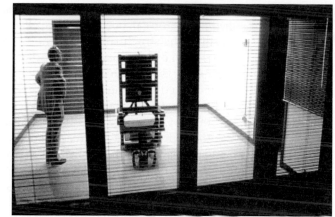

The new documentary is not beyond staging events for greatest effect—just as older documentries had done. Mr. Death: The Rise and Fall of Fred A. Leuchter, Jr., *by Errol Morris (1999)*

tially funded by the government, has therefore had to prove itself a neutral party. In both script and execution—the concentration on still images, newsreel, or nature footage, and close-ups of noncontroversial scholars—PBS and its cable imitators create documentaries apparently free of ideology—of the driving force of a cultural or political idea. In fact, because no work of the human imagination is without ideology, these remnants of the Griersonian ideal tend toward a centrist position, carefully treading the admittedly dangerous waters of governmental interference (including the withdrawing of funding) but, at the same time, keeping away from issues that some might consider "controversial"—a word that usually means that someone might disagree with what they see.

Commercial and cable television have spawned various documentary mutants, sometimes called "docudramas," which are actually fiction films about historical events, and the tremendously popular (at least in the early 2000s) voyeuristic documentaries of people on a tropical island or locked in a house, shows that allow the nonadventurous to see carefully controlled adventures, or stressful situations, without themselves being stressed.

THE GENRES OF FICTION FILMS

The malleability of the documentary appears to be greater than the fiction film genres we are familiar with. Fiction films seem more bound by the rules and conventions imposed—self-imposed—very early in the history of film than the more independent (and much less seen) work of documentarists. Even so-called independent filmmakers must adhere to generic rules if they want their films to be distributed. But these restrictions can sometimes be superficial. Many filmmakers expand, manipulate, or otherwise subvert generic expectations in ways that refresh the genres or, sometimes, destroy them. However, before change or destruction can occur, we, as well as the filmmakers themselves, need to understand the structures that might be changed. To do that, we need to move backward in film history when genres were a bit more straightforward.

Genres are such complex things that I want—for the sake of clarity and in order to see in strong detail how their structures, themes and variations work—to focus on two of them, melodrama and film noir, while referring to a number of others. One of the genres, melodrama, is very old and predates cinema. The other, film noir, is relatively new and particular to film. These case studies will allow us to examine a range of structures and meanings across the history of film.

Melodrama can be understood as a genre and a master narrative, an overarching narrative form that controls all films that aren't comedies and that had an existence before film was invented. Film noir, on the other hand, is original to film and is also a kind of hybrid. It developed out of detective fiction, the gangster film, thirties French cinema, the thriller, and melodrama itself. Film noir occurred at a very specific moment in the history of film as a response to specific cultural events. Its uniqueness has made it one of the most imitated forms in current cinema, and its name is one of the few terms from French criticism that have entered common usage. Curiously, at the time of the creation of noir in the early forties, nobody knew they were inventing what would become one of the most celebrated of genres.

Melodrama

As we noted earlier, melodrama is not original to film. Its origins are historically defined, and its evolution is clear and orderly. As a popular form it is even represented by a popular stereotype. Because it is the dominant serious dramatic and narrative form of so many cultures, it contains within it the seeds of its own parody. In popular usage, "**melodrama**" is often used to describe an exaggerated, emotionally overblown situation. But in this case, parody turns out to be a form of flattery (or self-protection) because melodrama has never lost its power to make grown people cry. It is the central cinematic form that creates empathy and identification. In its most popular guise, as television soap opera, it demands the attention of millions of viewers around the world.

Melodrama is about feeling or, more accurately, about provoking emotions, perhaps more intense than what are called for by the story being told. The desire to provoke emotions, and, for the audience, to have them provoked, was a driving force in the development of American cinema's classical style. Its formation and the development of film melodrama went hand in hand. Knitting the viewers' gaze within the narrative space of a film; emphasizing glances, faces, hands (D. W. Griffith especially liked close-ups of women's hands, wringing, twisting); and finding ways to mold the viewers' response into a narrative flow of despair, loss, anxiety, hope, and eventual triumph, suffered or instigated mainly by women, helped filmmakers establish a style of visual, narrative, and emotional continuity. Exaggerated as they might seem to us now, the gestures of silent film melodrama were in fact a refinement, even a rethinking, of their stage originals, providing an emotive language of look and gesture that created and maintained a connection with viewers. An intimacy between the audience and the representations of actors on the screen was greater than that achieved when live figures gesticulated on a distant stage. These looks and gestures and the way they were edited together became conventionalized codes that triggered conventionalized responses, predictably, time and time again. In their predictability lay their security. It lies there still. The gestures and looks are less broad now, but still codified. It must be so, because melodrama is about security, about the safe expression of overwhelming passion, safe because confined within the known bounds of cinematic codes. Circumscribed, predictable, closed, the codes of melodrama can permit extravagant stories to be told, stories that articulate deep, subjective passion and terrors, which are always contained within the bounds of the master narrative.

Broken Blossoms   D. W. Griffith was a central figure in the development of the contours and contents of film melodrama. He was a man of conservative, populist, Southern character, and his background and ideology colored his films. His racist film *Birth of a Nation* (1915) not only expanded the narrative scope and running time of theatrical film but celebrated and managed to revitalize a then dormant Ku Klux Klan. Griffith spent much of the rest of his career attempting to atone for the appalling social-political results of his "masterpiece." His racial attitudes were matched only by his attitudes toward gender (though it should be emphasized that these attitudes were shared with large parts of the contemporary culture). Women, in most of Griffith's films, fulfilled conventional roles of wives and mothers. They were weak and got into trouble, often at the hands of desperate, angry men. They needed saving by good, virile men. One of the essential, primary structures of narrative film, the cross-cutting editing pattern that links a sequence of captivity and a sequence of rescue, is based on this response to gender difference. The pattern was not invented by Griffith, and it was used in comedies as well, but he fully exploited it, made it essential to melodramatic construction, and climaxed it, in fact, in the great rescue scene of *Way Down East* (1920) where the woman—passive, trapped, stranded on rapidly dispersing ice floes—awaits rescue by her man, who is desperate to arrive before she dies.

Griffith helped institutionalize this formula—made it a permanent part of the language of melodramatic cinema—and he could also reverse it. In *The Mother and the Law,* a film made right after *Birth of a Nation* and included as one of the stories in *Intolerance* (made in 1916, the first of the films he made to atone for the racism of *Birth of a Nation*), it is the woman who leads the rescue of her son, imprisoned because he is wrongly accused of labor violence (Griffith's populism occurs in other films, like the 1909 short film *A Corner in Wheat,* where he takes the side of labor against business). Such a reversal in gender expectations is nowhere as startling as in *Broken Blossoms* (1919), a melodrama in which gender positions are set askew, and both the male and female characters suffer an enormous amount of repression. *Broken Blossoms* was another film made to help Griffith redeem himself for *Birth of a Nation,* and it sets some basic patterns for the family melodrama that have persisted, with much variation but little fundamental change, to the present.

Griffith's overt theme for the film is a rather weak-willed wish for "universal brotherhood." What the film crucially investigates is miscegenation (interracial sexual relations) and brutality to women. The central male character is a Chinese man, played by a white actor (Richard Barthelmess), who is referred to in the intertitles as "The Yellow Man." He comes to London—a mythical movie-set London, a place removed from any reality, a perfect mise-en-scène for this fantasy of domestic terror—on a religious mission to calm the savage white man. He lives an isolated life in the East End ghetto. He takes no part in the pursuits of opium smoking, which Griffith portrays in an extraordinary tableau, showing men and women lounging sensually in a smoked-filled opium den, and maintains a spiritual aloofness as a small shop owner. His revulsion from violence, his features and gestures, the very way he holds his body are strongly marked as female. That is, they are marked by what the culture recognizes as feminine—small, mincing gestures; hands and arms drawn close to the body; a nonaggressive personality.

"The Yellow Man" is doubled by the film's female character, Lucy. In gesture and demeanor she is his mirror image, and they are even composed by the camera in similar ways. Though white, Lucy is also an outcast, a poor, withdrawn, helpless creature of a monstrous father, the prizefighter "Battling Burrows," who beats her with ferocious violence. The melodramatic triangle set up by these figures is fascinating in its complexity and in the ways it reveals basic principles of the genre. Lucy is oppressed by a paternal figure of such violence that she attempts to escape him by turning to the gentle, feminized male—a

In Broken Blossoms *(1919) vulnerability and sensitivity are marked by gender and race. The two main characters are drawn to each other in an impossible attraction. They become reflections of each other.*

vulnerable, regressive figure like herself—for comfort. But the comfort she receives is also threatening in its otherness.

Melodrama must create a world of threat, not only to its characters but to its audience, before it resolves itself. Filled with desire of his own, "The Yellow Man" turns Lucy into a fetish object, making her up to look like an Asian doll and placing her on his raised bed. This really frightens her—and us. In one close-up from her point of view, "The Yellow Man's" face moves toward her filled with lust—a shot that will be echoed later when "Battling Burrows's" face moves toward Lucy, filled with violent hatred. But "The Yellow Man" has sublimated his lust and is no threat to her; he worships her. The look on his face actually reflects her own fears. Everything, the erotic in particular, remains repressed. In melodrama, sexuality and desire must be sublimated into something else. In *Broken Blossoms,* their sublimation results from the cultural prohibition against miscegenation and the fact that protection is stronger than the need for sexual satisfaction.

The sublimation turns "The Yellow Man" into a maternal figure, a strangely desexualized but somehow still erotic maternal figure who both worships and cares for the battered Lucy. But this adoration and care is no match for "Battling Burrows." The tension of the narrative is built when he finds his daughter. The brutality of the crazed patriarch will destroy the apparently innocent pleasures of this odd couple. He drags Lucy back to their hovel and beats her to death after she flees to the confines of a closet. "Battling" breaks down with an ax the walls she hoped would protect her, the camera capturing Lucy's entrapment and exposure through a sequence of point-of-view shots that is chilling and unrelenting. It is a scene so grueling and so expertly done that Hitchcock does homage to it in the shower scene in *Psycho,* as does Kubrick in *The Shining* (1980) when Jack breaks down Wendy's door with an ax.

It is typical of melodrama to create an experience of such extremity, a cruelty so enormous, that it seems impossible to correct it. But it must be corrected, because without closure, without recuperating the situation, the internal melodramatic world would be in perpetual disruption. It might be useful to think of melodrama spatially, as a kind of bell-shaped curve. The narrative starts out with a forced and weakened harmony between the characters. Events become complicated as when, for example, an abused white woman and an Asian man seek affection for each other. These complications raise the emotional graph to sometimes unbearable peaks. But these excesses must be themselves subdued—melodrama is always about subduing the excess it creates—and a kind of harmony is reestablished by the film's end. Often, when the narrative situation appears to have no probability of closure, the film will simply kill off its participants, which is what happens at the end of *Broken Blossoms.* Griffith tries to create a standard intercut sequence of rescue. But "The Yellow Man" doesn't arrive in time to save Lucy. She is murdered, and he shoots "Battling Burrows" and then himself.

Melodrama is structured on the containment and release of desire. It calls for the end of repression and then reimposes it at the end. That is because melodrama is essentially a cautionary form. Yes, it says, people live constricted and hurt lives. They want more, should have more. But too much more will damage the fragile emotional equilibrium, the sets of oppositions, the dominant and regressive states that the culture needs to survive. So melodrama always enacts, at its end, a process of recuperation, bringing its characters back to a kind of cultural health or, more accurately, a "health" prescribed by the dominant values, and the dominant fictions, of the culture. Melodrama is an expression of the master narrative of closure and equilibrium, of bringing characters and culture into a manageable steady state; and if it cannot recuperate its characters into a steadier state than the one in which they began, or if they cannot be recuperated because they have transgressed too far, it will enforce an equilibrium through their absence and kill them off, usually in the name of their being too good or too bad or too damaged to survive.

As a dynamic genre, depending upon a close interaction with the people who view it, we can almost say that melodrama has a life of its own. "It" can do things to characters and to viewers. All genres can do things, because they are prescriptive mechanisms. Within a genre, certain actions can and *must* be taken by or occur to certain characters, and the narrative that directs their lives must follow a proscribed path.

Broken Blossoms deals with one of the ultimate cultural transgressions, miscegenation. And while the film pretends a tender understanding of how "The Yellow Man" and Lucy find comfort in their bizarre, asexual union, it cannot possibly allow that union to prevail or endure. Melodrama is self-censuring. It always assumes to know how much passion and transgression the audience, within its cultural constraints, will or should manage. In the process of built-in censure, it will also gauge the maximum emotional capital it can cause the audience to use in exchange for the images they are watching. So, while Griffith has his three characters killed off because the triangle was simply more than cultural reality in the late 1910s could bear, he manages to wring from his viewers as much sympathy, or even empathy, as they can muster or commit.

Caution and exploitation are two of melodrama's main attributes. If tragedy—the dramatic form that preceded melodrama—asked of its audience a profound recognition of great human achievement undone by greater human limitation, melodrama asks for a less lofty but more emotional recognition of the necessity to contain all aspirations within comfortable and known boundaries. "Asks" is wrong, though. Melodrama demands. For melodrama to work, an audience must be told what to feel and when to feel it; viewers must be hooked and reeled in. Narrative movement must be unstoppable and not allow any questions to be asked. If, at any point, melodrama permits an opening through which the viewer can look and say, "This is ridiculous, such events, such suffering could or should never occur," the structure would fall to pieces. Melodrama demands continuous assent and uses all the force of the continuity style to get that assent. It sutures the viewer into its fabric and makes the viewer's emotional response part of that fabric's pattern.

The pattern is often enough based on very primal stuff. Simple human need for emotional comfort in the face of outrageous brutality is the baseline of

Broken Blossoms. But elaborated into a narrative of interracial romance, gender diffusion, and a grotesque representation of an abusive father, the baseline is built up just to the point of collapse. Griffith's delicacy and restraint (not qualities he shows in many of his other films) and the constant fascination of his mise-en-scène—the mythic constructions of East End London streets; the conversion of "The Yellow Man's" room into an exotic, erotic temple; the oppressive grunge of "Battling Burrows's" room—keep the viewer contained within the narrative. The simple cutting, the connections of gaze and response, ease the viewer into this mise-en-scène of gender hysteria. The sexual ambiguities, the continual threats to Lucy of violence and rape, even her ghastly attempts to smile at her beastly father by pushing up the corners of her mouth with her fingers, fascinate because of their very outrageousness. Melodrama turns the outrageous into the plausible and asks us to believe that plausibility is close to reality.

Now, Voyager   Melodrama throws pain and dissatisfaction in our faces, insists we can do better, and then, in the end, takes it all back, assuring us that we'll be fine if we only modify desire and deflect pain somewhere else—or end it with death. In 1942, Warner Brothers made a rich and complex melodrama called *Now, Voyager,* directed by Irving Rapper. With Bette Davis, one of Warner's major players, as its star, it combines an Oedipal narrative with the story of Cinderella to create the classic structure of melodramatic proposal and denial. A superb example of the classic Hollywood continuity style, *Now, Voyager* knits its pieces together within a narrative of such perfect continuity that the viewer is compelled across its parts into an illusion of a seamless flow of events. *Now, Voyager* substitutes an oppressive, upper-class mother for *Broken Blossoms'* brutal working-class father. Mother is always shown rigid and dominating the frame, even if it is only her fingers, ominously taking up the foreground of a composition, impatiently tapping on a bedpost. The subject of her oppression is her daughter, Charlotte Vale, seen early in the film as a mousy, gray, emotionally arrested, neurotic middle-aged woman. The film plays out the introduction of Charlotte as long as it can, in an interesting display of the intimacy filmmakers knew existed between viewer and film. Audiences already knew very well what Bette Davis looked like from her many other films: she was a major star who had gained even wider recognition by unsuccessfully attempting to break her contract with the studio because she did not like the roles she was being given. Viewers could be depended upon to have read stories of her lawsuit and also to have read publicity that stressed how ugly she was made to look early in the film. Therefore, *Now, Voyager* takes its time introducing her and, when it finally does, shows her legs first, descending the stairs, to further heighten expectation.

The film posits two men who come to Charlotte's rescue, each one a "foreigner," each one offering a different kind of assistance and release. One is a psychiatrist, a figure with a mixed history in American film. The cinematic role of psychiatry and psychiatrist reflects the profession's mixed reputation in the culture at large. Feared and admired, looked to as someone to deliver us from emotional pain, or as a personification of individual defeat and helplessness, or as the embodiment of evil influence, the psychiatrist can help or destroy. In *Now, Voyager* psychiatry is salvation, and its incarnation in Dr. Jaquith—a wise, ironic, and self-contained Britisher—enters Charlotte's mother's house at the very beginning of the film and rescues Charlotte. He is an asexual individual, emotionally potent but no romantic threat. Because the sexual is so foregrounded in melodrama and placed as a primary cause of most of the characters' activities, the genre often needs clean divisions between those for whom sex is a central issue and those for whom it plays no role. These nonthreatening figures (very often represented as the woman friend of the central character) are mediating forces. They act a bit as our presence in the film, guiding, threatening nothing, seeing everything, assuring the success of the main character. In *Now, Voyager,* Jaquith figures as a pleasant, though aloof, patriarchal counter to Charlotte's mother—understanding, supportive, curative where she is negative, mean, and destructive. Though the film does not show the details of her cure, Charlotte is indeed transformed by her stay at Dr. Jaquith's sanitarium and emerges, as if from a cocoon, to appear as the glamorous Bette Davis everyone in the theater would have been familiar with—as familiar as now we would be with Julia Roberts.

Jaquith helps execute the Cinderella myth embedded in this particular melodrama. The genre demands, however, more than physical and emotional transformation. Sexual transformation must occur as well. Jaquith provides the paternal guidance. Jerry, an architect with a European accent, provides the sexual awakening. Charlotte meets Jerry on a cruise. This is an important moment in her life. In a flashback to an embarrassing moment in her past, on another cruise, we learn the reason for her repression: her mother caught her making love to one of the ship's crew. The incident is coded to indicate that the mother's oppression of Charlotte's sexual awakening had lasting effects on her sexuality, constricting her, bringing her to that condition so abhorred by melodrama—and the culture that melodrama addresses—of being an old maid.

In melodrama, repressed sexuality is a standard starting point, liberated sexuality its apparent goal, moderated sexuality its favored closure. *Now, Voyager* pursues this path with relentless determination. In Brazil (Latin America being a stereotyped place of the erotic in classic American cinema), Charlotte and Jerry fall in love and make love, in the spaces of a fade-out between a glowing fireplace and its afterglow embers—a lovely substitution for the physical contact the censors forbade showing on the screen. Their affection is signaled by one of those great Hollywood inventions that hooks a film into our imagination. Jerry begins a habit of lighting two cigarettes in his mouth. One is for himself; the other he hands to Charlotte. The gesture is repeated many times in the film, and, with the recurring theme music on the sound track, it becomes a correlative of the couple's passion. The critic Thomas Elsaessar points out that in film melodrama, music and mise-en-scène often express the excess of emotion experienced by the characters. The lighting of the two cigarettes in *Now, Voyager* and

Cinderella in melodrama. Charlotte, in her ugly, repressed state, with Dr. Jaquith.

Charlotte liberated, beautiful, romantic with Jerry. Now Voyager *(Irving Rapper, 1940)*

the swelling sound track that accompanies it are excellent examples of gesture, movement, and sound that express to us a world of emotion.

As if in response to her daughter's romance, Charlotte's mother feigns illness and a crippling fall in an attempt to reclaim her daughter, who wavers momentarily and, out of touch with Jerry, thinks she will marry a local Bostonian of good family. She also discovers that Jerry is married. This decline and dangerous reversal are an important part of melodramatic structure, which depends upon graphing our emotions in predictable patterns. Having shown Charlotte a way out of her misery, melodrama insists on letting her—and the viewer—know that a return to the darkness is not far out of sight. Suspense and fear for the central character are constructed by means of comparing where she was, how far she has come, and how tentative her liberation remains. The female character of melodrama is always on a precipice, with the narrative line acting as a kind of tightrope, and we are depended upon to agonize over the chances of her falling back to where she was.

So tentative is Charlotte's situation that she winds up back in Dr. Jaquith's sanitarium, where a series of events occurs that is less important as a matter of story than indicative of what melodrama must do to recuperate its characters, even at the expense of strained credulity. The intolerable paradox of melodrama is that the liberation of its characters is also their transgression. To make themselves free they break culture's rules and have to pay. Through Jaquith's intervention and Jerry's intimacy, Charlotte achieves a degree of sexual freedom and emotional maturity. But a narrative and cultural tension is thereby created. As far as our identification with the character in her narrative is concerned, her freedom is a relief and our emotions soar with her. Charlotte has become an independent agent. But in terms of what is culturally allowable, what she has done is impossible.

In film, and perhaps still in the culture at large, a woman cannot express an independent, joyful sexual freedom outside of marriage without paying some price. Certainly, in the early 1940s, when restrictions on the representations of sexuality in film were stronger than they are now, Charlotte could not be permitted to go much further in her explorations of independence. But, in fact, little has changed. In the wake of the feminist movement there have been many films about liberated women. Most of them always compromise their female characters in one way or another. If such a film is a comedy, the strong-willed woman will be convinced that marriage is the only final outlet for her energies. This is not surprising, given the fact that, as a genre going back to Shakespeare and earlier, comedy ends in marriage. Marriage remains the ritual representation of harmony and rebirth in most cultures, the joyous reproduction of the family, and the unstated representation of sexual containment. If the film is a melodrama, the unrepressed woman is as often as not depicted as crazy or evil, threatening the man and his family. Think about three Michael Douglas films, *Fatal Attraction* (Adrian Lyne, 1987), *Basic Instinct* (Paul Verhoeven, 1992), and *Disclosure* (Barry Levinson, 1994).

Crazy if repressed, crazy if unrepressed, melodrama catches women in a double bind and allows few escapes other than death or a falling back into some barely tolerable compromise. The latter is what happens to Charlotte in *Now, Voyager*. In Jaquith's sanitarium, she meets a depressed little girl, the double of Charlotte in her former state. She nurses the child back to mental stability and discovers she is Jerry's daughter, product of an unhappy marriage in which Jerry nobly remains because his wife is an invalid. The metaphor of sickness and health overwhelms the film. Disease is melodrama-friendly, because it represents people in extreme states. Curing disease, or succumbing to it, parallels melodrama's accordionlike structure of repression or restriction, expanding outward to emotional or physical health and then collapsing again into a more culturally acceptable situation of moderated health and constrained emotional activity, or death. James L. Brooks's *Terms of Endearment* (1983), which seems to begin as a romantic comedy, ends with the onslaught of fatal disease that reawakens a mother's love for her daughter. Karl Franklin's *One True Thing* (1998) coaxes a daughter away from an independent life to care for her dying mother. The local fiction of any given melodrama is less important than the dominant fiction of sickness in body or mind that produces sacrificial acts on the part of one family member or another.

As the reigning metaphor of *Now, Voyager,* the cycle of sickness and health is passed from one character to another—to Charlotte, her mother, Jerry's wife, and his daughter. Charlotte gets well. But her cure is entirely local. She's happy, but her happiness does not satisfy the film's or the culture's melodramatic requirements. Individual happiness is never sufficient for melodrama. Perhaps because it has never completely shaken off its class origins, perhaps because audiences find insufficient gratification in a character whose happiness is complete, melodrama must do something to temper events. A selfish indulgence in sexuality might do well for Charlotte the fictional character, but it does not satisfy cultural demands for self-sacrifice and moderate behavior, qualities found if not always in life then in the ideal representation of life in melodrama. Melodrama mediates between desire and social probity, what we want and what the culture thinks it should allow. Its characters must conform to the impossible de-mands to be free *and* restricted, liberated *and* domesticated, sexual *and* chaste. For Charlotte, and all her predecessors and heirs throughout the history of film worldwide, a series of internal mediations is the only means to salvation. She must bring her desires down to a manageable level and recontain her passions in a semblance of respectability.

She will not marry Jerry. She will not return to her mother's domination. She chooses to become a surrogate mother. She will care for Jerry's daughter, subli-mating her passion for him through the child. Sex is out. Marriage is out. Sacri-fice is the key. Liberation from emotional repression is gained by means of another kind of repression. "Don't let's ask for the moon," Charlotte tells Jerry, after he lights two cigarettes and asks if she will be happy, "we have the stars." Why ask for passion, when our ideal love is mediated through the innocence of a child and the perfection of being close and separate at the same time? This is not happiness, only its perpetual promise. The music swells.

Melodrama's insistence on self-sacrifice or self-denial is a trait even more re-markable than its excessive emotions or piling up of incredible coincidence. It is more remarkable because self-sacrifice is largely an invisible trait. Hysteria and passion can be made visible in the mise-en-scène and audible on the sound track. Self-sacrifice is an internal condition, the external manifestation of which is usually *not* doing something rather than taking a visible action. Therefore, un-less the act of sacrifice is the ultimate one of dying, melodrama asks us to build our own response to the negative gesture of the character, to Charlotte's with-drawal from adult contact in order to love Jerry through his daughter. Some-times, if a film is part of a larger social movement, the negative sacrifice can be given positive, even political overtones. Rick gives up his beloved Ilsa to Victor Laszlo (played by Paul Henreid, who is Jerry in *Now, Voyager*) and turns to Cap-tain Renault (Claude Rains, who plays Dr. Jaquith) for the greater good of the war effort in *Casablanca* (Michael Curtiz)—the great melodrama Warner Broth-ers released the same year as *Now, Voyager.*

All That Heaven Allows   An important melodramatist of the fifties, Douglas Sirk (a German-born filmmaker, who made films in that country before coming to the United States in the late thirties) was especially talented at portraying complex attitudes of sacrifice and denial on the part of his male and female characters. Sirk appreciated the power of mise-en-scène to echo their emotional life. He used a lush, sometimes glowing, **Technicolor** palette and carefully arranged his characters in compositions that symbolically represented their states of feeling, in shadow, behind partitions, reflected in mirrors, surrounded by spectral light.

Sirk's *All That Heaven Allows* (1955) presents a proper, upper-middle-class, suburban widow, played by Jane Wyman, who falls in love with a nursery man, close to nature, in touch with his feelings. The man, Ron, is played by Rock Hudson, near the peak of his stardom, when the reality of his homosexuality was not permitted to interfere with the obsessive heterosexuality of the roles he played. The complaints and snobbishness of friends and family make the woman falter in her emotional commitment. She understands the rightness of her feelings and goes after him, only to see him fall and get seriously injured. In the last scene of the film, she is seated by his bedside. The doctor assures her that only with her constant care will her man get better. The unseemly sexual passion of an older woman is reduced to the nurture of a mother's protection. Rather than in the bed, the woman is now protectively sitting by its side, looking after her lover turned invalid/child. Outside, a deer, Sirk's sentimental image of innocence and hope in the film, plays by the window.

In *Now, Voyager,* after freeing herself from her mother's domination, Charlotte willingly falls under Jerry's by becoming his daughter's surrogate mother. Women sacrifice their desires for freedom and self-expression by reclaiming a cultural respectability that affirms the gross imbalance of conventional gender behavior. Even in contemporary melodrama, where the conventional ideologies of family and self-sacrifice have become ever more strongly posited, we see women gaining freedom and then returning to the family fold, often to look after a dying parent. Women are still seen as instigators and victims, as in *The Blair Witch Project*, which poses as a horror film but is really a melodrama of distraught and failing femininity. Other contemporary melodramas return to the vulnerable male syndrome we saw operating in the fifties. James L. Brooks' *As Good as It Gets* (1997) has a deeply flawed, profoundly neurotic male character at its center, a writer suffering obsessive-compulsive disorder. To this nerve-wracking center is drawn a simple waitress who must give herself to the man's often obnoxious behavior in a great act of self-sacrifice. Through her sacrifice, the man softens: he is—and this is a typical melodramatic trait—"redeemed," which has become Hollywood language for "behaving a bit better."

Melodrama must do what all Hollywood genres do, articulate the ideological norms of the culture, which are always, simultaneously, shifting and remaining the same. While film's master narratives remain fairly stable, its genres respond to ideological changes, though slowly, often reluctantly. Ideology is *not* reality (just as the film image is not reality) but a representation agreed upon by a large number of people. Ideology is not monolithic but, like the culture that adopts and acts upon ideology, always under negotiation and undergoing change or accommodation. It is a complex, shifting array of representations and is given form, expressed in the culture's dominant fictions. If the Jack Nicholson character in *As Good As It Gets* must be convinced that he has to soften somewhat, the Helen Hunt character must show how she can toughen up to accommodate and save him. Women save men emotionally, just as in action film men save women physically. A film that attempts to recognize new feminist values of gender autonomy and the softening of the cultural imperatives that make men tough must—as if the genre had a power of its own—compromise this recognition. In melodrama something always has to be given up. But this event has its equivalent in our daily lives, in which we give up things constantly. Unlike everyday life, however, the sacrifices of melodrama too often diminish the female character.

The long struggle over the social, economic, and political imbalance in gender relations that has taken place across the culture has often focused on issues of ideological representation. That is, discussion of gender is many times a discussion of how gender is seen and spoken about in art, literature, and popular culture. As often as film has attempted to come to terms with this discussion, it has just as often been resistant to presenting images and narratives that break away from the ideological mainstream. The problem is clear in the way film melodrama insists on recuperating its characters, its female characters especially, through acts of self-sacrifice or domestic passivity. It is clear in the way it almost always insists that heterosexual marriage is the most perfect closure to romance. Indeed, whether dealing with gender, race, or class, film's master narratives and specific genres render visible the culture's dominant ideologies, and its dominant fictions of imbalance, amelioration, and expediency. For women the imbalance is interpreted through the playing of a supportive or sacrificial role. Gays are interpreted less as individuals than as comic or melodramatic stereotypes. Class difference is almost always stereotyped. The very rich are usually portrayed as villainous, while the poor are seen as noble in their suffering and urged to be happy with their lot. The cliché that money can't buy happiness and riches bring sadness is offered over and over again. think only of *Citizen Kane* and *The Godfather*, Part II (Coppola, 1974)—films that seem to be complicit with larger ideological notions of stability that urge us not to want more than we have because we will only be unhappy. Only in matters of race—and then only rarely—has film taken something approaching a progressive approach, urging recognition of injustice and a desire for things to be better.

The Western

Film grows out of ideology and feeds back into it. Sometimes, when the ideology shifts radically, a genre can either vanish or go into a recessive state. The Western film is an interesting example of a genre that bent and then snapped under shifting ideological pressures. The Western began practically at the same time as narrative film itself was invented and continued composing our myths of the American frontier and the white man's destiny—the inexorable movement of European civilization westward to the Pacific. It drew on nineteenth-century literature of the West, but quickly established its own generic patterns. The settings of chaparral or desert, of small, dusty frontier towns bordering on vast, open land created the simulacrum of the culture's wilderness fantasies— the creation of a West that may never have existed. Narratives of white settlers fighting savages, of heroic gunmen protecting small communities from outlaws, confirmed our belief in the rightness of expansion and in the structuring authority of law and order. Western melodramas of women creating the cultural hearth in a barren land where men broke horses and shot Indians and outlaws and then returned to the domesticity they helped secure reassured us that our contemporary centering of the woman in the house was correct.

Only when historical realities became too overwhelming, when foreign wars put a lie to the notion of manifest destiny, when women fought against the patriarchal center and the "savages" fought against their demonized images, did the ideologies that supported the Western genre begin to falter. John Ford, the master director of Westerns, began questioning some tenets of the genre as far back as the forties. In the fifties, his film *The Searchers* questioned the battle of the white hero against the savage Indian, though not the community that battle helped to create. Three films of the late sixties and early seventies—Sam Peckinpah's *The Wild Bunch* (1969), Arthur Penn's *Little Big Man* (1970), and Robert Altman's *McCabe and Mrs. Miller* (1971)—shifted the genre's conventional myths of male heroism, the role of Indians, and the place of women on the frontier. They turned tables on the genre.

The Wild Bunch declared the end of the all-male community of gunfighters propounded by the Western and showed the violence of gunfighting as a terrible tearing up of the body. It also did what few earlier Westerns attempted: it examined the politics of violence, the male bond, and the taking of sides. *Little Big Man* turned the relationship of Indian and white man on its head, declaring that the "savages" were really the "human beings" and the white men crazy. *McCabe and Mrs. Miller* showed the Western community as a cold place of mutual betrayal, the hero as the joke of his own legend, and women as the marginalized, self-protective maintainers of rationality and sexuality. *The Searchers* showed the Western hero, embodied in the figure of John Wayne, as racist and vaguely psychotic. *McCabe and Mrs. Miller* showed him (here in the more vulnerable embodiment of Warren Beatty) as a grown-up who is still an adolescent, who believes in the Western myths in the face of every proof that it's money that drove westward expansion, not romantic ideals. Out in the real world, the Vietnam War devalued any lingering notions the culture may still have held that expansionism was good and the destruction of indigenous peoples something that the dominant culture needed to do. With this ideological shift, the Western could no longer provide adequate representation of cultural beliefs in manifest destiny and aspirations to control the social and political rights of others. The Western reached its height of popularity in the fifties, when the culture was busily trying to reaffirm its prewar beliefs and mythologies and began to show strains even then as the mythologies came under question. It has now all but disappeared. Only the exaggerated, often inverted references to generic principles in the Westerns of Clint Eastwood seem to maintain a hold on viewers. The feminist variations on the Western, mentioned earlier, have served mainly to point up how a genre, once fallen, can become subject to experimentation.

Because the Western mythologized history, it was at risk when the culture's ideas of history changed. Cinematic melodrama is in a somewhat different position. It attempts to avoid history (though there are such things as historical melodramas) and absorbs the external world into the interior. In melodrama, the personal replaces the political and the genre becomes a kind of history of the culture's unconscious. Therefore, melodrama has made itself immune to the forces that have undone the Western. Melodrama offers the pretense of timelessness, even of universality. This allows it to survive, but not unchanged. Douglas Sirk changed melodrama by exaggerating its already exaggerated characters and mise-en-scène. He almost turned melodrama into self-parody, though his good commercial sense prevented him from taking it to the point where the structure might implode. Other changes in the fifties allowed melodrama to focus on the sufferings of sensitive, vulnerable, and repressed men. Again, the structuring principles of the genre weren't changed. If anything, they were reinforced by proving themselves flexible and able to embrace all manner of suffering.

Melodrama today has shown a few signs of bending to cultural changes. Always on the conservative side, domestic melodrama still focuses on the heterosexual family, especially on the reunions of children and parents. Prison melodramas, popular in the thirties, have returned, with such films as *The Shawshank Redemption* (Frank Darabont, 1994), *Dead Man Walking* (Tim Robbins, 1995), and *The Green Mile* (Frank Darabont, 1999). But the postmodern urge to mix genres has also had its effect in films that mix comedy and melodrama. The popular 1998 film *There's Something about Mary* (Bobby and Peter Farrelly) proves the way the two seemingly antithetical genres can coexist.

Film Noir

In the mid-1940s a new genre developed, though it might be more correct to say that it invented itself. The genre, which was named "**film noir**" some years after it appeared, changed some elements of melodrama and disrupted some Hollywood stereotypes about gender and the inevitability of sacrifice and suffering. Hollywood didn't know it was making a new genre as the elements of noir were put into place. Neither filmmakers nor film viewers were aware, at least on a conscious, articulate level, that a new story was being told to them in a new visual style. It was the French in the 1950s who finally recognized that something was happening and gave it a name. But this does not mean that film noir was born out of nothing. Like any other genre, it came forth as a response to cultural need and developed out of cinematic elements already in existence.

During the Nazi occupation of France (1940–1944) there was an embargo on American films. *Citizen Kane* wasn't seen in Paris until early in 1946, five years after it was made. At war's end, American films flooded into France, a country that has had a deep and serious love of cinema since its invention. An eager group of young intellectuals—including François Truffaut and Jean-Luc Godard, who would go on to be immensely influential filmmakers—began watching these films with an intense interest. They had a good location in which to do this, the Paris Cinémathèque, run by Henri Langlois, who showed whatever films he could get his hands on, twelve hours a day. They watched everything they could and especially loved American films, the spoken language of which they couldn't understand. They learned what they needed from the visual narrative, the images and their construction. They noted across the films of the mid-forties a darkening of visual style and a darkening of thematic content. After a series of French detective stories called *Série noire,* one of these critics gave the name "film noir" to this new kind of film. But noir went far beyond the detective genre.

Expressionist Roots of Noir   Three main currents fed into the development of noir: German Expressionism, the hard-boiled detective fiction of the thirties, and the cultural turmoil of World War II. Noir's visual style harks back to the Expressionist movement in German film, literature, theater, and painting that flourished after World War I. **Expressionism** grew out of the cultural and psychological scars left on the people of Europe by World War I and was fed by a growing interest in psychoanalysis and a desire to make art more responsive to individual and cultural anxieties. A basic premise of Expressionism was that mise-en-scène—the visual space of the film (as well as of fiction, theatrical presentation, and painting)—should express the stressed psychological state of either its main character or, more universally, the culture at large. Edvard Munch's painting *The Scream* (1893) best exemplifies this effect, though it actually predates and influenced the Expressionist movement. This painting of a figure on a bridge, standing in front of a violent multicolored sky, hands held up to a face contorted in anxiety and terror, is a dominant image for the twentieth century. It encapsulates the Expressionist desire to make the world a reflection of the interior anguish it has caused.

Carl Mayer and Robert Wiene's *The Cabinet of Dr. Caligari* (1919) is the best-known film of the Expressionist period. A tale of madness, somnambulism, and seduction, it takes place in an artificial world of deformed houses, windows out of skew, shadows painted on the floor—a place of the dream: imprecise, hard to locate, distorted and full of darkness. Darkness becomes the key to the cinematic version of Expressionism. Darkness dominates the light, which may survive only as pools punctuating the blackness. Horror, too, is a lasting legacy of the movement. Expressionism's first major appearance in Hollywood was in the great series of horror movies produced by Universal in the early thirties. The first major American version of *Dracula* (directed

The Expressionist mise-en-scène in Robert Wiene's The Cabinet of Dr. Caligari *(1919). Note how the decor and the shadows are painted on. Perspective is forced, as if this were a painting. Note also how this image (and the film) presages the elements of the horror film.*

by Todd Browning) and *Frankenstein* (James Whale) were released in 1931. An approximately sixteen minute version of Frankenstein was filmed by the Edison Company in 1910. *Dracula* had already been made as a German Expressionist film by F. W. Murnau called *Nosferatu* in 1922. *Caligari* and *Der Golem* (Paul Wegener, 1914) prefigured Whale's *Frankenstein*. The Universal horror films were enormously popular. Nothing like them had been seen by American audiences. These dark visions of mythic European worlds invaded by monstrous figures of destruction had a similar (if belated) effect on American viewers as their predecessors had had on post–World War I European audiences. They articulated the master narrative of a calm and orderly world shattered by an unknown chaos and of nature gone awry through human meddling, and they created a new genre and sequels that go on and on.

The shadowy mise-en-scène of frightening monsters who are deformations of the human form, sexual predators who represent some of our darkest desires to do evil and triumph, brought to America the basic stylistics of German Expressionism. But monster movies were not the only examples of the Expressionist style in thirties Hollywood film. Josef von Sternberg created a heavily shadowed mise-en-scène throughout his thirties work in films like *Morocco* (1930), *Dishonored* (1931), *Shanghai Express* (1932), *Blonde Venus* (1932), *The Scarlet Empress* (1934), and *The Devil Is a Woman* (1935). Though born in Vienna, Sternberg was American by upbringing. He was deeply influenced by the Expressionist style, and he made his groundbreaking film, *The Blue Angel* (1930), in Germany. Many other filmmakers fled Germany to take up work in Hollywood during this period. One of the great Expressionist cinematographers, Karl Freund, photographed (among many other films) Murnau's *The Last Laugh* in 1924 and Fritz Lang's science fiction film *Metropolis* in 1927. He came to America and was cinematographer for the first *Dracula*. By the end of his career, he was cinematographer for *I Love Lucy*!

But despite the horror films and the work of Sternberg and the German émigrés, dark, shadowy mise-en-scène (a version of **chiaroscuro**, a term from art history that means painting with light and shadow) was not a dominant mode in the thirties. **High-keyed lighting**—in which the entire set is evenly illuminated—prevailed. Some Depression-era films did express the cultural darkness of the period, but most acted as an important antidote, their images of light and their bright, comic narratives performing a social function that would have been less well served had they all adopted the brooding, fearful darkness of the Expressionist mode.

Citizen Kane   *Citizen Kane* changed all that. Orson Welles was a man of the theater (and radio) before he came to Hollywood in 1939. He had done many theatrical experiments on the New York stage and came to filmmaking with a desire to translate radical theatrical styles of lighting, sound, and composition to the screen. He was particularly interested in the Expressionist use of shadow, and *Citizen Kane* has a dark mise-en-scène that uses shadow as a thematic device. *Kane* is a film about the impossible attempt to define a complex personality—a definition attempted by five people who think they know

Charles Foster Kane and whose stories make up the film's narrative. Kane himself remains often literally in the shadows. The film's mise-en-scène is dark and deep. The combination of chiaroscuro lighting and deep-focus cinematography, in which everything from close foreground to far background is in sharp focus, creates a mysterious world in which space is both inviting and threatening, where everything seems to be visible but little is seen that helps us to understand the central character.

Citizen Kane was not a commercially successful film. Because its story was too closely modeled on the life of the journalist and millionaire William Randolph Hearst, it was in trouble from the start. At one point, Hearst almost talked another studio, MGM, into buying and destroying the master negative. He was successful in preventing the many newspapers he owned from carrying advertising for the film. But even though its popular appeal took many years to form, its appeal to movie professionals was immediate. Directors, cinematographers, and production designers were taken by its radical style, which depended so much on the visual structures of Expressionism. The influence of Welles and his cinematographer, Gregg Toland, on the style of forties cinema was enormous. Darkness descended on Hollywood filmmaking.

Hard-Boiled Fiction   *Citizen Kane* was the main conduit into film noir, fed by the tributary of German Expressionism as well as some late thirties French film. Another source of influence came from literature. In the 1930s, a popular school of detective-fiction writers emerged, the most famous of whom were Raymond Chandler and Dashiell Hammett. Their work became known as the hard-boiled school of detective fiction, and they were masterful at creating visions of a dark, corrupt underworld of dopers and robbers, of sexual exploiters and an omnipresent immorality infiltrated by their cynical but morally secure detective characters—Hammett's Sam Spade and Chandler's Philip Marlowe. Their detectives were unheroic but persevering, cunning but flawed and vulnerable, barely surviving their exploits with their moral centers intact.

A third figure connected with this school did not write detective fiction. James M. Cain told stories of sleazy, lower-middle-class families falling apart under the pressures of infidelity, murder, and general moral corruption. Almost all his novels—*Double Indemnity, Mildred Pierce, The Postman Always Rings Twice*—were made into films in the forties. Cain's work and that of the hard-boiled school did not fit well with the Hollywood of the thirties, however, burdened as it was with its self-imposed censorship code and need to provide ideological uplift for a Depression-ridden culture. But this wasn't for lack of trying. Warner Brothers had acquired rights to Hammett's *The Maltese Falcon* very early on and filmed it twice during the thirties, once as a Bette Davis vehicle. They didn't actually get it right, though, until 1941, when John Huston directed the film with Humphrey Bogart as Sam Spade. During the thirties, MGM was more successful with Hammett's *The Thin Man,* which the studio made as a series of **screwball comedies**—bright, fast-paced narratives about an upper-class married couple who drink a lot and verbally spar with each other while they do a bit of detective work on the side.

The Maltese Falcon   The 1941 version of *The Maltese Falcon* was not a comedy, though it did have a more ironic and wry tone than its predecessors. It is also somewhat slower paced and more intensely composed and cut than most films of the thirties. It maintains much of Hammett's tough-guy dialogue, and it catches the sense of an infinitely corrupted world that was difficult to do in thirties studio film. Visually, while the film was darker in tone than was usual during the preceding decade, it did not employ the deep chiaroscuro that would occur in films after the appearance of *Citizen Kane*. That darkness began to take over about 1944.

Murder, My Sweet; Double Indemnity; Scarlet Street   The third current that made film noir possible occurred outside of film. The darkness of noir owes much to the darkening mood of the culture during and right after the war. Noir's themes of male isolation and weakness, of female treachery and murderousness, grow out of a multitude of insecurities occurring in the American psyche—events we discussed in Chapter 4. These themes infiltrated film noir through both form and content. The genre's visual darkness and its obsessive damaged men reflected the culture's anxious postwar state.

Three landmark films solidified the look and the thematics of the new genre in 1944 and 1945. RKO, the studio that made *Citizen Kane*, produced an adaptation of Raymond Chandler's *Farewell My Lovely*, directed by Edward Dmytryk, that they called *Murder, My Sweet*. (Presumably the name was changed because the film was a vehicle for Dick Powell, a lead player in musicals, who was attempting to broaden his acting capacity; the studio feared that audiences would think the original title would be interpreted as another Dick Powell musical.) *Murder, My Sweet* is among the best of the Chandler adaptations. Powell delivers Philip Marlowe's voice-over narration with a grim irony, while the world the characters inhabit is bathed not in thirties light but in darkness only occasionally relieved by light. "I'm a little man in a dirty job," Marlowe says at one point, a comment that exemplifies the reduced existential circumstances of the noir male in a world he cannot quite see through, cannot accurately detect.

In the same year, 1944, the German director Billy Wilder made *Double Indemnity* for Paramount. Based on a James M. Cain novel with a

Domestic noir. The palpable slats of light from the venetian blinds become a visual convention in forties cinema. Billy Wilder, Double Indemnity *(1944).*

screenplay by Raymond Chandler, it synthesized noir's essential generic elements—bitterly ironic dialogue, a weak male character who falls prey to a female predator, and a mise-en-scène not quite as dark as *Murder, My Sweet* but unrelentingly gray and claustrophobic. The film contains some rare (for its time) exterior footage: a nighttime city street is pierced by the headlights of a careening car and the spark of a workman's blowtorch; a gray suburban Los Angeles street, its cracks filled with veins of black asphalt, adds to the pervading atmosphere of limited, sleazy lives. Interiors are dusty and gray. The living room of Phyllis Dietrichson—the woman who lures the poor insurance salesman, Walter Neff, to murder her husband and then shoots him and is shot by him in turn—is cut through with light coming from behind venetian blinds. The light makes palpable the swirling dust in the air. The image of the shadowy slits of light from venetian blinds occurs in almost every forties film from this point on.

Double Indemnity can be read two ways. It is either a misogynist film about a terrifying, destroying woman, or it is a film that liberates the female character from the restrictive and oppressed melodramatic situations that render her helpless. Feminist critics are divided in their views of the film and the noir genre as a whole. If it is in fact a film that gives its female character more strength and control, it no longer situates her as the secure center of the family but its destroyer; it marks a shift in the dominant fiction that speaks of women's passivity. However, the fact that both she and her doomed male prey die at the end diminishes its radical potential. What is unambiguous is the film's attitude toward such sacred cultural institutions and generic mainstays as the protective family and the brave, heroic, self-possessed male.

Walter Neff is dying from the very beginning of the film, which is narrated in flashback as, slowly bleeding to death from Phyllis's gunshot, he dictates his sorry tale onto a recording machine in his office. And while Neff is never self-pitying and remains verbally dexterous and self-deprecating in his story, he is also clearly a loser, whose lust for Phyllis undoes his reason and self-control. Phyllis, we learn, creates families in order to destroy them. The family into which Walter comes, as an insurance man trying to make a sale, are a bunch of snarling whiners. Phyllis's husband is fully worthy of the death she plans for him. She manipulates first him and then Walter through a morally (and visually) gray world of cheap houses, crowded office buildings, supermarkets, and dark railroad tracks where Walter dumps the husband's body. There is as little sentimentality in this narrative as Hollywood could allow.

The following year, Fritz Lang, another director from Germany and an important figure in the Expressionist movement, made a film called *Scarlet Street*. Here, a meek, henpecked husband, Christopher Cross (played by Edward G. Robinson, an actor from the early gangster film days, who plays Walter Neff's boss and would-be friend, Keyes, in *Double Indemnity*), becomes sexually in thrall to a young woman named Kitty. His enthrallment is climaxed by the kind of image Hollywood loves to use to indicate male debasement: he paints her toenails. Painting is a major issue in this classic noir film. Chris Cross is a would-be painter, and Kitty has her boyfriend, Johnny, pass off Chris's work as hers. Chris kills Kitty in a rage, and Johnny is sentenced for the crime. The meek man is given power only through his reaction to being played a chump, and though Johnny deserves killing for many reasons, his execution is the cause of overwhelming guilt, borne by the ironically named Chris Cross.

This grim little narrative is given considerable substance by Lang's ability to reproduce the desire and paranoia, the failure and miserable triumph of his meek and hopeless main character. The narrative is given existential portent in its climax, as Chris becomes a kind of eternally guilty everyman. He becomes a street person, wandering a city that is empty of other people. He is the only man alive, carrying his despair alone.

Scarlet Street announces a universal anxiety and a reduction of individual agency that are usually associated with great modernist literary fiction. Its point is made over and over again by film noir. The world is dark and corrupt. Women are predators. Men are either violent and brutal or the passive, unwary prey of the violent or the sexual. Any way out is hard to see. As one film noir character says, "I feel all dead inside. I'm backed up in a dark corner and I don't know who's hitting me." All of this is remarkable in a cinema usually devoted to the bright and harmonious or to the safe excesses and reassuring closures of melodrama. While none of the filmmakers had a term for the genre that rapidly took over production across the studios, the darkness reigned, and by the mid-forties, most films from Hollywood that were not comedies shared some noir characteristics, even if only the core image of a room banded by shadows of light coming through venetian blinds.

Noir's Climax   Noir lasted through the early fifties, climaxed by four films that were very self-conscious of what they were doing. Nicholas Ray's *In a Lonely Place* (1950) combines elements of noir with the male melodrama we discussed earlier. Humphrey Bogart, who had helped form the male noir character in *The Maltese Falcon* and *The Big Sleep* (Howard Hawks's 1946 adaptation of Raymond Chandler's novel, the screenplay of which was cowritten by William Faulkner), constructs a figure of repressed rage, a screenwriter who lives in the shadows of his own uncontainable violence. He is recessive and aggressive at the same time, and when he emerges into the light and falls in love, he is undone by his rage. *In a Lonely Place* is as complex and moving an analysis of male angst and the turmoils of gender as exists in the canon of American cinema. This is the rare American film that allows the fact that love may not, actually, conquer all; that differences in gender response may be insuperable; and that the central characters and their narrative may not be resolved.

The Wrong Man   Alfred Hitchcock's *The Wrong Man* (1957) took a "true story" and created a quasi-documentary style to narrate the events of an ordinary family man accused, arrested, and tried for robbery. His wife sinks into madness as a result of the events. Much of the film—visually as dark and claustrophobic as Hitchcock ever made—doggedly follows the process of its central character's incarceration and trial. It has a slow, almost trancelike pace and refuses to mitigate its characters' unrelenting misery. Even more than *Scarlet*

Street, made over a decade earlier, it uses the structures of noir to address the loss of individual power and identity in the post–World War II world.

Loss, powerlessness, the inability to pull out of oncoming chaos—the elements of a bad dream drifting from the individual unconscious into the culture at large—had marked noir from its beginning. Now near the end of its first cycle, these noir elements spoke to the fifties with even more immediacy. In a decade characterized by extreme governmental interference into the intellectual freedom of the country, by big corporate growth, by the construction of a myth of a superenemy ready to infiltrate the very fabric of the culture, fifties paranoia was addressed quite profoundly by film noir as it was addressed somewhat less profoundly by the alien invasion science fiction film, a major fifties genre.

Kiss Me Deadly Robert Aldrich's *Kiss Me Deadly* (1955) used the private detective version of film noir to address Cold War issues directly. The film is based on a novel by Mickey Spillane, who wrote vulgar, violent, woman-hating detective fiction that was enormously popular during the fifties. Aldrich's screen version of Spillane's detective, Mike Hammer, removes much of the vulgarity, turns the sexual violence into a peculiar kind of prudery (even sexual reticence), but leaves the physical violence much intact. *Kiss Me Deadly* is about the search for a mysterious box that contains nuclear material. When opened, the box roars, screams, and glows with a deadly light: Quentin Tarantino got the idea for the mysterious suitcase with the golden light in *Pulp Fiction* from the mysterious box in *Kiss Me Deadly.* The box is discovered and opened by a curious woman—the film plays on the Pandora myth with a special fifties misogyny—and it blows up the world.

Noir is usually about implosion rather than explosion. But as the poet T. S. Eliot pointed out in the twenties, the end of the world does not have to come with a bang. A whimper is more likely, and a whimper is what's heard in *Scarlet Street* or *The Wrong Man* or *In a Lonely Place. Kiss Me Deadly* turns the whimper back into the more conventional bang. When light pierces through the noir darkness, the world comes apart. When the detective finds out the secret he's been looking for, he gets fried. This is the peculiar double-edged paranoia of the fifties. Men will collapse into lonely isolation, or, if they really find out the world's secret, they and everything else will be destroyed.

Touch of Evil Between implosion and external destruction, there is another possibility. Create a world that appears as an ongoing nightmare of dizzying perspectives, long, dark streets, bizarre individuals careening around an unstable landscape of strip joints, hideous motels, oil fields, barren gray intersections, and open sewers. In other words, update the Expressionist vision to address the modern age. This is what Orson Welles does in *Touch of Evil* (1958), the last film noir of the genre's first cycle. It is fitting that this climactic film should be made by the director who originated the genre seventeen years earlier. Welles had been away from the United States, making films in Europe, for almost eight years and returned to find a project based on a second-rate novel about corrupt police, starring Charlton Heston as a Mexican cop. He took the challenge and created the most intriguing and inventive film noir to date. Filming mostly in the streets of Venice in Los Angeles, and inside actual buildings, Welles turned

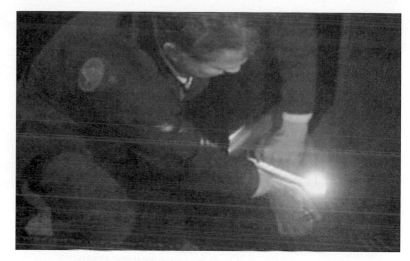

*An example of intertextual allusion. The blinding light of an atomic
device hidden in a box in Robert Aldrich's* Kiss Me Deadly *(1955).*

*Quentin Tarantino is thinking about Aldrich's bomb when he has Jules open the mysterious suitcase
in* Pulp Fiction *(1994).*

the "real world" into a bad dream of a border town trafficking in corruption, a
local cop who plants evidence to catch his man (the cop is played by Welles
himself, puffed up, limping, and growling), and a sappy, moral Mexican official
out to save his country's name and protect his American bride.

Touch of Evil is, in part, an outsider's view of mid-fifties America just coming
out of the grip of Joseph McCarthy and the anticommunist, evidence fabricating
witch hunts—a morass of moral and political corruption. It is also an ironist's
attempt to play sympathy for the devil. Welles's Hank Quinlan, the corrupt

cop—a Joseph McCarthy surrogate—is, in fact, weak and spiteful, out for revenge against "my dirty job." The world Welles creates for these characters, on the other hand, is of Welles's imagination only, insinuated by his camera, which tracks, cranes, cants, sinks far below eye level and then rapidly cranes high above the characters. The long opening shot of *Touch of Evil* tracks a car moving through the dark labyrinth of a Mexican-American border crossing. The shot lasts for almost four minutes and is one of the most famous long takes

The apotheosis of film noir. The urban landscape: dark, vertiginous, threatening. Orson Welles, Touch of Evil *(1958)*

in contemporary cinema. The camera articulates the characters and the audience's perceptions of them by means of dizzying, off-center compositions and enfolds them in its dark, nightmare world. It is the definition of how mise-en-scène can be created.

Noir's Rebirth   There was not very much further one could go past *Touch of Evil* in creating a dark, decaying, Expressionist mise-en-scène. The genre was spent, and films were beginning to respond to television in ways that made noir obsolete. The deeply shadowed black and white of the forties was giving way to a more evenly graded spectrum of gray tones in the fifties. Then in the sixties, black and white gave way to color. Since film noir was so essentially dependent on the dark end of the black and white spectrum, a move to color would seem to mark the end of its visual life, despite at least one notable noir color experiment, Henry Hathaway's *Niagara* (1953). But color turned out to be a very flexible medium. To understand why, a short history of color film is necessary.

Film had always been tinted and toned in the silent period, with a red tint signifying passion, blue standing for night, gold for day. Experiments with a more "realistic" color stock began in the early twenties, and the three-color Technicolor process was introduced in the early thirties. Color remained a specialty process until the early sixties, used mainly for musicals and fantasy films (that's why the Oz portions of the *Wizard of Oz*, 1939, are in Technicolor). Realism required black and white. We have been discussing all along how conventionalized film is, how it is based on repeated patterns and recognizable structures. This is nowhere more apparent than in the fact that "reality" for film before the sixties meant black and white cinematography. Of course there is nothing inherently "realistic" in either color or black and white. The latter was considered "real" only because it was the dominant mode and color wasn't. But that changed in the sixties. By the early sixties, television began to broadcast in color, and, because the final distribution point for any film is the television screen, by the end of the decade, all films had to be made in color.

The influence of film noir was powerful, and young filmmakers, many coming out of film school in the late sixties and early seventies, felt a response similar to that felt by those French intellectuals in the early fifties: the discovery of something extraordinary in the style and content of American film from the forties and early fifties. They began to revive noir, rethink it in color, and use noir as a way to make color cinematography responsive to their imaginative needs. Arthur Penn made a key film in the noir revival in *Night Moves* (1975), and Martin Scorsese was at the center of the revival. *Taxi Driver* (1976) captures the dark Expressionism of original film noir, with its creation of an urban landscape that reflects the paranoia of its main character more thoroughly than any film since *Touch of Evil*. The genre named by the French became, by the seventies, a genre recognized by many filmgoers. By the eighties, *TV Guide* was referring to film noir in its listings. In 1984, there was a nightclub sequence in *The Terminator*. The club is named "Tech Noir."

Genre Resilience   A peculiar circle is drawn. Genre is a shared experience. Filmmakers create their films within the generic boundaries in which audiences find comfort and affirmation. Noir does not create comfort, yet quickly became a recognizable pattern—of gloom and despair. What's more, noir was not created in the usual generic sense. Rather it grew, almost unconsciously, from a variety of factors that were not directly under filmmakers' intellectual control. Noir—even more than the Western, the romantic melodrama, the science fiction film, or most conventional generic structures—was formed by viewer response and recognition and was defined by critics rather than filmmakers, first in France, then in America. Once noir was defined—that is, once critics discovered that it existed and analyzed it, and young filmmakers understood its vitality as a visual and narrative form—it was revived, restructured, and once again began to infiltrate other genres. Films as various as Alan J. Pakula's *Klute* (1971), the first two *Godfather* films (1972, 1974), Roman Polanski's *Chinatown* (1974), Pakula's *All the President's Men* (1976), Ridley Scott's *Blade Runner* (1982), and *Alien³* (David Fincher, 1992), to name only a very few, rethought the form and structure of film noir and reworked it for contemporary needs. Noir continues today in films ranging from Oliver Stone's *UTurn* (1997), Curtis Hanson's *L.A. Confidential* (1997), to Alex Proyas's *Dark City* (1998), a science fiction film whose title comes from a 1950 film noir.

Proyas turns the noir city of dreadful night into a dream of alien mind control, which turns out to be the unrealized desires of the city's inhabitants, themselves quite possibly the dreams of the aliens. All of noir's attributes, from the encompassing darkness to a nightclub scene that is almost a prerequisite in any forties noir, as well as specific borrowings from Fritz Lang's early Expressionist films, are at work in *Dark City*. David Fincher uses the noir mise-en-scène to extrapolate into the visual spaces of his films the darkness and fears of his characters. In *The Game* (1997) and *Fight Club* (1999), characters move—almost as they do in Welles's *Touch of Evil*—through a landscape of the mind, a contemporary San Francisco haunted by the ghosts of the sixties in *The Game*, the angry, violent dreams of a cultural schizophrenia in *Fight Club*.

The key to genre is its ability to be reworked. This may appear to be a contradiction. Earlier I said that the key to genre is the way it maintains itself through a variety of variations over a long period of time. Indeed, there is a point beyond which generic boundaries cannot be stretched, or they will break and the genre will fall apart. But genres are malleable and can infiltrate one another. The Western, along with the war film, was refigured in *Star Wars,* for example. Sometimes, as in film noir, genres can stretch the boundaries of the master narratives and revise their dominant fictions. For some filmmakers, testing the boundaries and even pushing them beyond the breaking point are ways to define a subjective approach to filmmaking, to move beyond the classical American style. By working from a generic base, filmmakers can find their voice, change viewer perceptions, change the genre, and, perhaps, change cinema.

European and Other Cinemas

Italian Neorealism   We have noted that American cinema is the dominant form across the world. It should not be surprising then to find that when filmmakers in other countries seek their own style, their own methods of seeing the world in cinematic terms, they begin by thinking about American film and how their work can be different. We saw this happening among the postrevolutionary filmmakers of Russia and see it again in post-World War II Italy, where a new style of filmmaking emerged that changed cinema the world over for many years. **Italian neorealism** was born of many economic, social, and political factors—not the least of which was the fact that the Italian economy and the very physical structure of the country were in ruins in 1945. Filmmaking as usual was neither possible nor desired. Italy was destroyed by the fascist regime, a dictatorial structure of corporate state control that managed and brutalized all facets of life, including filmmaking. (Italy's main studio, Cinecittà, was inaugurated by dictator Benito Mussolini.) After the war, Italian filmmakers linked the commercial cinema of prewar Italy with all that was bad about the fascists. They also saw a link to Hollywood film in those fascist comedies and melodramas about romance among members of the upper middle class—called "white-telephone" movies because of their overdone decor. They knew that all of this production, with its reliance on elaborate sets, stars that were removed from the life of ordinary people, stories that addressed the lives of people who could not possibly exist in the day-to-day world—the whole artifice of middle-class fantasy—had to be overthrown. In its place would be a new genre of film that addressed poor people in their daily lives, peasants in the countryside, workers in the streets and in their apartments and meeting halls.

Stars and studios, sets, and the elaborate tricks Hollywood used to fabricate complex, unreal images would be jettisoned. Gone too would be stories about doomed love affairs among the rich and the indulged emotions of bored women and heartless men. Instead of the studio, films would be made on the street, on location, amid the traffic and the people of the cities, or in the countryside. Instead of movie stars, ordinary people or semiprofessional performers would be used. Their faces would not be familiar or associated with other films. Hollywood cinema, and the cinema of fascist Italy, were altogether an act of evasion. People went to movies to see movie life, not the life of the world. Do away with these conventions, strip generic formulas and generic responses, get to the people, and film would in turn communicate back to the people images of life as it is.

It's important to repeat that the neorealists were not interested in making documentaries, even though they influenced documentary filmmakers. They wanted to continue using fiction as a means to structure an ordered narrative. But for them, the narrative and the mise-en-scène would appear to grow out of the present circumstances of history and place. Many of the films they made had an immediacy and texture quite unlike anything ever seen before. Roberto Rossellini's great war trilogy, *Rome, Open City* (1945), *Paisan* (1946), and *Germany, Year Zero* (1947); De Sica's *Bicycle Thieves* (1948), *Miracle in Milan* (1950), and *Umberto D.* (1951); and Luchino Visconti's *La Terra Trema* (1948) were raw, even unpolished films of great power and clarity. They spoke about Italian life during and after the war. *La Terra Trema* was one of the few films ever made that addressed the poverty and hopelessness of disenfranchised rural life. All of the films have a roughness and directness that move the viewer beyond the form of the film to the movement of its story and its characters. But unlike Hollywood films, which also take us beyond their form and into their content, neorealism addresses poverty and desperation, the social life of the poor, and the difficulties of forming supportive communities in a way Hollywood genres rarely permit. Unlike the classical Hollywood style, these films demand our visual attention. By filling the screen with images of a shattered and destructive world, they ask us to observe what we have never seen in film before.

Bicycle Thieves   And yet Italian neorealism is, basically, melodrama. Hollywood melodrama is about the politics of subjective suffering—individuals oppressed by gender, domesticity, unrealizable desires to escape. Italian neorealism is about the suffering brought on by political and economic events, as well as the lives affected by them. The characters of neorealism are deeply oppressed, not by domesticity or gender but by war and poverty. *Bicycle Thieves,* for example, has a simple premise: a very poor man gets a job putting up advertising posters. In a key sequence, he pastes up a poster of the very famous late-forties movie star Rita Hayworth. It is a kind of symbolic act that demonstrates his distance, and the film's, from the world of Hollywood glamour. In order to do his job, he needs a bicycle to get from street to street. To get the bicycle, he hocks the family's linens. He is happy at his new job. Then his bicycle is stolen by someone in even worse economic shape than he is. The rest of the film follows his search around Rome in a hopeless attempt to find the bike and restore his life.

Ricci, the main character (played not by an actor but by a laborer), is seen amidst family and comrades in the houses and streets of Rome. The camera will often move away from him to observe passersby and the life going on around him. At one point, when he is putting up his posters, two beggar children wander by and the camera casually stops looking at Ricci to follow these two along the street. The American continuity style insists that narrative and visual focus remain at all times on the central figures of the story. The world around them is often only suggested or caught in quick cutaways. In neorealism, the world that surrounds the characters is given equal space with the characters themselves. Neorealism's mise-en-scène is created by the interplay of city or countryside, people, and the central characters who emerge from the community. Ricci is one story among others. But his story, finally, is about anguish and hope, which are irresistible. De Sica, no matter how he tries to link Ricci with his surroundings, still finds that he must focus on his character's emotional state, though he never lets us forget that it is tied to the class and economy in which the character lives. He communicates these emotions and creates empathy in his audience by one of the most standard of melodramatic means, triangulating the viewer between the main character and his little son, Bruno. The child clings to Ricci's hand throughout his search for the stolen bicycle. His misery and tears echo his father's despair and amplify it. They finally entrap the audience as much as any other melodramatic device like death or a dog, both of which De Sica uses in his later film, *Umberto D* (1951).

Neorealism in America   This is not to undercut the power of the neorealist movement or the extent of its influence, which was enormous. It is important, though, to stress how powerful genres are, especially melodrama—so powerful that melodrama maintained its hold on a filmmaking movement whose original aim was to overthrow the structure and ideology of cinema's past. Neorealism was absorbed into American filmmaking very quickly because of its melodrama and because its style of exterior shooting was so novel. It influenced—of all things—the gangster genre. By the late forties, some films were being promoted as shot "on location," where the action "actually takes place." *The Naked City*, filmed in 1948 by Jules Dassin, was not a neorealist film by any means. Neither was it filmed entirely on location. There was still the need to manufacture images in the Hollywood style. But it used exterior sequences to a somewhat greater degree than many previous films, and it led the way for gangster films and films noir to use the streets more than the back lots, to generate images out of the material of the world rather than putting them together in an optical printer.

The exterior shooting influenced by neorealism also reflected some economic realities. Italian neorealism emerged from the wreckage of the postwar economy and political culture. More subtle wreckages occurred to the United States after the war. What Hollywood faced was a decline in movie attendance (and therefore a falloff in revenues), the end of many binding contracts between studios and their personnel, accompanied by the blacklisting of many key creative personnel—including Jules Dassin, who directed *The Naked City*, and Albert Maltz, who wrote it. The power of the studio, manifested in its total control of the filmmaking process, was waning. Filmmakers began to form independent production companies and to shoot their films outside the studio. One of the results was a movement out onto the streets. Shooting on location in the United

States was not only a matter of aesthetics and probably never, as it was in Italy, a question of ideology.

The French New Wave   Exterior shooting was the closest American filmmaking came to the neorealist movement. The young French critics—the same ones who discovered film noir after seeing many American films from the late forties—looked also at *Rome, Open City; Bicycle Thieves;* and the other neorealist films coming from Italy. They recognized in both forms a departure from the classical Hollywood style and new ways to imagine cinematic space. When they made the move from film viewers and film critics to filmmakers, they found that, by combining the gangster/noir style with neorealism, they could shake up the very foundations of genre and the way we think of film. They shot on the streets, using new, little-known actors. While they did not make their films about the working class, like the neorealists, they did look at the lives of the dispossessed and the marginal.

Jean-Luc Godard   Most of these young directors started their careers by making interesting variations on the American gangster film. Jean-Luc Godard, who became the most influential filmmaker since Orson Welles, made his first full-length film a celebration of the gangster genre called *Breathless* (1960). Godard would go even further—Godard was always going further—and in 1965 made *Alphaville,* a film that places the noir detective inside the science fiction genre and has its tough-guy hero travel the universe in his Ford Galaxy. (This should not give the impression that Godard was idle between 1959 and 1965. After *Breathless* and before *Alphaville* he made seven feature films and a number of short ones. Every one, and all that followed, experimented with genre, narrative form, and all the basic conceptions and preconceptions of cinema.) François Truffaut, the best known of this group of innovators, made his second film an homage to noir called *Shoot the Piano Player* (1960).

These films were neither imitations nor parodies. They were homages, energetic celebrations of the American films that nourished their directors' imaginations, and they were vehicles for rethinking how genres work and how audiences respond to them. Their films interrogate the ways genres operate and, further, the ways in which films told their stories and developed mise-en-scène. For Godard, the gangster or the private eye became a figure of existential anxiety (not that far from Chandler's Philip Marlowe), who seeks out identity and speaks philosophically about who he is and how he is to be known. The latter becomes the key question for Godard: how do we *know* what we see in a film and learn about characters? What is the nature of the cinematic image and the genre-driven cinematic narrative? When we see the same characters in roughly the same story, with basically the same outcome in film after film, are we lulled into a sense of acceptance, of ideological complicity with the filmmakers and their work, both of which request our uniform response? Can genres be altered in a way to make us ask questions rather than respond with the same feelings?

Godard's answer to these questions was to take genres, the cinematic image, and the narrative apart, in order to make us look and understand that what we were seeing was just an image ("This is not a just image," Godard would say, "this is just an image") and that these images were freighted with ideological and cultural baggage. His films break all the rules: they give up straightforward continuity editing, avoid over-the-shoulder shots, gaze at length from a position directly in front of the characters, who talk not only to one another but to the audience. His narratives shift mood and direction, closure is not promised, and loose ends, popping out all over the narrative, need not be tied up at the end.

Michelangelo Antonioni   Other filmmakers followed suit in the sixties and seventies, continuing to ask questions about the Hollywood style and Hollywood genres and answer them in their films. If they didn't use the gangster film as their object of interrogation, they turned to melodrama. In Italy, following the neorealist movement, filmmakers examined the world inhabited by their characters, now more often middle rather than working class. They articulated the spaces around the figures, the architectural structures they lived in that defined their social and emotional life. Michelangelo Antonioni, for example, investigated the melodramatic mise-en-scène so that the world surrounding his characters not only expressed their anxieties but manifested the repressions that caused them, in a strange and powerful combination of Expressionism and neorealism. Antonioni was the great modernist poet of urban space in which architectural geometry delineated the barriers of the spirit. His quiet, oppressed women and jumpy, unfocused men wander through architectural landscapes that don't so much dwarf them as carry on a visual dialogue with them.

Unlike the classic American cinema, Antonioni does not privilege the figure in the frame. He insists that composition be about the relationship between the human figure and her surroundings and that emotion emerge from that inter-

Architecture and composition define the figure. Red Desert *by Michaelangelo Antonioni (1964)*

action. His camera is a distant, sometimes disembodied observer, whose movements make us wonder who authorizes the gaze in a film. Who is looking at whom, and why? His films rely on the eloquence and articulateness of the image more than those of almost any other filmmaker. They are the poetry of the figure in the urban landscape.

Antonioni—in films such as *Il Grido* (1957), *L'Avventura* (1960), *La Notte* (1961), *The Eclipse* (1962), *Red Desert* (1964), and *Blow-Up* (1966)—broke many rules. He substitutes composition for the cut, forcing the viewer to look *at* the frame rather than across it from one action to the next. He changes the internal dynamics of melodrama. Instead of transposing excess emotion from the individual to mise-en-scène and back again, he makes the individual part of the mise-en-scène and asks the viewer to inspect both very carefully. Emotional excess is replaced by a shifting visual dynamic. Emotion emerges from our comprehension of these dynamics and is never removed from intellectual awareness. The cinema reclaims its obligations to the visible, and melodrama is restrained by an active engagement of the viewer's eye and mind.

Yasujiro Ozu   Antonioni is not the only filmmaker to force the viewer's eye to observe composition and make the human figure only one aspect of a complex mise-en-scène. Orson Welles and Stanley Kubrick do the same. Hitchcock does it and, subtly, often without showing his hand, so does the great director of Westerns, John Ford. In Japan, Yasujiro Ozu made many domestic melodramas that addressed the quiet change of culture in that country after the war. Films as moving and beautiful as their titles—*Late Spring* (1949), *The Flavor of Green Tea Over Rice* (1952), *Tokyo Story* (1953), *Early Spring* (1956), *Late Autumn* (1960)—examined the Japanese middle-class family from an ironic, quiet distance. Ozu places his camera in the "tatami" position, low on the floor, emulating the traditional seating of a Japanese at home on a tatami mat. But this emulation does not define the point of view of a particular individual in the frame. It is, rather, a cultural gesture, looking at the world from a Japanese perspective. That perspective includes a respect for space, an interest in rooms and surroundings that is

The middle-class Japanese family, scene from the "tatami" position—that is, from a mat placed on the floor. Tokyo Story *(1953)*

not confined to the narrative of a particular film but speaks the narrative of the culture as a whole. As I indicated earlier, American films rarely maintain interest in or focus on spaces that have no human figures in them. Ozu loves these spaces, because, even though no figure is present, they were humanized, made by people to live in; and therefore they retain and define human presence, even in their absence. His camera gazes at a room before someone enters it and after she leaves. He cuts away from the main narrative line to create a montage of the city, a train passing, a rock garden, clothes hanging on a line. Ozu's world is defined by its particular cultural articulations.

But there is no mistaking the melodramatic base of Ozu's films. They are about families in turmoil. Parents die, daughters marry, fathers get drunk, sisters are mean, the domestic center does not hold. None of these situations is addressed with the hysteria and overstatement beloved of American melodrama, nor is the viewer asked to deliver emotion on the basis of a character's death or the redemption of a misguided soul. The viewer is asked only to observe and put things together and to recognize within Ozu's mise-en-scène a harmony that transcends the particular upheavals of the domestic.

Rainer Werner Fassbinder   If Ozu sought a greater cultural harmony out of local family melodrama, the German filmmaker Rainer Werner Fassbinder looked for melodrama to deliver insight into history and politics and to discover in the family a microcosm of large power structures in the culture. Fassbinder was one of the more remarkable figures to appear in European cinema during the 1970s. He started making films in 1969 and directed thirty-nine of them—including multipart series for television—before his premature death in 1982. A large, punk, openly gay man, Fassbinder brought together a remarkably talented stock company of cast and crew, who set out to rethink American film melodrama as a mode of addressing the politics of the family and the state.

Fassbinder's idol was Douglas Sirk. Sirk's over-the-top, bigger-than-life melodramas pushed the genre to its limits, made the viewer aware of how the excesses of emotion, and the spilling over of those excesses into the mise-en-scène, were the marks of the genre's artifices rather than imitations of life. Sirk pushed the melodramatic boundaries. Fassbinder attempted to reflect them back in on themselves and exploit them not as reflections of the personal but as statements about the political. In Sirk's *All That Heaven Allows*, an upper-middle-class, suburban widow defies family and friends to marry a much younger, down-to-earth nurseryman. Fassbinder remade the film in 1973. *Ali: Fear Eats the Soul* takes the essential banality of Sirk's premise and turns it into political and social allegory. Sirk had tried to transcend the banality of his film's story by creating a complex mise-en-scène and by turning the film into a commentary on sexual repressiveness and the fifties' concerns over conformity. Fassbinder goes further, creating instead of an upper-middle-class matron as the central female character, an old German washerwoman, a widow whose husband was a member of the Nazi party; instead of a handsome young nurseryman, a homely, bumbling Moroccan, an immigrant worker, suffering the indignities, scorn, and oppression faced by people of color who are brought in by a rich culture to do the dirty work.

The old German woman and the young, black immigrant fall in love and marry. Fassbinder makes this all so touching that we have to shake ourselves to realize how perfectly absurd it is. It simply couldn't happen. But then, the conventional absurdities of ordinary melodrama could never happen either. The narrative structure of *Fear Eats the Soul* only points up these absurdities and makes us examine our assumptions about them. The film invites us to come to understand how much we take for granted in melodrama, and how much goes unexamined. Emmi and Ali—the unlikely couple—are visited by a string of humiliations. Emmi's neighbors scorn her; her family reviles her. They take out their anger on her possessions. In *All That Heaven Allows*, Carrie's children buy her a television set to keep her mind off her lover; in *Fear Eats the Soul*, Emmi's son kicks in the television set to show his anger at her impending marriage. The local grocer won't sell his food to Ali. And people stare. Fassbinder makes the staring almost comic and absolutely unbearable. He will show people frozen in a stare; he will create tableaux of staring—staged, artificial, and obvious—to make his point. This couple is so transgressive, all anyone can do is stare at them.

Then he reverses the situation. Suddenly, Emmi's children realize that mother is a good resource for babysitting; the neighbors want Ali to help them move furniture; the grocer, realizing that his business is being hurt by supermarkets, welcomes Ali at his shop. But as outsiders change their tune to fit their own needs, Ali and Emmi go through a reverse change and become their own exploiters. Emmi shows off Ali's muscles to her neighbors and refuses to allow his friends to visit the apartment. He, in turn, flees to the arms of the woman who runs the

Visual rhyming. Rainer Werner Fassbinder observes his characters trapped within the oppressive gaze of other people. Here, Emmi, who has married a Moroccan migrant worker, is badly treated and isolated by her coworkers.

Later, when another worker arrives on the scene, Emmi and her friends isolate her and the shot composition is the same. Ali: Fear Eats the Soul. *(1974)*

local Moroccan bar. Earlier Emmi was cast out by her coworkers. Now she joins them in taunting and isolating a foreigner who has joined her cleaning crew at the office. Fassbinder makes a special point of this by literally rhyming a shot. Earlier in the film, his camera looks at Emmi sitting alone on the stairs, eating her lunch, as her coworkers group together making fun of her. She is composed between the spokes of the banister, as if imprisoned. Later, when Emmi joins her coworkers taunting the newcomer, this poor soul is framed by the camera in exactly the same way Emmi was. Oppression returns like rhyme.

For Fassbinder, oppression is not something internalized. Repression is not only sexual. Unhappiness is not always the result of a bad romance or a failing marriage. Repression and unhappiness are social and political phenomena; they are about power and one-upmanship—about how someone with a little power exercises it by oppressing someone with even less. This cycle of oppression and hurt is itself contained within a larger cycle of power and repression exercised by the state. Emmi and Ali have a reconciliation. They meet at the bar for Middle-Eastern immigrant workers where they first found each other, and they dance. A happy ending threatens until, suddenly, Ali collapses on the floor. In *All That Heaven Allows,* Cary, realizing that Rock Hudson is indeed her only love and key to happiness (a doctor has told her that her headaches and depression are a result of repressing her desires), pursues him in the snowy countryside. Before he hears her calling to him, he falls off a cliff. The film ends with her assuming a maternal position at his bedside, while a doe plays in the snow outside. Ali's collapse has nothing to do with despair over losing Emmi. He is suffering from an ulcer. The doctor at the end of *Fear Eats the Soul* offers no hope and tells Emmi that Ali will never get well. His condition is a common physical response of immigrants to the terrible conditions and humiliations they face in their host country. The humiliations and the ulcers will keep occurring until he dies. The film ends with the image of Ali in his hospital bed. There is no deer at the window, only the hard Munich skyline.

The Influence of Brecht   Fassbinder does not merely invert melodramatic principles and structures or turn them inside out; he shows how they can be made to work. Instead of absorbing the political into the personal, he shows how personal suffering and emotional repression can be understood as political events on the micro and macro levels. He also shows how melodrama can be made to work on an intellectual level by inviting the viewer to step back a bit and look with some detachment. Fassbinder does this by borrowing principles from the influential left-wing playwright Bertolt Brecht, who said that the work of art should not mystify or make itself invisible but rather open itself up to interrogation. For Brecht, the more invisible the style, the more the viewer is fooled into believing the illusion. The more fooled, the more he is taken advantage of. The more visible, the more the viewer understands how form and ideology operate, and the work of art becomes a tool for understanding larger structures of power in the culture. Brecht would have the playwright (and, by extension, the filmmaker) build into his work effects that create distance between it and the viewer. Fassbinder does this by creating outrageous narratives with characters who are quite unattractive by Hollywood standards. Then he employs an unusual visual style. His lighting is often very low, so figures don't stand out with the presence we expect in a Hollywood film. He frames his characters in doorways and within rooms so that we become conscious of the framing of the camera and how that framing comments upon the characters and their situation. He will stop dramatic action and have his characters look up and stare at the camera, forcing us to recognize the artificiality of the scene. He will repeat actions and compositions, as when he rhymes the shot of Emmi isolated on the stairs. He will exaggerate actions and make melodramatic coincidences obvious. He is unafraid to make the melodramatic structure totter and even fall, so that he can rebuild it from a new perspective, a public and political as opposed to a private and personal perspective.

The Brechtian influence on Fassbinder (and earlier on Jean-Luc Godard) was important in the reconceptualizing of genre and the continuity style. Since the main function of the classical Hollywood style is to make viewers unconscious of there being any style at all, the Brechtian reworking of the style serves the opposite function. The result is a consciousness of film and its stories as something *made*, not something natural, given, and present. The viewer, forced to come to terms with form, will then be willing to think through why the form is so constructed, why she is asked to look a certain way, at certain things—why she is asked to look at all.

Visual Pleasure

This coming to terms with form is nowhere more important than when we consider how movies make us look at gender. One of American cinema's master narratives is, as we have seen, the confirmation of woman's male-dependent, passive role. It forms the basic pattern of melodrama, and it drives comedy. Laura Mulvey, who wrote an influential essay called "Visual Pleasure and the Narrative Cinema," pointed out that the classic Hollywood style is structured through the way the gaze of the camera, of the male characters in the film, and of the viewers watching the projected image in front of them is directed at the female character. She is, as it were, fixed by the male gaze that drives the narrative. She is objectified, her subjectivity transferred to the male gaze.

In melodrama, the woman is fixed by the process of the narrative itself, hurt, kept down, offered a possibility of release, and then returned to the domestic fold, wiser but still kept down. "Don't let's ask for the moon . . . ,we have the stars." The melodramatic narrative does not permit her to ask, "Why not ask for everything?" She is there only to be looked at with pity or compassion, admired for her beauty, worried over if she is too demanding or energetic, and then recouped or killed off. More often than not, she is simply the mechanism of the melodrama's sexual economy, its parceling out of desire, sacrifice, and redemption around the fulcrum of the female character. She is the object of the gaze: it gives her value and takes it away. In the work of maverick filmmakers like

Fassbinder, Godard, Chantal Akerman, or the American Todd Solondz in his film *Happiness* (1998), that gaze is wrenched away from the suffering woman to some other perspective, to an ironic look at people who damage themselves and others, and are somehow attractive and repulsive at the same time, as in "real life." Such filmmakers move us away from identification—a key necessity of melodrama—to a position where we are allowed our own self-possession, where we are allowed to understand.

Master narratives, dominant fictions, and the genres that are made from them are never immutable. They remain in force through a kind of inertia, which is broken when an energetic, curious cinematic intelligence comes to examine them closely. And this, after all, is the power of cinema. Though owned and created like a manufacturing process, there are often spaces through which individuals squirm through, making films that not only break with convention but prove that the language of cinema—its technical, formal, generic conventions—is really quite flexible. What we see every day on our screens is not what we *must* see.

Film, Form, and Culture: The CD-ROM

A visual analysis of one genre, film noir, is offered in the new *Genre* segment of the CD-ROM, and an example of thirties documentary is given in *Montage*. Examples of Griffith's work appear throughout the CD and especially in *Mise-en-Scène* and *Camera*, where his use of framing and space are addressed. Other aspects of directorial style appear in the *Point of View* and *Lighting*.

NOTES AND REFERENCES

Master Narratives and Dominant Fictions   The term "dominant fiction" is suggested by Kaja Silverman in *Male Subjectivity at the Margins* (New York and London: Routledge: 1992). For a theory of the *end* of master narratives in the postmodern age, see Jean-François Lyotard, *The Postmodern Condition: A Report on Knowledge,* trans. Geoff Bennington and Brian Massumi (Minneapolis: University of Minnesota Press, 1984).

Master Narratives: Censorship   David Cook presents an excellent history of Hollywood censorship in *A History of Narrative Film,* 3d ed. (New York: W. W. Norton, 1996), pp. 280–84.

Genre: Generic Origins   François Delsarte was a nineteenth-century Frenchman who codified dramatic facial expressions and gestures in the nineteenth century. There is some interesting discussion about the tension between genre and individual expression in Leo Braudy's *The World in a Frame,* which has been previously cited in Chapter 2, and by Robert Warshow in his essay "Movie Chronicle: The Western" in his book *The Immediate Experience* (cited in Chapter 4) and the collection *Film Theory and Criticism* (cited in Chapter 2).

Genre: Generic Patterns   A lively history of the Warner Brothers gangster film and biography of its stars is in Robert Sklar, *City Boys* (Princeton, NJ: Princeton University Press, 1992).

Genre Analysis   A good theoretical discussion of film genre is done by Steven Neale, *Genre* (London: British Film Institute, 1983). See also Robin Wood's "Ideology, Genre, Auteur," in *Film Theory and Criticism*.

Documentary   A useful history of documentary is Richard Meran Barsam, *Nonfiction Film: A Critical History* (Bloomington: Indiana University Press, 1992). A strong analysis of Leni Riefenstahl's work is in Susan Sontag's essay "Fascinating Fascism," in *A Susan Sontag Reader* (New York: Vintage, 1982). For current theory on nonfiction film, see Bill Nichols, *Representing Reality : Issues and Concepts In Documentary* (Bloomington : Indiana University Press, 1991). The quote from Grierson comes from *Grierson on Documentary*, ed. Frosyth Hardy (New York: Praeger, 1971), p. 289. For an interview with the Maysles brothers, see my "Circumstantial Evidence" in *Sight and Sound* (Autumn 1971).

Melodrama   There are two excellent anthologies of essays on melodrama and film: Marcia Landy, ed., *Imitations of Life: A Reader of Film and Television Melodrama* (Detroit: Wayne State University Press, 1991); and Christine Gledhill, ed., *Home Is Where the Heart Is* (London: BFI Publishing, 1987). The standard essay is Thomas Elsaesser's "Tales of Sound and Fury: Observations on the Family Melodrama," reprinted in the 1992 edition of *Film Theory and Criticism* and in *Home Is Where the Heart Is*.

Ideological Norms   Ideology is a complex topic and so is much of the writing on it. One place to start would be Terry Lovell, *Pictures of Reality: Aesthetics, Politics, and Pleasure* (London: BFI Publishing, 1980).

Film Noir   So much has been written on noir, but the best remains an essay by the screenwriter (of *Taxi Driver*, among others) and director Paul Schrader, "Notes on Film Noir," *Film Comment* 8 (Spring 1972). A good visual analysis is offered by J. A. Place and L. S. Peterson, "Some Visual Notes on Film Noir," in Bill Nichols, ed., *Movies and Methods*, vol. 1 (Berkeley and Los Angeles: University of California Press, 1976), pp. 325–38. See also Frank Krutnik, *In a Lonely Street: Film Noir, Genre, Masculinity* (London and New York: Routledge, 1991); and James Naremore, *More Than Night: Film Noir In Its Contexts* (Berkeley: University of California Press, 1998). For a feminist reading, see E. Ann Kaplan, ed., *Women in Film Noir* (London: BFI Publishing, 1980).

Expressionist Roots of Noir   The best work on German Expressionism is Lotte Eisner's *The Haunted Screen*, trans. Roger Greaves (Berkeley and Los Angeles: University of California Press, 1973). An interesting cultural study of the thirties horror film is in David Skal, *The Monster Show* (New York: Penguin Books, 1994).

Double Indemnity   Walter Neff is played by Fred MacMurray, until this time an actor in light comedy. Like Dick Powell, he used a noir film to change his style. Phyllis is played by Barbara Stanwyck. For discussion of whether noir elaborates a destruction of the women-based family or merely recuperates it, see Claire Johnston, "Double Indemnity," in the previously cited *Women in Film*

Noir, pp. 100–11; and Joyce Nelson, "Mildred Pierce Reconsidered," in Bill Nichols, ed., *Movies and Methods,* vol. 2 (Berkeley and Los Angeles: University of California Press, 1985). The quotation "I feel all dead inside . . ." is from Henry Hathaway's *Dark Corner* (1946) and is quoted in Frank Krutnik's *In a Lonely Street: Film Noir, Genre, Masculinity,* p. 101.

Touch of Evil   There is a wonderful sequence in Tim Burton's film *Ed Wood* (1994) in which the momentarily dispirited director of very bad films goes into a dark bar in the middle of a bright Hollywood day. He finds Orson Welles sitting in a corner working on a script. "Tell me about it," Orson tells Ed Wood. "I'm supposed to do a thriller at Universal, but they want Charlton Heston to play a Mexican!" The long take at the beginning of *Touch of Evil* is lovingly parodied in the opening of Robert Altman's film *The Player.* Altman makes his shot even longer, and the characters who move around in it keep referring to Welles's film.

Noir's Rebirth   Original Technicolor used three black and white negatives that were filtered to respond respectively to the primary colors, red, green, and blue. These negatives were then pressed with dyes during the printing process and, in combination, laid down a full color image on the positive film. By the early fifties, Eastman Kodak developed a single-strip color process. This became the standard and three-color Technicolor disappeared. This was a shame. The original Technicolor was very stable. Eastman Color is not, and most films made between the late fifties and the mid-eighties fade if not properly protected.

European and Other Cinemas   A good survey of postwar European and international cinema is in Robert Phillip Kolker, *The Altering Eye* (New York: Oxford University Press, 1983).

Italian Neorealism   On Mussolini, Cinecittà, the history of neorealism, see Peter Bondanella, *Italian Cinema: From Neorealism to the Present* (New York: Frederick Ungar, 1983).

The French New Wave   The best discussion of the movement remains James Monaco's *The New Wave: Truffaut, Godard, Chabrol, Rohmer, Rivette* (New York: Oxford University Press, 1976).

Fassbinder   Some of Fassbinder's crew are now active in America. His cinematographer, Michael Ballhaus, now works for Martin Scorsese and has filmed such diverse projects as *Goodfellas* and *The Age of Innocence.*

The Influence of Brecht   Brecht's theoretical writing is collected in *Brecht on Theatre,* trans. John Willett (New York: Hill and Wang, 1979).

Visual Pleasure   Laura Mulvey's essay is widely reprinted and can be found in *Film Theory and Criticism.*

6

OTHER SCREENS: THE FUTURE OF THE IMAGE

Even after all the careful analysis we have done about the forms and history of film, we must come to a realization that it is, in fact, a dying vestige of an old technology. Dying, after all we said about its vitality and ability to change? It is doubtful that its master narrative conventions as well as the innovations of individual filmmaker who looks for nontraditional means of story telling will die, but certainly the old nineteenth-century techniques of spreading photosensitive chemicals on a plastic surface, running the plastic through a camera, developing the negative in a chemical bath, editing the resulting images together with glue, printing a positive, distributing them to theaters, and then projecting them on a screen will. Like almost everything else in the film business, this will all change because of economics and new technologies. In the late twenties and again in the middle of the twentieth century, image recording and delivery—the ways in which the images and their narratives reached their audience—underwent some modifications. By the end of the century, the basic technologies and economies of the screen began changing in radical ways. Sound was added to film in the late twenties because film attendance was in a slump and a novelty was needed. In the fifties, a new screen had already overshadowed the movie screen: television. The studios responded by widening the size of the theater screen.

By the early 2000s, the computer screen promises to overshadow both, and Hollywood will meet it in two ways. It will continue to make films like *The Lawnmower Man* (Brett Leonard, 1992), *The Net* (Irwin Winkler, 1995), or *The Matrix*, that warn against the dangers of cyberlife, just as it made fun of television in the fifties. And, as it did back then with television, it will get into the computer business—with a vengeance that will put an end to celluloid-based film.

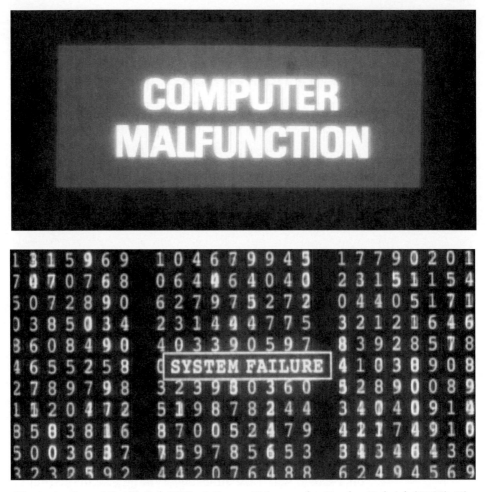

Cinema's view of the digital: 2001: A Space Odyssey *by Stanley Kubrick (1968);* The Matrix *by Andy Wachowski, Larry Wachowski (1999)*

With the merger of America Online and Time-Warner, we have an inkling of how the computer and the movie screen will begin to merge as a business. George Lucas will "film" the next *Star Wars* on digital tape. He has already experimented by showing the last episode, *The Phantom Menace* (1999), in a digital version. In other words, the "film" was projected from digital tape. As soon as the technology and the economics are worked out, all the studios will be making and distributing films this way—the digital way. They will be shown in theaters from either tape or discs that are cheaper to make and distribute than 35 mm film, or broadcast directly to theaters from satellites.

Almost everything concerning the image that we have been speaking about will change. It will look different from 35 mm, be made differently, composed, lit, and in general structured differently. Whether the content of the narratives constructed by the images will change is another matter. The example of television does not give much hope.

TELEVISION

Television, of course, was the second new screen after movies. But TV was less a technological change than a cultural and economic upheaval. Like film, television is an analogue process, which means that the light waves reflected from a surface, such as the human face, are recorded on a chemical surface in intensities that are proportional to the original light source. But in television, instead of processing the surface with chemicals, the light is transformed into electronic signals. These signals are transmitted through the air, received by the television set, and reconverted into electrons that activate the phosphorous surface of the television tube, which responds to them by reproducing images whose electronic waveforms are analogous to those that originated the process.

The technology of television parallels the technology of film, and film is, more often than not, the primary material that television transmits. But beyond that, TV and film are very different. Film represents the outside world, not because a film narrative necessarily takes place in the outside world but because, before the late sixties, in order to see a current film, you had to travel into the outside world. Going to see a movie meant going out of the house. It was a communal, urban experience. After World War II, urban communities began to change. Middle-class people left the city in great numbers. At the beginning of this migration, before the growth of suburban malls where movie houses were relocated in miniaturized form, going out of the house to see a film declined as a social event. Television became the means to satisfy the driving need for visual narratives.

Film was always available on television: old movies, filmed series, and movies made for television were there almost from the start. Live television drama had a relatively short life, and Hollywood-made production took over by the late fifties. In the brief period of live drama—from the early to the mid-fifties—television produced a number of writers and directors—Rod Serling, Paddy Chayefsky, Arthur Penn, John Frankenheimer, and Delbert Mann, for example—who went to Hollywood and were important influences in the movies. Some live television dramas were turned into films that took a hard and tightly composed look at working and lower-middle-class characters: *Marty* (Delbert Mann, 1955), *12 Angry Men* (Sidney Lumet, 1957), *The Bachelor Party* (Delbert Mann, 1957), *Days of Wine and Roses* (Blake Edwards, 1962). This direct interaction was short-lived.

But no matter what the source of the programming, our reception and perception of television are very different from what happens to us in a movie theater. The space is different: domestic rather than public, inside rather than out. The focus of concentration is different: television is situated as a piece of household furniture to be stared at; it is usually watched in the light and with other things going on in the room. The screen is different: it is small and lit from behind, its resolution is low, the image is fuzzy and full of noise. Television does not elicit the concentration demanded from us in a dark movie house. On commercial channels, programming and advertising contend for our attention.

Commercial Structures

The commercial structure of movies is, in a sense, subtle and deep. As we have seen, there is a quiet, profit-driven negotiation between filmmaker and film viewer that is maintained through all the processes of production and reception. In television, a kind of pay-as-you-go process was instituted very early on. Instead of individual funding for individual productions, money would come from advertisers. They would invest in a program not on the promise of delayed returns in the form of gross receipts but in the hope that viewers would buy the products that were advertised on the shows. In the early days of television, until the late 1950s, advertisers minimized their risks by producing the very shows they sponsored. The television program was another product of Kraft Foods or Firestone Tires or General Electric and was used to advertise those products.

By the late fifties, most production was turned back to the networks and their independent suppliers. Advertisers bought time on particular programs, or simply bought time periods, and their commercial presence thrived. But no matter the mechanism, the presence of the advertiser and the production of programming to support the advertised product constitute the essential dynamic of television. The programming does not stand on its own but is interlaced with commercials. In these commercials, the viewer may be exhorted to buy a product by a spokesperson or a disembodied voice that accompanies images of people using the product. Or the viewer may be engaged by miniature narratives, small stories of sexuality, of loss and desire, of inadequacy and fulfillment, of false cynicism and real manipulation, often in a style that is quite different from the classic continuity structure of the main program.

The Television Gaze

Watching a film is a self-contained, integral narrative experience. In a sense, it advertises itself through the continuity style that propels us forward and keeps us engaged. Watching a film or other programming on television is not integral but fragmented. As a television viewer, one watches and takes part in multiple narratives: the main program, the commercial interruptions, and the domestic dramas going on in the room, all of them folded one within the other. In this way, television becomes a kind of communal experience, though different from film and the movie theater. You go out to a movie and choose a specific film to go to. You stay in for television, and you are less likely to aim for a particular show than simply to "watch television." The light television creates on its screen may be there for many other purposes than simply making its images visible.

Stylistically, television is sometimes more eclectic, even more adventurous, than film. While most of the narrative material follows the rules of the continuity style, there are exceptions and there are structural conventions that are unique to television itself. News programming and some commercials, for example, have developed a style of audience address unlike anything in narrative film. News readers face and look into the camera, making eye contact with the audience (who are, of course, mediated by camera and screen). This is largely denied to practitioners of the classical style in film. The gazes of film work by indirection. The straight-on gaze of the news reader or advertising spokesperson, however, is instituted to create another kind of intimacy.

The television screen was promoted, from the early fifties, as the window on the world, the place where isolated suburbanites or besieged city dwellers could see into the outside without having to be there. Movies ask people to come out to the theater where they can see the melodramatic, the fantastic, and the uncanny and be moved. Television delivers the friendly, the frightening, and the informative directly. The person who delivers the information, whether of a man made disaster or a new refrigerator, looks right out at you, confidently. In your private, domestic space, the face on the screen can pretend intimacy and evoke a narrative of participation and proximity, an invitation into a fantasy world of threat and violence (the news) or desire and pleasure (the commercial).

The News and the Gaze

As television and the world it pretends to represent progressed and the need for ratings and advertisers overcame good programming sense, the information it delivered got uglier, more vulgar, violent, and desperate. The look remained, becoming a demand for attention, a conspiratorial invitation into the shocking and dismaying. In commercials it became a mock-ironic beseeching look, asking us to consider that the value of one product was greater than another. The gazes of the news presenter, the host of a tabloid program or talk show, or the spokesperson for a commercial product are perverse examples of Walter Benjamin's theory of the loss of aura. Few things in life should be as intimate and moving, as subjective and unique, as direct eye contact with another person. But the eye contact of a television talking head is without uniqueness, without intimacy. His or her stare is for everyone and for no one in particular. It is, finally, a stare for the camera, which is translated to the screen. The viewer stares back, not at the head but at the screen. The result is a narcissistic interaction of mutually noncomprehending gazes.

Benjamin hoped that loss of aura would mean increased access, an ability to see more deeply and communally into the world. Removing the sacred presence of the artist and the ritual aspect of looking at "great works" might allow proximity, even active insertion of social imagination into works of all kinds. But television's lack of aura creates a wider gulf between the viewer and the world than film does, precisely because the direct gaze of the talking head or the hysterical boyfriend on Jerry Springer and the constant supply of information *seem* to provide a look into the wide world. Quite the opposite occurs. The view is shallow, not deep. It is directed by a belief—on the part of news and other producers—that violent and antisocial events interest the largest number of people. It is a paranoid and antisocial view; and rather than provoke people to look deeply into the world, as Benjamin hoped movies would do, television—especially the television of news, talk, and tabloid programming—promotes a paranoid view. Television wants people to stay home and watch television.

Narrative Programming

Narrative programming on television can sometimes have a different effect. Dramatic programs and made-for-television movies sometimes tackle current social problems, the latter occasionally from a woman's perspective. Theatrical film addressed social issues, long ago (capital, credit, and community were themes of *It's a Wonderful Life*); television has taken up the responsibility. Cable and broadcast movies are sometimes concerned with political issues, even moral problems. Serials (programs with an open narrative line that continues from one episode to another like soap operas) and series (programs with a continuing set of characters in somewhat different narrative situations in each episode like situation comedies) may not address social issues, but often offer interesting exceptions to the classical continuity style and the stereotypes so often present in theatrical film.

Soaps   Closure is a key element of the classical Hollywood style. In finally pulling closed all open narrative threads, recuperating any transgressive actions back into the cultural mainstream, the classical style creates a sense of uniqueness, the impression that what we have seen is a contained and one-of-a-kind story. It offers satisfaction, the assurance that everything is now OK.

Television serials and soap operas work in quite the opposite manner. The main narrative work of the soaps is to keep its narrative going, to never let it end! Every installment of a soap opera opens more questions, spins out more narrative threads, generates more trouble for its characters than it can ever close or solve. Another part of soap opera's work is done through its slow narrative rhythm and its concentration on female characters, intimately engaging its viewers. Soap opera is an extension of melodrama, which, as we saw, is often constructed around a woman repressed by her family, inhibited, unhappy, briefly liberated, and then, through an act of great sacrifice, brought back into the domestic fold in harmony with the moral demands of the culture. Soap opera greatly expands the liberation and sexual questing of the female characters by delaying their recuperation into the normal scheme of things for as long as it can. It allows a considerable latitude in the behavior of its characters and demands a long-term attention and commitment from its viewers beyond that required for any film and most other television programming. The slow pace of soaps, their lingering on character and details of the gaze, their exaggeration of goodness and villainy help integrate them into the lesser melodramas of daily life. They become part of life's routine.

Series   Series are the mainstay of evening television programming. They demand a peculiar kind of "now you see it, now you don't" response. Although they are broadcast every week, with the same characters, who regularly demonstrate the same characteristics in the same physical surroundings, both the characters and the programs also present the illusion of being reborn in each episode. In situation comedy, the events in one episode rarely recall the events in the previous one. The only continuing thread is the way characters will respond to a given stimulus. The characters and their narratives seem to live in a closed universe. Their narratives are like miniature genres, which can be depended upon, in episode after episode, to deliver variations on the same ideas, the same lines, the same physical and emotional responses, the same viewer reaction. They are the same each week, only different. The breaks in this convention are rare enough to be striking, as when a character on *Seinfeld* mentions something that happened on another episode. *The Simpsons,* the postmodern animated series that embraces and mocks popular culture in complex ways, parodies the amnesia effect of television series. Homer's boss never remembers who his employee is, no matter how many close experiences they have had.

More than movies, series (sitcoms especially) attempt to address the world many of its viewers live in. They are family or work oriented—though when they deal with work, they try to turn the workplace into a surrogate family—and they look at small issues, small "situations." They can, these days, be very vulgar and exploitative in their references to sexuality, but they can also be comforting in their familiarity and their repetitive pattern, their sense of sameness and difference, their reassurance that, whatever happens to their characters, they will respond always in the same way.

Flow

It is possible to think of the whole of television as a genre, and its sitcoms, melodramas, commercials, news, tabloids, music videos, "reality" shows, and nature programs as subgenres of a general, overriding structure in which images and the viewer's attention are casually locked into an assenting gaze. This is a structure of enormous elasticity where disparate images and stories, facts and factoids, representations of sexuality and merchandise, or merchandise as sexuality, the steady gaze of the news anchor or the nervous, twitching camera movements that, borrowed from MTV videos, are now commonly used for commercials and coming attractions all flow together. These bits and pieces are mediated by the television screen, which is gazed at by millions of people, all of whom seem easily to absorb the flow. The British cultural theorist Raymond Williams developed the concept of **"flow"** when he was trying to make sense of American television's homogenized disorder, the seemingly random, jarring movement of styles and stories, sameness and difference and constant interruptions, a movement that invites intimacy and refuses it at the same time. Flow is the coherence of the incoherent, a representation of life in bits and pieces. A reflection of the postmodern world.

Williams' notion of flow is somewhat analogous to the continuity style in film, a way to make coherent sense out of the fragmentary. But in the case of television, any illusion of continuity must come from the viewer with little assistance from the structure of what is being viewed. Unlike film, whose self-contained pattern of fragments follows the clear rules of continuity, television breaks programming down and interrupts it continually with few apparent rules of continuity. For the flow of parts to cohere, the viewer has to will it into coherence or accept the fragments as they move past his nonattentive eye. Curiously, television viewers seem not to want the flow to cohere as completely as in a movie, and, in fact, they sometimes add another layer of disruption. Channel surfing, in which the sixty or so channels of an average cable hookup are moved through in random disorder by means of a remote control, is a popular act of televiewing that is both a sign of desperation and a welcoming of the incoherent. Channel surfing allows the viewer to impose a subjective disorder on the chaotic flow of images and information, narratives, and advertising supplied by the producers of television. It creates a curious intimacy by turning externally produced chaos into personal chaos—another kind of negotiation between the viewer and the text.

Nothing like channel surfing is available when watching a film in the movie theater (perhaps, moving from one theater to another in a multiplex). My guess is that surfing rarely occurs when a film is viewed on cassette or laserdisc. Film is conventional in its demands for linear attention no matter what the venue, whether mall theater or domestic space. When we watch a film on cassette or DVD, it can recede into the background the way television often does. But when we give it our attention, it holds us through its length, if it's not boring, the phone doesn't ring, and no other domestic demand occurs that would be absent in a movie theater. The television screen becomes a convenient surrogate for the movie screen when the self-defining, self-cohering images of a film narrative are projected onto it—though with DVDs, there is the opportunity to move to different scenes in the film. When *television* is projected onto it, however, that coherence disappears, and the screen reflects as much our own restlessness as it does the fragmented programming and mix of styles sent over the air or through cable.

Cultural studies has embraced television as the form that is most amenable to viewer negotiation. Because the television screen is placed in an intimate, domestic space, the desire to make it a part of our subjective lives is strong, as we've just seen. Because television is the major diversion of the culture, watched by almost everyone, it becomes both private and communal intellectual and emotional property. Of course in reality no one owns television but its owners—General Electric (NBC), Rupert Murdoch (Fox), The Disney Company (ABC), Time Warner (HBO), Viacom (Paramount Pictures, MTV, Comedy Central), Westinghouse (CBS)—and most of these are involved in many other communications operations such as filmmaking and publishing. These companies sell their broadcast time to advertisers—except for HBO and other cable networks that get their fees from subscribers—and programming decisions remain far above viewers, who are represented in the abstract by viewership numbers, the Nielsen ratings (based upon relatively small viewer samples), and focus groups. But the desire on the part of viewers to make an accommodation, a negotiation, is very strong, and a kind of ownership grows at the home end. People talk about "my shows," fans appropriate *Star Trek* and rewrite episodes, sometimes as pornography. Celebrity trials become major cultural preoccupations. Watching soaps and sitcoms and quiz shows and "reality" programming becomes part of a life's routine, and some of us may feel deprived without them.

Televisual Pleasure

The television screen becomes a cultural mediator far different from the movie screen. Film delivers large emotions in intense bursts. The television screen reflects and refracts small, lingering, persistent, even obsessive concerns. Its fictional programming goes on and on, and viewers' capacity to look at a series of programs over and over again seems as limitless as the broadcast outlets these programs find. *I Love Lucy, MASH, Star Trek* (in its many incarnations) are shown and watched with a fascination that indicates a desire to own the pleasures and imaginations of these programs and reexperience them endlessly. Situation comedies build their own dominant fictions of a closely knit family or, more often, a contentious but ultimately warm workplace community that's like a family, but without its oppressive blood ties. These are stories that speak to people about desires that are hard to fulfill in life.

But it is not sufficient to explain the popularity of such programs by reducing them to substitutions for the experience we want but can't seem to find any place else but on television. More important are the touches of humor and imagination, the characters that represent traits we find endearing or those we imagine we could emulate, the narrative structures that play intricate changes on some basic themes—the way films that belong to a genre do: these are the determining characteristics of the form and structure of television narratives. So is their intimacy, their omnipresence in the space of domestic life, and their ability to be retrieved, almost at will, from local stations, cable channels, and videotape. Television is available, emotionally as well as physically. It is with us and of us. We ignore it and embrace it. We shore up its fragments for our pleasure.

FROM ANALOGUE TO DIGITAL

The play of intimacy and industry remains a key to understanding television and why its screen has become the site of the obsessive gaze of millions of individuals and of multi-million-dollar mergers and high corporate aspirations. Intimacy also plays a determining role in the most recent screen to occupy domestic space, the computer screen, where new kinds of representations—

some nonnarrative (in the conventional sense), some with peculiar, suppressed, or labyrinthine narratives—are addressing and even creating new audiences, communities, and cultures. In order to understand what this means, and to begin a transition from our discussion of the analogue to the digital screen, we must first recover some terrain.

Film and television are analogue processes: the light and sound waves that originate from the subjects being photographed are, on a physical level, related to the light and sound waves that light the screen and that vibrate the loud-speaker. The digital image does not have physical continuity with whatever originates it. Light or sound from the source object is translated into information that is *not* analogous to the source. Input—light, sound, a request for a withdrawal from an automatic teller machine, or a search through a library catalogue—is translated into the common language of the binary. This is code, represented at its base by zeros and ones that operate the electronic switches that make computers work and act upon any information fed into them. That is why the very word "information" has stretched the limits of meaning, signifying not knowledge or ideas but the almost ineffable process of input to output, what goes into the computer and is digitized, compressed, and sampled and what comes out, the characters and graphics displayed on a screen.

Digitized information, because it is reduced to a relatively simple binary language, stripped of all excess and redundant material, is easily manipulable and can be copied repeatedly with no degradation. This makes it perfect for moviemaking. Let's for a moment go back to our discussion about how film-makers construct a shot. Wherever possible, a shot is built up from a number of elements that do not have to be in front of the camera at the same time. In predigital times, a human figure would be photographed against a blue screen. Later, a painter would make an elaborate, real-looking image of a backdrop. In the effects laboratory, these two shots would be projected onto another strip of film, resulting in a composite image of a character on a road, on a cliff, in a cityscape, moving, flying, and so forth. This is a complex, multistep process in which, among other things, the image is degraded as it is rephotographed over and over.

Digitizing images reduces the steps and does not degrade the final result. Digital manipulation of images allows anything to be done by artists and programmers at graphics terminals. Real movement can be created out of still figures, and figures can be created that exist nowhere in reality. Digital artists can place a figure in any kind of environment. In Spielberg's *Jurassic Park* (1993) and *The Lost World* (1997) all the dinosaurs that are not mechanical models are digital designs matched with human figures. Almost everything seen in the sky in *Independence Day* (1996), including the flying saucers and the airplane sorties against them, is digitally created. Films use digital design in more subtle ways as well. Crowd scenes can be created by simply duplicating figures digitally; the head of one actor can be pasted upon another; stunts can be constructed on a computer terminal with a minimum of actual human activity. Digital image manipulation and replacement have pretty much replaced optical special effects, just as digital "automatic dialogue replacement" (ADR) has replaced sound dubbing, so that filmmakers can construct the best reading of lines after the film is shot, perfectly synchronizing sound to lip movements. The result of all this is that what you see and hear in a film is even less authorized by the exterior world than it was before. The feather, that image of grace and simplemindedness, drifting down to Forrest Gump's foot, is a digital effect.

Storage and Distribution

What can be done on the micro level of the shot can be done on the macro level of the film itself, and so digitization becomes a distribution as well as a creative process, changing the way films are seen and where. Entire movies can now be digitized into electronic files, the way a term paper is digitally stored on a word processor. To be sure, the process is more complicated, and the computer resources that are needed for the process are enormous. But in the realm of the digital, storage and transmission problems are rapidly solved. With the solutions will come different kinds of ownership, availability, and access. If dozens, or hundreds, of films can be digitally stored on a computer, and if that computer can be accessed over a television or phone company cable or via satellite, viewer habits will undergo a major change. The introduction of DVD, which are the size of CDs and can store enormous amounts of digitized material, will make movie watching even more of a portable experience than it is now with videotape.

Availability and access will expand. On a more profound level, the aesthetics of the image will change. Digital HDTV (high definition television), currently under development, creates an image made up of 1,125 lines of scanned resolution, as opposed to the current resolution of 525 lines. Although the HDTV image is still made up of scanned lines, as opposed to the fine chemical grain that makes up the film image, the number of those lines, along with the digital sampling that removes any extraneous visual "noise," renders an extremely well resolved image that is capable of reproducing a gradient of color and brightness quite astonishing in its subtlety. It does not look like film. The quality of light and shadow is different; it has another kind of visual presence. When HDTV becomes available, a new kind of cinematography, or videography, will emerge that will allow imaginative film or video makers to create images as intricate and subtle as any on film.

As we've noted, the studios are already thinking about the economies that can be realized in broadcasting HDTV images directly to theaters rather than the current practice of striking prints of a film and shipping them around the country. The result will be that, when we go out to the movies, we will, in effect, be going to see television, though with a projected image of more visual subtlety than is now available on television. The content may very well remain film content. There may not be commercials that interrupt the narrative, though they will continue to exist inside the film, in the form of recognizable products, easily identified, a practice that has been going on for some time. But the image will be a video image, projected on a large, wide screen.

HDTV promises a video image of high resolution and large size, but neither it nor any other new delivery and distribution systems promise anything radically new in content or any experimentation in narrative structure. Indeed, all previous technological developments in film and television suggest that the old narratives will remain pretty much the same. The pessimistic view is that the movie screen and the television screen will become almost identical. What is projected on them will increase in spectacle, because the creation of large, explosive effects seems to be the direction that digital rendering is going in commercial film. What the images and narratives speak to us about, however, may exist within the old generic contours, driven by the same master narratives that have controlled film from its beginnings. The economics of large technological change almost always result in a conservative approach to the content delivered by new media.

THE THIRD SCREEN

Pessimism is countered, however, by the computer screen itself, which has rapidly found its way into the home and is competing with television as the primary screen in the domestic space. So much so that television and film companies are making deals with computer companies (Microsoft co-owns the NBC cable outlet MSNBC) and almost all shows have Web components. (*The Blair Witch Project* gained its popularity first from a web site!) A main reason for the popularity of the computer screen is that it affords the greatest amount of control, the most solid interaction between the viewer and the material viewed. This is a direct, intimate control, unlike the process of negotiation that goes on with the unyielding images of film and television. The computer monitor looks a lot like a small television. Technically, part of its operation is like a television set in that electrons activate phosphors on the back of the picture tube and images of text or pictures appear on its viewing surface. However, here the similarity ends. The way those representations get to the monitor, what they represent, and who owns and controls the creation and reception of them are quite different from film and television.

Despite the fact that computing requires technical knowledge and active participation, which might logically have led to the argument that it could not be considered a popular art or part of the mass media, its popularity has grown and grown. Although there still exists a frustrating "digital divide" that limits access to personal computers by economic class and by education, the number of all users, of all races and genders, grows exponentially. Although the numbers of machines in use and access to the Internet grow yearly, their penetration into the home is nowhere near that of television. Figures still hover around the 60 percent range of American homes with Internet access, as compared with nearly 99 percent for television. The largest growth in use in early 2000 was by women. However, these figures change when put into economic contexts. Far fewer poor and minority families own computers, but nearly all groups own one or more television sets. Still, working or playing at the computer is becoming a major preoccupation for many, and it makes up in intensity what it lacks in numbers of people whose lives it directly affects. The computer screen and all it represents have become a cultural, political, and economic force; it has changed us in some profound ways, some of them not for the better; and it will change more as more people get access.

Other Narratives

The computer screen offers creativity and inclusion in a process. Unlike a television program or a movie, what is displayed on the computer is not an ongoing story that positions us to respond emotionally at just the right moments, but an invitation to work, to be included in, or placed in control of, a process. The conventional film or television narrative sutures us into its forward momentum, even when the latter is chopped up with commercials. Our interaction with the computer screen lacks the linearity of a classically constructed story with dramatic characters. The drama is made by us; we are the character interacting with the machine and with the words and images it helps us generate.

Human–computer interaction is ongoing, in process, and demands an active participation as opposed to a simulated one. It involves knowledge, specifically attained as opposed to passively absorbed. We learn the codes and conventions of film by watching films; we know how to interact with the computer by learning specific skills. This knowledge and the processes involved in working with the computer and its screens are subdivided into different kinds of interactions. These vary from relatively passive ones to the complexity of programming new screens, creating new computer applications and multimedia projects. Surrounding all this activity is the phenomenon of the Web, the ability of one computer screen to access thousands of others, on which different processes, different representations of data, can be observed and different interactions can be performed.

Computer Games

Computer games are on the passive end of the scale, requiring more reflex than thought. In many ways, they constitute the closest analogy to movies and television. Games are, in fact, the computer venue in which movie studios are investing much time and money. They are often created as tie-ins with movies, and original computer games are made with movielike narratives. These are based on the action-adventure genre—often with second-string actors appearing in digitized videos within the games, some of which are mere blood sports, with destructive responses expected from the user and representations of violence shown on the screen.

There is an interesting correlation between these games and the primitive period of film. One of the legends about early cinema—a story told over and over regarding the Lumière brothers' film of a train leaving a station—was that the audience, so inexperienced with cinematic images, pulled back in fear at the sight. There is, of course, no likelihood of this reaction occurring in the face of the digitized, pixilated figures of a computer game. In fact, there was probably no likelihood that the Lumières' audience reacted in this way either. The legend is more important than the reality. But computer games do attempt to simulate a kind of primitive reflex reaction by allowing the viewer to contend with elements of a program (represented by images of warriors or monsters on the screen) that will do various things in response to various kinds of input. If you click the mouse or move the joystick at the right moment, in the right place, the program will respond by graphically representing on the screen a digitized figure spouting blood. There is emotion involved, based on the anxiety of timing the response at precisely the right moment, and satisfaction of sorts at seeing a figure seem to drop dead because of your action (or disappointment at seeing the figure representing you expire). But the interaction goes no deeper, takes no part of the complex structures of interactivity that the computer offers. Game playing is simultaneously a little more and a great deal less than a movie experience, reduced in size, with a crippled mise-en-scène and a considerably restricted internal narrative. It is the nickelodeon version of computer interaction.

Myst and its sequel, *Riven,* created by Rand and Robyn Miller, use the computer game model—moving around the screen to find the answer to a riddle. But it removes most of the violence, adds a mise-en-scène that owes something to cinema, makes use of complex computer graphics capabilities, and elaborates a pattern of process, uncertainty, probability, logic, and open-endedness that is as close as we currently are to a program that expresses native computer potential. *Myst* and *Riven* speak a language and engage us in a narrative that is possible only on a computer screen. And this is an important event. Computers began as machines to replace and make easier jobs that used to be done by other means—typing, decoding, managing data, doing math, moving money (which is just another kind of data). Now computer–user interaction can produce images and events that are not substitutes but original creations in a discourse that can only be spoken by the machine in relation to the user.

Artists and filmmakers are also turning to the potentials of computer expression. Chris Marker is a longtime French avant-garde filmmaker who is best known for his short science fiction film, *La Jetée* (1962), made mostly of still images and the source for Terry Gilliam's *12 Monkeys* (1995). He recently made a CD-ROM called *Immemory,* which uses vast numbers of images and text woven into a pattern of discovery, dream, and thought, involving cinema, animals, war, and other human experiences in a complex hypertext, where each link takes the user to unexpected images and sounds. Like *Myst,* though with less of its game-playing aspect, *Immemory* brings the conventions of narrative into a kind of computer-driven crisis. Part museum, part journey, part associative poetry, *Immemory* is an object of discovery.

All of this offers more answers to some important questions about computers and narrative. Can computers tell stories at all? Can they narrate as opposed to being part of a larger cultural narrative? That is, can they—should they—represent a series of events in time in which characters are created, given a context,

The French filmmaker Chris Marker's CD-ROM, Immemory.

placed in a world, have things happen to them, which are then resolved back into equilibrium that allows their world to be closed off? Can they provoke us, as viewing subjects, to enter this narrative web, evoke in us anticipation and desire? Can they make us want things to happen simply to see how they will be resolved?

Conventional computer games do some of this. They set up a chase and pursuit model with a set of rules. By and large, they do this within a limited loop: chase, kill, be killed. The variations on the genre are limited. The narrative is bound not by what the computer is capable of but by the limits of the genre of the game and the restrictions set by the assumed desires of their players— mostly adolescent males. The computer is capable of doing much more. More accurately, imaginative designers and programmers, artists like Chris Marker and others, are capable of making the computer reach for something approaching a new language and, therefore, require the user to do more work, as well.

Interestingly, computers are, at their binary fundamentals, makers of narratives. A computer program is a kind of script, a set of instructions that make the machine perform, take user input and calculate it based on the information available to the program, move through that information, do recursive actions so that some things happen over again and others don't, branch, loop, and finally display the results of calculations on the screen.

A script for a film is interpreted as the director, editor, actors, production designer, composer, and cinematographer translate the words into images. A second interpretive act occurs when the film is viewed. Each viewer responds according to the cinematic and cultural codes structured into the film's narrative and his or her subjective reactions. These reactions have little effect on the narrative being constructed on the movie screen, except in the way it is interpreted. The script that is a computer program, on the other hand, can respond in varying ways. It can, within the limits of its construction, incorporate user response and change its calculations—where it branches, loops, whether something done in one place has repercussions on another part of the program—and represent the result of its calculations on the screen. These images can be addressed in turn and can make the program respond in different ways.

This should be obvious if we consider something as ordinary as a word-processing program. The program on the computer I used to write this book helped dictate the book's form, structure, and to some degree even content. It allowed me to type in whatever text characters I wanted and helped me put them in the form of chapters, paragraphs, caps, italics, notes, and so on. It responded to my needs, acted the way I wanted it to act. It can do many things, except supply the words I need (though even in this case I can open the computer's thesaurus database and find analogous words for a word I highlight). When I manipulate images on the computer, the program does much more. It samples colors down to the smallest visual unit on the screen—the pixel—and can alter it. I can clip a figure from one image and paste it into another. Here, the computer is in a complex mode, reading its program (its script), the information I give it, and working out new images as a result.

Computers and the programs that drive them do not have intelligence in the sense that they can originate ideas (though this has long been a dream of one branch of computer science, artificial intelligence). But they are manipulable in that they can take one piece of information and, if they have been instructed how to do so, produce a number of different results. This is the basis of computer program structures that operate on logical elements: if … then … /and … or … /true/false/yes/no. Within these and other parameters, they can manipulate user input to produce a variety of different results. The results themselves can then be changed to create new results, which can then loop back to alter the foundation of whatever created the original results in the first place. The more intricate the program, the more articulate the graphical representations on the screen; and the more latitude given to the user to alter them, the more complex the interactions can be.

These are some of the principles that lie behind *Myst*, *Riven*, and *Immemory*. The structure of the program represents what appears to be an endless series of alterations, each one having a ripple effect so that a choice in one place creates consequences in other places. This would be interesting in an abstract, mathematical sense were it not for the fact that these programs work their changes through graphical representations that are the closest the computer screen has come so far to creating a mise-en-scène—images of imaginative worlds. The designs of *Myst* and *Riven* bear a visual relationship to the art of 1950s science fiction magazine covers and are articulated in the blue/green colors best suited to the limited range of some personal computers and articulated with objects that can be addressed by the user: switches, buttons, dials, cranks, books, pictures—the moving of any of which has an effect in some other screen, some other structure of the program, another imaginary, graphical space. As in a movie, musical themes are associated with various places, rooms, and worlds, spaces and times through which the viewer moves in search of the answer to a riddle, which itself has to be discovered before we know where we can begin to look for the answer.

This mise-en-scène is remarkably humanized, though without representations of human figures. A video of a man, talking incoherently, can be located in one of the books in the library of *Myst*. Winged figures, reminiscent of the mythic Icarus, who flew too close to the sun, can be seen floating from the sky on some of its screens. But the worlds of *Myst* are unpeopled landscapes, a fact that becomes part of the mystery. (There are a few more figures in *Riven*, but there, too, the player is the most important presence.) The mystery—the plot of this particular digital world, about kidnapping and ancient family feuds—is of considerably less interest than its process. The "people" of *Myst* are its players. The main character, the subject of the work, is the person operating the program during any particular session. The main narrative movement is the exploration of images and devices. Like some movies, the plot is simply less intriguing than the narrative process that creates it. The best part is the process of investigation, inventing a narrative within the wide-ranging bounds provided by the program, moving through the graphic images of imagined worlds.

In *Immemory*, the images vary a great deal in style; and navigation, though not worked like a game, is deeply hidden. Marker is not so much interested in where you click, but why, and what you will see when you do. He wants the user to make not narrative as much as a pattern of sights and sounds, to become the author's author.

Hypertext/Hypermedia

Process—in which the viewer/user is both subject and object, in control of the screen, searching for data, images, connections, following branches and links, pursuing paths, being led down blind alleys, coming up with specific or diffuse results—is something almost inherent in the form and structure of the computer. In 1965, a Harvard graduate student named Ted Nelson coined the word **"hypertext"** to describe an idea he had of computer-generated nonlinear connections or links between data. Such links would allow the user to connect disparate parts, connect big and small chunks of text and images, open one set of text to reveal others, move in ways other than straight lines, link data continuously and extensively. He called his project Xanadu, after Samuel Taylor Coleridge's magical kingdom in the poem *Kubla Khan*, and after the unfinished castle, filled with the world's art treasures, in Orson Welles's *Citizen Kane*. True to its conception, the project was never completed.

But the idea of hypertext and hypermedia caught on. *Myst* is a kind of hypermedia creation. Some works—like Michael Joyce's *afternoon, a story*, Stuart Moulthrop's *Victory Garden*, and Carolyn Guyer's *Quibbling*, and the poems and novels in the hypertext issue of the online journal *Postmodern Culture*—have attempted a new fiction in which blocks of prose or verses are linked in apparently arbitrary ways that alter the conventional linearity of the literary narrative, providing alternative ways of reading, alternative possibilities of how and where texts and textuality may exist. Hypertext fiction has not quite reached the status of a literary movement, and it is more provocative theory than good literature.

Outside of word processing (in which the user is actively creating words), plain text is not the most inviting of representations to look at on the computer screen for long periods of time, even if it can be manipulated into curious patterns that allow the reader to create variable narrative structures.

Hypertext fiction needs to be linked into the larger concept of hyper- or multimedia, the ability to represent relationships between images, text, and sounds in a design that provides links between them, allows the user to discover or make connections, and displays contiguities of ideas that might not be obvious or possible in traditional linear, page-bound presentations. Hypermedia is a methodology for exploring insides and outsides, of seeing into the margins, of opening the linkages between different kinds of representations, and explaining one class of representation (a visual image, for example) by means of another (a sound or words). In a hypermedia project, a word or a block of text can be linked in various ways to other words and can be associated with an image. Parts of an image can be divided and linked to verbal description; a sound or voice-over narrative can accompany, embellish, or contradict the elements on the screen.

Film, Form, and Culture: The CD-ROM

If *Myst* or *Immemory* is a kind of multimedia presentation that calls upon complex, covert links between image, language, and sound, the CD-ROM that accompanies this textbook is an example of multimedia used for analytic purposes. The study of film has always been hampered by the difficulty of access to illustrative material. Before the computer, it was next to impossible to quote from film, the way a literature teacher and critic can quote from a novel or poem. The cinematic text is physically removed from the viewer; it can't be held in the hand like a book; its sequences are difficult—and on the printed page, impossible—to access. Although videotape and laserdisc media have made it easier to control the visual text, showing a sequence on a printed page, the way lines from a poem or a reproduction of a painting can be shown, has remained elusive.

This is an elusiveness that constrains our ability to understand how the form and structure of film work. Still images don't do the trick and are hard to authenticate. Unless they are clearly frame enlargements—that is, photographs made from an actual frame of a film, as they are in this book—they are usually production stills, posed photographs of a film's stars that may have been made outside the main production. These were common throughout the studio period and are still made. They are not quotations from the films.

The ability to digitize film images, to turn their rich, analogue visuals into the common binary language of computers, puts them in the same class as any other computer file. They become the equal of text file and can become integrated with it. They can be addressed, altered, programmed, and designed into a larger textual entity. Earlier, we spoke about the ways in which Hollywood filmmakers are using computers to do the kinds of image manipulation that was formerly done by optical printing. Similar kinds of manipulation can be done on smaller desktop computers, and the result is a new kind of control of the moving image that leads to a new and more authoritative analytic and critical understanding. Digitized motion picture images can be incorporated into most advanced word-processing programs. Although they can only be seen with the document on a computer screen, there they provide instant examples, clarifications, and authentications for the prose analysis. In the CD-ROM that accompanies this book, digitized sequences from films become one part of a larger interactive design; they are used as examples and their mysteries revealed. Taken out of the ongoing narrative flow of the film, isolated and broken down, they become part of another text, a hypermedia text in which image is linked to image, to analysis, example, and redefinition. As you will see, it is possible to open a critical dimension within the image so that by interrogating it (by a mouse click), information is divulged. Images in the CD-ROM from Eisenstein's *Battleship Potemkin*, Welles's *Citizen Kane*, and Pare Lorentz's *The Plow That Broke the Plains* have animated lines diagrammed within them—the way a football commentator on television diagrams a play—to show how the filmmaker uses space and mise-en-scène to define character and narrative. All the moving images can be paused and stepped through, as if a VCR or DVD were incorporated into the computer screen. Abstract principles like point of view and genre—and general concepts like continuity cutting, montage, lighting, music, sound and the work of the camera—are made visible. Idea and image are put in the reader's control.

The Computer and the Text

The hypermedia event, no matter what its subject, is a creation of dimensions, an elaboration or invention of contiguities and connections, a way of creating an intertextuality of word, image, and culture in space by opening up linkages and associations that move in many directions. At the same time, it concentrates diverse materials in accessible ways. A central tenet of cultural studies is that people and the things they do never stand in isolation from each other. Texts are large, coherent events that include not only a single book, a film, or a television show but the various events going on around them, all directly or indirectly connected. Social attitudes and situations, ideological currents, newspaper reports, fashions, music, the history of the moment, and our own responses are all part of a larger textuality that is, in turn, a part of the culture. Hypermedia enables the creation of a text that can pull together these various textualities and explicitly or implicitly make links between them. It is a text of texts that makes range and depth part of its properties, and access an ongoing, interrogative process.

The creation and use of multimedia put the viewing subject in a situation unlike any other textual event. It gives the viewer control of a variety of large amounts of data that can be structured in intriguing and imaginative ways. It creates a sense of connection and exploration; and, in its networked, global form, it is creating a new kind of community, a kind of universal culture, in which subjectivity, identity, and participation are in the process of being redefined.

Modernity and the Internet

In Chapter 4, we discussed the concept of modernity and defined it as the movement of technological advancement; increased urbanization; rapid fragmentation of dependable, cohesive structures (such as family, religion, a dominant race or ethnicity, and government); and the falling away of individual agency. Modernity can be figured as a movement away from a center, and that "center" can be understood through a variety of representations: religion, the extended family, the small community, the ideology of free will and independent action. Computer technology is a bridge from modernity to postmodernity. It allows us a way to experience and manage the transition. It shows ways to break away from the centers and create new configurations of the individual in the world that are both liberating and nostalgic, freeing and constraining. Film and television make us nostalgic about the simpler times that exist only in its images, offering us ways to dream ourselves out of the confusions of the modern world. Computer networks let us see modernity and offer us ways to navigate through it.

Modernity is developed on the ground of communications. The ability of people to be in immediate contact with each other offers ways to transcend local community and construct the global one that is essential to the processes of decentralizing culture. The invention of printing in the fourteenth century was a primary event in the spreading of information and ideas, the diffusing of the authority of the individual by making his words take the place of his presence, spreading those words beyond his voice, his ideas beyond his control. Printing helped conquer space by making ideas and information movable and independent of an individual. This was when aura began to diminish.

In the nineteenth century the process received another boost. During the last half of the nineteenth century, the railroad became a way for physical decentralization, allowing people relative ease of movement across a country. In the twentieth century, the car and the airplane took the place of the railroad and provided international access for many and local mobility for almost everyone. At about the same time, the cinema became an imaginative and emotional means of expansion, a means to access images of other spaces, other kinds of behaviors. Telegraphy and the telephone created—like the book and the film—a curious hybrid of movement and stasis. Through them, a person could reach another, distant place while remaining physically rooted in her original location. The telephone permitted the voice, the most forceful of communicative agents, to transmit its presence and intimacy. It broadened community and, like the railroad, increased commerce. Telegraphy and the teletype allowed the transmission of writing and images and therefore the communication of detailed information, structured, authoritative, and official, in the way speaking never could.

Telephone and telegraphy, like movies and television, are part of the analogue realm—continuous waveforms of information, transferred from point to point. The transportation, quality, management, and storage of this kind of communications were bulky and limited, subject to the constraints of space and to the "noise" that is introduced by factors as various as sunspots, poor equipment, and distance. "Noise" is a concept in communications theory that stands for any kind of interference in the transmission process, physical, ideological, corporate. The digital reduces noise on many different levels. By transforming the analogue into the binary, image, sound, and text can be sampled and compressed as numbers rather than waves. Physical noise can be removed, and, as we've seen, degeneration in quality is eliminated. Most important, because large parts of the digital repository of information are open, accessible to all who have the rather simple (if still somewhat expensive) equipment necessary to find and see them, the ideological "noise" of ownership and information control should be somewhat diminished. However, as we have seen in recent years, especially in the music world, ownership of digital files has become a major issue. Still, though computer communication is hardly as universal as the telephone, and corporate constraint continues to raise its ugly head, where it is available, it offers opportunities of access and content, individually controlled, that no other communicative form has.

The great repository and distribution system of digital communications is the Internet. Although it is a product of modernity, it is also a model of what postmodernity is about. The Internet is an idea without a location, a thing with no single physical presence, a way of moving ideas, visual images and sounds, and a lot of text around the world, from screen to screen, with as little noise as possible. Early on, the Internet defied capitalist rules of ownership, because it wasn't owned. It was originated by the U.S. Department of Defense in the 1960s, taken under the partial stewardship of the National Science Foundation, and became governed by a loose confederation of universities, government agencies, and corporations. Ownership did not define the Internet; access did. The Internet is, in its simple reality, many computers—called servers—linked together through a complex addressing protocol that makes each one of them identifiable and addressable by any other. An individual who can access a network directly or by a phone hookup can connect to some or all of the Internet, find those servers, and look at what they have to offer.

This, of course, is its major limitation, the place where noise enters the system in the form of economic and class barriers to access and the growing ownership of web sites by corporate interests, crowding out public and academic access. This is partly because though unowned in the normal corporate senses of the word, the Internet costs money. Those costs are usually borne by universities or corporations. Any student who is assigned an address and has access to a machine with a modem or direct connection can access the network. For around twenty dollars a month, anyone else with a computer and a modem, and a local company that provides an Internet connection, can get access. Pay-for-use dial-up services, like America Online, provide some Internet connections. In many communities, public libraries, churches, and community centers are providing access. The advent of high-speed cable modems and telephone-delivered DSL (direct subscriber line) services is making that access quicker and easier—and more expensive. The poor, minorities, those living in the inner city or outer rural areas still find access very difficult.

For those who can access the Net, and despite the growing corporate control, there are various genres, various ways of representing, communicating, and receiving data, each with its own conventions, structures, and protocols. Newsgroups provide a large and sometimes bizarre variety of ongoing discussions, from computer programming to paramilitary rant. Some newsgroups constitute the male-only barroom of the digitized world, where aggression, vulgarity, and old rituals of gender exclusion are played out with uncensored ferocity. More propriety is shown on listservs, which are also discussion groups but made up of subscribed members, grouped usually by academic interests. Listservs are easily formed and made local, so that your college class, for example, can create a listserv in which members can discuss related topics with one another.

These means of personal communication, combined with electronic mail, which uses the Internet to send individual messages between people with server access, make the digital a personalized realm, and a comfortable one as well. Although, as in any community effort, loud and angry voices sometimes threaten to overtake conversations, niches have quickly developed, giving them a place where they can be either attended to or ignored. The spaces that remain are filled with people exchanging information, making contact, talking, a faceless, spaceless community in which subjectivity is redefined by intellectual and emotional interests, where one can simultaneously be audience and participant.

Were these the limits of the Internet, it would remain the province of university researchers and people who like to chat about everything from politics to sex and guns. What has brought it into prominence, made it a part of the cultural landscape where it is vying with film and television for the attention of both individuals and the corporate world, is another means of depositing and retrieving data across thousands of servers, called the World Wide Web. The Web was developed by computer scientists as an easier means of transmitting images and sound along with printed text across servers around the world. So easy, in fact, that almost anyone who has Internet access can design a "home page" and put it up for the world to see. The home computer can become a distribution site.

Web sites work in hyperlink fashion. Sites are linked to other sites, often continents away, through a mouse click; images yield texts and texts images. Experimentations with every kind of material occur. Individuals put up pictures of their children; there are online collections from most of the major museums in the world; advertisements for local flower shops; scientific and humanities research; those large corporate sites that supply everything from moving images of recent film releases to software updates. These exist along with literary texts, photographs, avant-garde art and literary experiments, pornography, government and medical information, bibliographies, library catalogues, scholarly journals—a world of broad though often, except in the case of full-length articles or books, narrow "information."

Every university, most of its departments, and many of their students and faculty have a web site. Special public services, such as forums for sufferers of particular diseases, groups and companies attempting to bring Internet access and information to African American and Hispanic and Latino communities as well as to older citizens, have sites. Rock groups, film festivals, and government agencies have web sites. Using special sites that provide search mechanisms, you can find the most general or particular information on the Web. It is an enormous, unruly assemblage, a place where many people go to look around and find, with time and patience, what they need. Because of its unruliness, it is sometimes an untrustworthy place. Much of the information is, as I mentioned, very thin; some inaccurate. Some literary texts posted on the Web are inauthentic. Many essays that appear to be scholarly may not have stood the test of review by academic peers. In a structure with no central authority—where almost anyone can be a producer—the facts and the narratives may be wrong or devious.

Any number of judgments can be made about the Web: the lazy person's shopping mall; a community for shy people; a passing fad for those bored with television; a useful, though limited, research resource and a very poor replacement for the library; a place for businesses, large and small, to make another buck; a space to exhibit and exchange images of all kinds—a postmodern space of sense and nonsense, the banal and, though not often, the profound. It might be useful to think about it on a slightly more abstract level. The Internet, and the World Wide Web in particular, are the current outposts of the postmodern, where subjectivities—the sense and the place of the individual self—shift and change. The Internet is an enormous and a small space where a person can assert herself by connecting to and communicating with (no matter in how limited a way) almost every computer in the world. Or a person can be absorbed by the images and words shifted around the globe from server to server and screen to screen. It is a place, like the movies, of myriad representations but, unlike the movies, of few stories in the conventional sense.

Like almost everything on the computer screen, the World Wide Web is a place of process in which everything happens but nothing is resolved. Unlike the movies, its images and words do not fall into closed, knowable fictional worlds (when fiction appears on the Internet, either it is of the hyper variety, which means that it is fragmented and without closure, or it is a reproduction of a traditional text, difficult to read in its entirety on screen). As we said earlier, what is narrated on the Web is the story of investigation and participation, the subject's progress through an open-ended system.

The representations on the computer screen are open, ongoing, and their constraints are much different from those of conventional story-telling media. Because of the interactive nature of the computer and its screen, the individual subject is turned into an active participant and agent. And with that turn, rules are changed. Mass media, as we've said many times, require a largely passive response. Despite the validity of the cultural studies argument about negotiating interpretations and engaging the text according to our determined desires to read what we want to read, much of our interaction with film and television is a passive reaction to its codes and conventions. Little passivity is possible in our interactions with the computer screen. We need to know what we are doing, actively seek things out, and often interact with what we find. No matter how strong corporate interference becomes, this will never change.

More than film and television, our engagement with the images on a computer screen is without aura. That startling idea of Walter Benjamin's, stated in the 1930s, is even more applicable now. With the advent of digital cultures, we are freer than ever to enter a community of ideas, of words and images—of representations—and find our way with less constraints than the older media. Benjamin wrote in "The Work of Art in the Age of Mechanical Reproduction":

> Every day the urge grows stronger to get hold of an object at very close range by way of its likeness, its reproduction.... To pry an object from its shell, to destroy its aura, is the mark of a perception whose "sense of the universal equality of things" has increased to such a degree that it extracts it even from a unique object by means of reproduction.... The adjustment of reality to the masses and of the masses to reality is a process of unlimited scope, as much for thinking as for perception.

For "masses" read "ourselves." We are the ones extracting images and ideas, our own subjectivities, and testing them in the digital, networked world in ways the makers of popular culture could have never imagined. Through the digital, reality is being adjusted, just as it was with the movies at the turn of the century. And, just like then, we are searching for new languages of expression, new ways to create the new realities.

The structure of the World Wide Web, the possibilities inherent in hypermedia authoring, the resources available to computer programming, may yield a language of inquiry, of humanity, of emotional resonance that could speak to us—or to which we may speak—with complexity and insight. This language will be of a different order of resonance and responsibility than the great works of film, the movies of Hitchcock, Kubrick, Welles, Scorsese, Godard, Antonioni, Bertolucci, Altman, Fassbinder, and all the others who have used their medium to probe and ask questions. But it will address and articulate our curiosity and desire.

All the tools we have to act, perceive, and create have the potential to ask questions and find new meanings, new realities; and the languages of the computer and the possibilities of its screens have no more inherent limits than any other. The limits exist only in those who use the languages, who make the images and read them. Someone once said that the computer is still looking for its D. W. Griffith. What that means is that we still await the imagination that can turn the language of the computer program and the images of the computer screen into articulate and coherent statements that speak to our selves, our history, our culture.

Film, Form, and Culture, the CD-ROM

The *Film, Form, and Culture* CD-ROM is itself one example of new media, in which film and analysis appear in a computer-created interactive environment.

NOTES AND REFERENCES

Television   The best source for a cultural study of how television infiltrated the home is Lynn Spigel, *Make Room for TV: Television and the Family Ideal in Postwar America* (Chicago: University of Chicago Press, 1992).

Commercial Structures   A good history of the development of commercial television is William Boddy's *Fifties Television* (Urbana, Illinois: University of Indiana Press, 1990). Mike Mashon's *A Word from the Sponsor: Madison Avenue and the Evolution of American Television*, forthcoming from University of Texas Press, clarifies television's early history.

Narrative Programming   For a good differentiation of "series" and "serials," and a discussion of narrative form in television, see John Ellis, *Visible Fictions: Cinema, Television, Video* (London: Routledge, 1992).

Soaps   For soap operas, there are two collections of essays: E. Ann Kaplan, ed., *Regarding Television: Critical Approaches* (Frederick, MD: University Publications of America, 1983); and Suzanne Frentz, *Staying Tuned: Contemporary Soap Opera Criticism* (Bowling Green, OH: Bowling Green State University Popular Press, 1992).

Flow   The citation for Raymond Williams is in Chapter 4.

From Analogue to Digital: Storage and Distribution   Here is a story about a film that combines digital replacement with advertising. *Demolition Man* (Marco Brambilla, 1993), a film set in the future, with Sylvester Stallone and Wesley Snipes, has sequences that take place in a Taco Bell fast-food restaurant. There were no Taco Bells in Europe—where American producers count upon a film making a lot of money—but there are Pizza Huts, which are owned by the same company, Pepsico. Pepsico paid to have Taco Bell appear in the film. The filmmakers simply did a digital replacement so that Taco Bell now appeared as Pizza Hut. No refilming was necessary, and Pepsico got advertising in its European markets. (See *The Wall Street Journal*, Dec. 2, 1993, p. B1.)

The Third Screen: Hypertext   The original group of hypertext authors were published on disc by Eastgate Systems. One of the best hypertext stories is Matthew Miller's "Trip" in vol. 7, no. 1 (September 1996) of *Postmodern Culture*. *Postmodern Culture* is an online subscription journal available at http://muse.jhu.edu/journals/postmodern_culture/.

Hypertext theory is outlined in J. David Bolter, *Writing Space: The Computer, Hypertext, and the History of Writing* (Hillsdale, NJ: L. Erlbaum Associates, 1991). Bolter's *Turing's Man: Western Culture in the Computer Age* (Chapel Hill: North Carolina University Press, 1984) is an interesting attempt at a cultural history of computing. A classic book on interactive narrative is Janet Horowitz Murray,

Hamlet on the Holodeck: The Future of Narrative in Cyberspace (Massachusetts: MIT Press, 1997). There is a discussion of Ted Nelson and the theory of hypertext called "The Electronic Labyrinth," by Christopher Keep and Tim McLaughlin, found at http://jefferson.village.virginia.edu/elab/elab.html.

Film, Form, and Culture: The CD   One must always be aware of copyright issues when digitizing movie clips.

Modernity and the Internet   Two collections of essays address the cultural contexts of the Internet: David Porter, ed., *Internet Culture* (New York and London: Routledge, 1997); and Mark Stefik, ed., *Internet Dreams: Archtypes, Myths, and Metaphors* (Cambridge, MA: Massachusetts Institute of Technology, 1996).

180-degree rule This rule holds that, from one cut to another, the camera does not cross an imaginary line drawn behind the characters.

anamorphic processes The camera lens "squeezes" an image onto the film. When unsqueezed by the projector lens, the ratio of the image is 1:2.35. Panavision is the most common proprietary anamorphic process.

aspect ratio The relationship of screen width to height. There are four ratios. "Standard" ratio existed from the early 1930s through the early 1950s and is 1:1.3. Two wide-screen ratios are 1:1.6 and 1:1.85. Anamorphic wide screen (Cinemascope, Panavision) is 1:2.35.

auteur French term for the film director who places a personal style on his or her films.

avant-garde Often used to explain works of artists that are personal, experimental, and not aimed at a wide audience.

backlighting Lights behind the characters that set them off from the background.

chiaroscuro A term from art history that refers to the use of deep shadow in the mise-en-scène.

cinéma vérité A version of documentary developed by the French in the late fifties and sixties that attempted to capture the ongoingness of everyday life without narration.

cinematographer (director of photography) Working with a film's director, the cinematographer lights the scene, chooses the appropriate lenses and film stock, and therefore carries a large responsibility for determining the look of a film.

classical Hollywood style The classical Hollywood style refers to a complex collection of formal and thematic elements that became basic to Hollywood filmmaking by the early teens. Continuity cutting—including shot/reverse shot and over-the-shoulder cutting—the 180-degree rule, happy endings, psychologically motivated characters, villains getting punished, women becoming wives and mothers are all associated with the classical Hollywood style. The continuity style is a subset of the classical Hollywood style.

close-up   The actor's face fills the screen. Also, medium close-up, where the actor is seen from the upper torso.

composition   The arrangement of characters and surroundings within the boundaries of the screen frame.

continuity style/continuity editing   Smooth, seamless editing that links shots so that the cuts appear invisible to the viewer.

crane   An apparatus that can lift the camera into the air and is therefore responsible for a crane shot.

cultural studies   A wide-ranging critical approach to works of imagination that examines them in light of the cultures they are part of and that create them.

culture   The sum total of the intricate ways we relate to ourselves, our peers, our community, our country, world, and universe.

deep focus   In deep-focus cinematography, all objects from front to rear of the composition are in sharp focus.

documentary   A film that records actual events, often creating dramatic impact through editing.

dolly   An apparatus that holds the camera but can, itself, move in, out, or from side to side. A dolly-in or dolly-out refers to a movement toward or away from a figure.

editing   The process of cutting film footage and assembling the pieces into an expressive, narrative structure.

editor   The person who assembles the shots of a film into its final shape.

establishing shot   Before a cutting pattern can begin, there must be a shot that establishes the whole space. Examples of establishing shots are the initial two-shot of characters in a dialogue sequence, or the image of an entire roomful of people, or of the city in which the film takes place.

Expressionist   This term originally referred to the style of film and theater in post–World War I Germany, where the mise-en-scène expressed the exaggerated, neurotic psychological state of the characters. Now it is used to refer to a mise-en-scène that is dark, distorted, and menacing.

eye-line match   Continuity editing dictates that, if a character is looking in a certain direction in one shot, she should be looking in the same direction in the following shot. This is crucial in the over-the-shoulder pattern, where the characters must seem to be looking at one another (even if both actors are not physically present at the same time when the shots are made).

fill lighting   Lights that fill in the scene, creating accents, removing or adding shadow.

film noir   A genre of film developed in the 1940s. Noir has a literary heritage in the hard-boiled detective fiction of Raymond Chandler and Dashiell Hammett and the novels of James M. Cain. Its cinematic lineage is German Expressionism and Welles's *Citizen Kane*. It is marked by a mise-en-scène of heavy shadow and narratives of weak men destroyed by predatory women.

flow   A notion developed by the British cultural scholar Raymond Williams to define the ways that disparate and incoherent elements, commercials, promotions, and the shows themselves move together seamlessly on television.

Frankfurt school   Short for the Frankfurt Institute for Social Research, founded in Germany in 1924, much of it devoted to the study of popular culture and its productions.

genre   A "kind" of story or narrative, made up of character types, plot lines, and settings common to all its members. Science fiction films and Westerns are genres, for example.

high-keyed lighting   Creates a bright, evenly lit scene.

hypertext   A digital work—a novel, poem, or website—that contains links to other sections of the narrative or other Web pages.

image track   As opposed to the sound track, the series of images that contain the film's visual content.

intertextuality   The way texts are interwoven or refer to each other in film, music, and the other arts. "Sampling" in rap is a kind of intertextuality.

Italian neorealism   Developed by the Italians at the end of World War II, a genre that defied studio conventions by filming on the streets, using nonprofessional or semi-professional actors to define a working class ruined by the war.

jump cut   The result of editing out unnecessary transitions so that continuity is replaced by rapid changes in space.

key light   The main overhead light that lights the faces and is reflected in the eyes.

long shot (long takes)   Characters and surroundings are shown at a considerable distance from the camera.

long take   In an average film, shots last six to nine seconds. A long take may last sixty seconds or more and contain rich narrative and visual information.

medium close-up   Character is shown from the shoulders up.

medium shot   Character is shown from the waist up.

melodrama   With comedy, the major genre of film, providing large arcs of emotion, often spilling into the music and mise-en-scène, and ending with the death of a beloved character or a closure in heterosexual marriage.

mise-en-scène   The use of space within the frame: the placement of actors and props, the relationship of the camera to the space in front of it, camera movement, the use of color or black and white, lighting, the size of the screen frame itself.

montage   A style of editing that juxtaposes shots to build dramatic tension. Sergei Eisenstein used montage as the basic structure of his films.

over-the-shoulder cutting pattern   A major component of the classical Hollywood style. A dialogue sequence (two people talking to each other) begins with a two-shot of the participants and then proceeds to cut from over-the-shoulder of one speaker to over-the-shoulder of the other. Occasionally a shot of one of the participants talking or listening will be cut into the pattern.

pan   The camera pivots on its tripod or dolly. A pan can be lateral (side to side) or up and down.

panning and scanning   The only way to show the entire width of a wide-screen film on television is to matte the top and bottom of the screen with black bars (the process is called letter-box format). Because many people believe they are seeing less of the film in this format (they are actually seeing more), television broadcasters and videotape distributors blow up the image to a square and move the focus around in that image to find what they think are the important elements.

point of view   Simply, the representation of what a character sees. But it also refers to the dominant "voice" of the film, the teller of the tale, similar to third-person point of view in fiction.

post-studio period   Since the late fifties, when the studios no longer controlled every aspect of a film's production.

producer   The individual who administers the making of an entire film, and often puts together its financing.

production designer   Conceives and elaborates the setting's rooms and exteriors that help give a film its visual texture.

rear-screen projection   The background of a scene is projected on a screen from the back, while the actors play their roles in front of the screen. Actors and the projection are photographed by a camera in front of them and the screen.

reverse shot   Cutting to the opposite side of the previous shot. In a dialogue scene, a reverse shot occurs when a cut is made from over the shoulder of one character to over the shoulder of the other character. If a character is seen looking at something and a cut is made to what she is looking at, that is a reverse shot.

screwball comedy   Films of the 1930s in which both members of a romantic—often married—couple carried equal weight with dialogue of wit, strength, and self-possession.

shot   An unedited, or uncut, length of film.

shot/reverse shot   Any pair of shots in which the second shot reveals what is on the other side of the previous shot. If, for example, the first shot is a hat and the second shot is a character looking at something, the character constitutes the reverse shot and we assume that character is looking at the hat.

silent era   From the beginning of film to the late 1920s, there was no recorded sound accompanying the image. Nonetheless, films were never shown without sound. A piano or, in a big movie palace, an entire symphony orchestra played a score that was often created especially for a particular film.

sound track   Either an optical or a magnetic strip along the side of the film that contains the recorded sound for the film.

studio system   Beginning in the early 1920s, the film studios developed a production process—with the producer at the head on any given film—and a style of shooting and editing that, despite many variations, remains to this day.

take   A shot made during the production of a film. A scene in a film is the result of editorial choices made from many differing takes.

Technicolor   A proprietary color process that used three strips of black and white film, each one exposed to either red, blue, or yellow light. These strips were then used to transfer color dye to impart a rich color to film that did not fade with age.

The New Wave   A group of French filmmakers—Jean-Luc Godard, Claude Chabrol, François Truffaut, Eric Rohmer, Jacque Rivette—who started as film critics, became filmmakers in the late fifties, and briefly revolutionized the look of cinema.

track   The camera moves on a transport mechanism like a tripod or dolly. This mechanism is put on rails so that the camera will move smoothly. A lateral track moves horizontally.

two-shot   A shot composed of two people.

INDEX

FILM, FORM, AND CULTURE CD-ROM

Contents

- Introduction—Film and Representation
  Define—Representation
  Steamboat Bill, Jr.
  Analyze—Buster Keaton: The Forms and Structures of Film
  Steamboat Bill, Jr.

1. CONTINUITY EDITING—The Classical Hollywood Style
   Define—Over the Shoulder Cutting and the 180-Degree Rule
   Analyze:
      The Classical Style
         Meet John Doe
      Continuity Editing
         Light Sleeper
      Unconventional Cutting
         Light Sleeper
   Discover:
      Intertextuality
         Light Sleeper
         Pickpocket

2. THE LONG TAKE—Orson Welles and the Construction of Cinematic Space
   View—*Citizen Kane*
   Analyze
      The Dynamics of Wellesian Space
         Citizen Kane
      Cinematic Space and the Story of Kane's Childhood
         Citizen Kane
      Compre
         Citizen Kane

3. MONTAGE—Sergei Eisenstein and the Dynamics of Editing
   Analyze
      Battleship Potemkin
         Hammock Sequence
         Plate Sequence
         Odessa Steps Sequence
      The Plow that Broke the Plains
   Compare
      Battleship Potemkin
      The Plow that Broke the Plains
   Contrast
      Continuity: *Light Sleeper*
      The Long Take: *Citizen Kane*
      Montage: *Plow that Broke the Plains*

4. POINT OF VIEW—The Look and the Gaze
    Analyze
        The Characters Gaze
            Vertigo
        Play of Glances
            Broken Blossoms
            Meet John Doe
        Complexity of Space
            Rear Window

5. MISE-EN-SCÈNE—Frame, Space, and Story
    Define—Mise-en-scène
    Analyze
        Broken Blossoms
        Vertigo
        JFK
    Discover—The Screen Frame
        Citizen Kane
        JFK
        The Trial

6. LIGHTING—The Expressive Substance of Film
    Define—Lighting Basics
    Analyze
        Sculpting with Light
            Meet John Doe
            Nothing Sacred
            Detour
            Vertigo
        Color and Light
            Vertigo
            Light Sleeper

7. CAMERA–Framing, Placement, and Movement
    Analyze
        Framing
            Broken Blossoms
        Camera Placement
            Intolerance
            Meet John Doe
            Vertigo
        Camera Movement
            Light Sleeper
            Meet John Doe

Synthesize
  Meet John Doe
  Detour

8. SOUND AND MUSIC—Sound and Image
  Sound
  Music—Analyze
    Vertigo
    Alexander Nevsky

9. GENRE—Style, Form, and Content
  Genre
  Film Noir
    Detour
    T-Men
    Raw Deal
    He Walked by Night
    The Trial